Parrots For Dummies®

Important Parrot Resources

The World Parrot Trust

www.worldparrottrust.org

This charity funds projects and promotes parrot conservation and welfare. Great information on parrot welfare and links to parrot resources.

The Avian Welfare Coalition

www.avianwelfare.org

The AWC is a working alliance of representatives from bird adoption, rescue, and sanctuary groups, humane societies, animal advocacy organizations, published research biologists, animal behaviorists, shelter and research veterinarians, and attorneys and other animal law specialists dedicated to the ethical treatment and protection of birds living in captivity and in their natural habitats.

Natural Encounters

www.naturalencounters.com

Cool site featuring one of the best-known trainers in the world, Steve Martin, who has pioneered the art of training a variety of birds and animals through positive reinforcement. The site contains lots of practical training information.

The Alex Foundation

www.alexfoundation.org

Very informative Web site for Dr. Irene Pepperberg's research on Alex, an African grey parrot, and two other greys. If you want to know about parrot intelligence, this is the site.

The Shyne Foundation

www.shynefoundation.org

This site details the benefit of free flight in parrots and shows you how to build a free flight habitat.

My Toos

www.mytoos.com

Thinking about getting a cockatoo? Please check out this site first!

The Gabriel Foundation

www.thegabrielfoundation.org/Home/

A nonprofit corporation promoting education, conservation, rescue, rehabilitation, adoption, and sanctuary for the needs of parrots everywhere.

The Association of Avian Veterinarians

www.aav.org

Find an avian vet in your area.

Avian Protection Society

www.avianprotectors.homestead.com

A group promoting the welfare of parrots everywhere. Excellent resource for adopting a parrot or for parrot behavior and welfare issues.

Foster Parrots

www.fosterparrots.com

Run by Marc Johnson, is dedicated to improving the lives of parrots as pets and in their natural habitats. You'll find information about rescue and adoption in this site, as well as lots of other good stuff.

Tropical Nature Travel

www.tropicalnaturetravel.com/travel/

Want to see parrots in the wild? This organization offers tours for just that purpose.

Free Parrots

www.freeparrots.net

A great parrot news site run by Harvard biologist Mike Schindlinger, who also runs the Oratrix Project, an in-depth study of the language of wild Amazon parrots.

Parrots For Dummies®

Items to Keep Your Parrot Away From

Avocados

Alcohol

Caffeine

Chocolate

Pencils

Pens

Toxic houseplants

Lead

Chipping paint

Glues

Candles

Air fresheners

Ionizers

Nonstick surfaces

Jingle bells

Cats and dogs

Ferrets and snakes

Standing water

Open windows

Household cleansers

Pesticides

How to Teach a Child to Behave Around a New Parrot

1. Use inside voices, but don't whisper.
2. Talk to your new parrot. Get it used to the sound of your voice.
3. Don't play with the bird too much in the first few days. Allow the bird to become acclimated.
4. Move slowly. Children tend to display sharp, quick movements which can scare parrots.
5. Be gentle. Never squeeze, hit, or throw the bird. Use slow, gentle movements.
6. Be compassionate and understanding. Teach your child that the bird is not a toy.
7. Teach your child not to be afraid of the bird. Fear will lead to an ignored and unhappy companion.
8. Don't stick your fingers in the cage or tease the bird.
9. If the bird is afraid, it's not personal. He's just being a bird.
10. Offer the bird yummy treats to make friends with it.

Copyright © 2005 Wiley Publishing, Inc.
All rights reserved.

Item 8353-0.

For more information about Wiley Publishing, call 1-800-762-2974.

For Dummies: Bestselling Book Series for Beginners

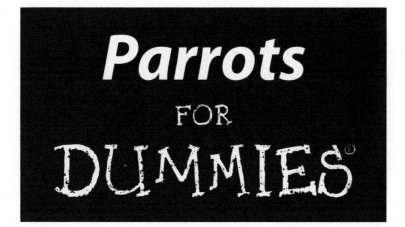

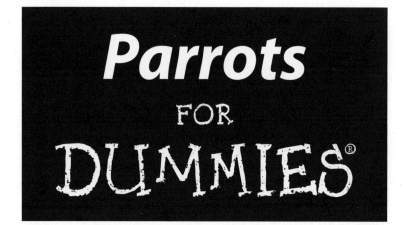

by Nikki Moustaki

Wiley Publishing, Inc.

Parrots For Dummies®

Published by
Wiley Publishing, Inc.
111 River St.
Hoboken, NJ 07030-5774
www.wiley.com

WILEY

About the Author

Avian Care and Behavior Consultant, **Nikki Moustaki,** M.A., M.F.A., is the author of 14 books on bird care and behavior, including *Parakeets For Dummies* and *Finches For Dummies*. In her practice as an avian consultant, she works with clients to heal the strained relationships between themselves and their feathered friends. Nikki writes for several magazines, including *Bird Talk* magazine and *Pet Product News*. She is the host of www.goodbird.com and regularly gives educational talks to bird clubs and societies. Nikki is also on the board of directors of the Shyne Foundation, a nonprofit free flight avian sanctuary (www.shynefoundation.org).

Nikki has been involved with birds since 1988, when she became very active in several bird clubs and began breeding and showing birds. She had several dozens of parrots at that time, many of them rescues, as her hobby grew. She worked in pet shops for seven years and eventually went on to manage an all-bird shop. These many years spent working in pet shops, breeding birds, and traveling to bird shows gave her unique insight into the various issues that people encounter with their avian companions. Aside from reading everything she could find about birds over the years, she acquired a variety of birdy mentors, including veterinarians, breeders, and rescuers, and received invaluable hands-on experience through them as well as through her own birds.

Nikki has kept lovebirds, cockatiels, budgies (parakeets), lories, macaws, Amazons, conures, Brotergeris, poicephalus, finches, and canaries. She became aware of the bird overpopulation problem around 1993, stopped breeding birds, and began helping in rescue efforts. Today, Nikki lives with various animals, including an African Grey parrot and a Meyer's parrot, as well as two schnauzers and a miniature poodle. She splits her time between New York City and South Florida.

Dedication

This book is dedicated to the loving memory of my grandfather, Soli B. Moustaki, who loved birds and who gave me my very first pair of parakeets when I was a little girl.

Author's Acknowledgments

Thank you to all of the people who have helped make this book a solid and informative piece of avian literature: Corbin Collins for his wonderful editing and snarky sense of humor; Tracy Boggier for signing it up and for being the cool chick that she is; Dr. Greg Burkett, D.V.M., for his invaluable advice (www.birdieboutique.com); Carolyn Swicegood for her cyber-friendship and her knowledge about avian nutrition and other great stuff (www.landofvos.com); Bob and Liz Johnson for being spectacular birdy mentors (www.shyne foundation.org); Dr. Irene Pepperberg for reading the intelligence chapter (www.alexfoundation.org); and to all of my friends who supported me throughout the writing of this book.

A huge thank you to all of the people who contributed their photos to this book. It couldn't have happened without you. A special thanks to Vicki Johnson and her caiques for going the extra mile to make sure I had all of the photos I needed. Thanks to Bridget Morrison for being there through thick and thin. Last but not least, thanks to all of the birds that have come through my life and taught me so much.

Publisher's Acknowledgments

We're proud of this book; please send us your comments through our Dummies online registration form located at www.dummies.com/register/.

Some of the people who helped bring this book to market include the following:

Acquisitions, Editorial, and Media Development

Editor: Corbin Collins

Acquisitions Editor: Tracy Boggier

Editorial Program Assistant: Courtney Allen

Technical Editor: Becky Margison

Editorial Manager: Michelle Hacker

Editorial Supervisor: Carmen Krikorian

Editorial Assistants: Hanna Scott, Nadine Bell

Cover Photos: © Martial Colomb/Getty Images/ Photodisc Green

Cartoons: Rich Tennant (www.the5thwave.com)

Composition Services

Project Coordinator: Maridee Ennis

Layout and Graphics: Carl Byers, Andrea Dahl, Joyce Haughey, Stephanie D. Jumper, Barry Offringa, Melanee Prendergast

Proofreaders: Jessica Kramer, Carl William Pierce, Aptara

Indexer: Aptara

Publishing and Editorial for Consumer Dummies

Diane Graves Steele, Vice President and Publisher, Consumer Dummies

Joyce Pepple, Acquisitions Director, Consumer Dummies

Kristin A. Cocks, Product Development Director, Consumer Dummies

Michael Spring, Vice President and Publisher, Travel

Kelly Regan, Editorial Director, Travel

Kathleen Nebenhaus, Vice President and Executive Publisher, Consumer Dummies, Lifestyles, Pets, Education

Publishing for Technology Dummies

Andy Cummings, Vice President and Publisher, Dummies Technology/General User

Composition Services

Gerry Fahey, Vice President of Production Services

Debbie Stailey, Director of Composition Services

Contents at a Glance

Table of Contents

Introduction

Welcome to *Parrots For Dummies,* a detailed guide to parrothood. Get ready to dive into the wonderful world of parrots . . . and the not-so-wonderful world of parrots. Though a parrot may seem like the "perfect pet," by the time you get done with this book you'll see that it isn't even a *pet* at all, but a wild companion to be respected, catered to, and cared for with extreme attention to detail. I know, that might sound over-the-top now, but keep reading, and I promise you that you'll understand what I mean.

About This Book

Every sentence in this book was written with the human/parrot relationship in mind. There's some info here about parrots in the wild, which is indirectly useful in your day-to-day relations with the parrot in your home.

Parrot care and behavior can be baffling. Most of it is counterintuitive — human intuition doesn't work well with parrots. You have to learn what they need and want, because recognizing those things aren't in your natural hard-wiring. You're programmed to read subtle cues in other humans and even in some other mammals — not so with parrots. But when you live with parrots long enough, and you take the time to understand them, your human intuition shifts, and you begin to think using *their* modes and standards.

Getting inside the mind of your parrot is important. It's not going to happen the other way around.

So by now you probably want to know about my qualifications. I have had parrots nearly all of my life (for *all* of my adult life), having bred them, rescued them, gone though just about every avian illness and injury with them, tamed and trained them, and lived with them as companions and friends. I worked in pet shops for most of my teens and early twenties, and managed an all-bird shop for a while. I learned a lot in those years, dealing with just about every species you can mention, and my personal flock grew as I took in many homeless parrots.

I became heavily involved in large and small bird clubs in my area and even wrote a newsletter for one of them for a couple of years. I had wonderful "birdy mentors" in those days, people who had been involved with birds for decades. I kept myself in the birdy loop, reading everything I could on the topic (and still do). My whole life was birds. Eventually, I became the birdy mentor too, and started my avian behavior and care consulting practice with my site, www.goodbird.com.

I write for national bird magazines and speak at bird clubs and shows, and I've written many other bird care books as well. I also train dogs and have many dog clients, which has actually helped me a lot in my bird practice through employing new techniques and learning models. I offer you a lot of birdy experience in this book, and I'm hoping to help you learn from my own mistakes and successes, as well as those of others. Most important, I'm interested in helping your parrots live happier and healthier lives. The information in this book will definitely do that if you apply it.

Conventions Used in This Book

I use *he, she,* and *it* interchangeably in this book when referring to parrots. I didn't want to settle on one pronoun, because all three are commonly used in the parrot community. In general, people usually assign a gender to their parrot when they first get it, usually starting with a name, and then they use the appropriate pronoun. This can backfire, however. Case in point is my African grey parrot, Hope, who turned out be male after I confirmed his gender with a DNA test. I mention this particular bird quite a bit in this book because he's my constant companion.

Foolish Assumptions

I wrote this book assuming that you're considering getting a parrot and that you're doing your birdy homework. I also wrote it for readers who already have a parrot and are looking for all the basic information to get started. This book will help both kinds of readers. It will also get you into some sophisticated methods of parrot care, taming, and training. Even intermediate and experienced parrot guardians will be able to take valuable tips and information from this book. So whether you're parrotless for the moment or you've got a whole flock, this book is for you.

Icons Used in This Book

Every *For Dummies* book has pictures in the margins called *icons* that helps you navigate the text of this book, and this one is no different. Here's the lowdown on what each icon means:

Gives you practical information that you can put into practice right away.

This icon is the most important one. It tips you off to dangers to your parrot's health and safety. Please heed these warnings.

Here's where I repeat important information, generally for clarification. This is good info to tuck away as you become more involved with your parrot.

How This Book Is Organized

Before you get started reading the meat and potatoes of this book, I want to let you know a little bit about how I've organized it. First, as with every *For Dummies* book, Chapter 1 is an overview of what you'll find in other chapters. The rest of Part I is geared toward helping you find the right species of parrot for you and then helps you figure out where to get the bird.

After that, Part II covers parrot housing and general care. Parts II and IV include important chapters that will help you keep your parrot alive and happy, and clue you into their behaviors. Then comes the taming and training in Part V, as well as a little bit of info on breeding and showing. Finally, in Part VI you'll find a few lists of ten important aspects of parrot care.

Following is a little more detail on each part in this book.

Part 1: Your Wild Child: Introducing the Parrot

Here you'll find information on many of the popular parrot species, including tips on how to choose the best feathered pal for you. From the tiny parrotlet to the giant macaws, you've got a lot to choose from. You'll also find a chapter on where and how to purchase or adopt your bird.

Part II: Bringing Home Your New Parrot

This is where I start getting into the practical nitty-gritty of sharing your home with a parrot. You'll find all the information you need on proper parrot housing and accessories. Bringing a parrot home is an exciting day if you're prepared for it, and you'll find a lot of good information here that shows you how to parrot-proof your home, as well as where to place the cage and how to properly interact with your parrot from day one.

Part III: Caring for Your Parrot

Possibly the most important chapters are contained in this part. Parrot nutrition is a controversial topic and certainly makes the difference between a healthy bird and a dead one. Hence, Chapter 8 may be the most essential chapter in this entire book. After that, you'll find chapters on grooming and on health and illness.

Part IV: Parrot Behavior Made Simple

Well, parrot behavior isn't simple, but these chapters attempt to explain why parrots do the funny and odd things that tend to baffle guardians. You'll get info on both normal and abnormal companion parrot behaviors, as well as advice for living in a multiple-parrot household.

Part V: Taming, Training, and Beyond

In this part, you'll find information on taming and training, and these may be the first chapters many people turn to when they get this book. After that, there's a chapter on breeding and a chapter on showing your birds in bird shows.

Part VI: The Part of Tens

The Part of Tens is found in every _For Dummies_ book. Here, three chapters give you tips on travel, advice on entertaining your parrot, and ten important things that your parrot should know.

Where to Go from Here

Chapter 1 is a good place to begin if you want to get a solid overview of the rest of the book so that you know what to look for as you read. If you want to dive right into things, start with Chapter 2. If you're looking for something in particular, the table of contents is a quick reference to a basic section. For a much more thorough reference, check out the index.

Part I
Your Wild Child: Introducing the Parrot

The 5th Wave   By Rich Tennant

"Honey! I told you to watch the bird.
This breed of parrot tend to be
real talkers."

In this part . . .

Welcome to parrothood! You're flying with the big birds now. Yes, there's a lot to know about parrots and a lot to do to keep one happy and healthy in your home. This part takes you through some of the toughest choices you'll make in parrothood. Chapter 1 gives you an overview of the essentials of what it's like to live with a parrot and points you to other places in the book where you can find more information. Chapter 2 details everything you can expect from parrot guardianship. Chapter 3 gives you a nice snapshot of some of the more popular parrot species, and Chapter 4 helps you find the best parrot possible.

Chapter 1

Meet the Parrots

*W*elcome to the wonderful world of parrots. Okay, it may be wonderful, but it's not utopia. There's a lot to know and a lot to do in order to make a parrot happy and keep it healthy in the average home. This chapter gives you an overview of this entire book and shows you where to look for the important information you'll need to get started with parrots.

An Introduction to Parrots

If parrots were human, they'd be supermodels. They'd want their spring water and their carrot sticks, and they'd want them *now*. Parrots are beautiful, temperamental creatures that need a lot of handling from a good manager — that's you, the parrot's guardian — to make sure they're treated right (Figure 1-1). It's in the fine print of the parrot's contract: You will do the bird's bidding, and you won't ask any questions.

Well, doing the bird's bidding sounds a little un-fun, doesn't it? I don't mean that you're the bird's servant, though it can sometimes feel that way. What I mean is that parrots have a lot of requirements that need to be met *or else*. The *or else* means high veterinary bills, a very unhappy parrot, and perhaps even a dead bird. The *or else* isn't a place you want to go.

You have to feed the parrot right, house it right, and give it your full and total attention. You have to provide it with toys, friends, things to do, health care, and everything else it needs. It's a complicated companion, far more so than a dog or cat. If you read this book cover to cover, you'll have a great handle on how to properly care for your bird.

From pet to companion

The first and most important thing to know about parrots is that they're not like other pets. They're *companions.* And you're not the owner. You're the *guardian.* This is the vocabulary I use throughout this book. The language you use to describe other people is how you perceive and relate to them, and the same goes for the language you use to describe the animals in your life. You can find out more about this in Chapter 2.

A little bit of wilderness

Having a parrot in your home is like bringing a little bit of the rainforest, grasslands, or plains inside. A parrot is a wild animal and always will be, no matter where it lives. When you live with a parrot, you have the unique responsibility of caring for a truly natural creature, one that hasn't been domesticated in any way. Captive parrots and wild parrots share the exact same instincts. See Chapter 11 for more details on how instincts inform your parrot's behavior.

Some parrots are indeed easier to care for than others. Which parrot you choose should depends on how much space and time you have. There's never really enough time in the day to give a larger parrot the attention it wants. Smaller parrots, such as parakeets and lovebirds, are often kept happily in pairs, which is a great option. Large parrots love each other's company as well. Since parrots are social, flock-oriented animals, they like to be together. Chapter 3 gives you the lowdown on which parrot species might be right for you (Figure 1-2). Chapter 4 shows you how to choose a healthy parrot from the right kind of place.

Figure 1-1:
These tame budgies are wonderful companions and are as close to officially domesticated as parrots get.

Photo by Priscilla Scmidt

Figure 1-2:
Parrots have some funny behaviors, like this caique eating a big cookie with one foot.

Photo by Shari Markowitz

Home Tweet Home

The average home must be modified to accommodate a parrot, whether it's a little budgie or a large macaw. You've got to parrot-proof your home the way you'd kid-proof it for toddlers. Parrots can get into even more trouble than toddlers, because not only can a parrot open the cupboard under the sink, but it can also get up to the cupboard above the refrigerator. It can eat through drywall, pick at the chipping paint near the window, and dunk itself in the toilet. It can get outside and never come back again. Parrot-proofing is crucial. See Chapter 7 for parrot-proofing ideas.

Making birdy comfortable

After you've parrot-proofed, you've got to find acceptable housing for your bird. In parrot circles, the idiom *bigger is better* is applied to bird cages, aviaries, and habitats. Birds are meant to fly, so it's great if you can offer a safe flying space. Flying is essential for healthy respiratory, muscular, and skeletal systems.

Where you place the bird's housing is also crucial. Parrots like a secure spot close to a wall, out of drafts, and in a room where there's a lot of traffic. It's a lonely and miserable bird that's relegated to the garage or a back room. Chapter 5 gives you lots of housing do's and don'ts.

Parrot paraphernalia

Once you've decided on housing, you need a lot of parrot paraphernalia. Fortunately, manufacturers of birdy stuff have gotten incredibly creative over the years, and there's a cornucopia of parrot accessories out there that will make your bird more comfortable, give him things to do, and perhaps even save his life. Check out Chapter 6 for your parrot shopping guide.

Parrot Care 101

There's a lot more to know about parrot care than tossing some seed and water into a cage and hoping for the best. Those days are over (thankfully). Much research has been done on parrot health and nutrition in the last couple of decades, bringing parrot people to a new level of awareness and allowing parrots to live longer, healthier lives. Though some species of parrots are long-lived, some with a lifespan of more than 80 years, most don't even make it past a decade. The information throughout this book shows you how to ensure that your parrot lives out its full lifespan. Most people think that budgies (parakeets) only live a few years. With the proper care, budgies can actually live to be well over 15.

Health care

Parrots are complex organisms that have very different systems than humans do. Things that don't bother humans at all can kill a bird instantly. For example, the fumes from nonstick cookware, avocadoes, and aerosol sprays are deadly for birds. But by far the most deadly thing for birds is lack of proper health care. Getting your parrot to a certified avian veterinarian is crucial to keeping it healthy and alive. Check out Chapter 10 for more information on illness. While you're at it, don't skip over Chapter 9: grooming.

Nutrition

By far the deadliest thing for most parrots is poor nutrition. A parrot that's suffering from vitamin and mineral deficiency has a weakened immune system and is susceptible to many diseases and ailments, not to mention behavioral problems. Read Chapter 8 for a lot of good tips on proper parrot nutrition.

Parrot Behavior

It's too bad parrots don't come with owner's manuals — well, until now. You've got a great one in your hand. But as with just about everything, you're going to learn about parrot behavior by trial and error. If your parrot bites you, hopefully you'll figure out what caused the bite and won't repeat the events leading up to the incident. Chapter 11 gives you some insight into wild parrot behavior and why your "wild child" behaves the way it does.

Normal behaviors

Some behaviors that seem really odd **are actually** quite normal. You can't try to understand parrots by using human intuition. It's very easy to anthropomorphize parrots, giving them human qualities. They definitely do some things that seem quite human. But for the most part, the things they do are all part of a complex communication that's really designed for other parrots. From body language to vocalization, your parrot's behaviors all mean something. The key is to get inside that feathered head and figure out what the parrot is trying to tell you. Check out Chapter 12 for more on normal parrot behavior, body language, and vocalization. Chapter 15 is all about parrot intelligence and will help you understand your feathered pal as well.

The parrot monster

Some of the behaviors that are normal for parrots can be annoying or baffling to their human guardians — screaming, plucking, biting, beak banging — it's enough to make a human guardian pull her own hair out. Because parrots aren't really meant to be kept inside a home, they can come up with some terrible behaviors due to frustration and loneliness. Chapter 14 fills you in on how to handle birds gone wild and gives you options for getting help.

Parrot Pals

Most people want a tame, hands-on parrot companion. Some people do have *watching only* birds, generally the smaller parrots, but when it comes to the medium to large parrots, it seems that guardians are really looking for a friend. That's great, actually, because parrots bond well to gentle, kind humans who have their best interest at heart and behave accordingly. But remember, the road to hell is paved with good intentions. You can't just *intend* to do right by your parrot — you actually have to walk the walk.

Making friends with your parrot

Check out Chapter 16 for advice and step-by-step tips on taming and training that will help you make good friends with your parrot and help you have the correct expectations. Most relationships go bad when expectations exceed actuality. In a parrot/human relationship, it's usually the parrot that loses, which is pretty tragic for him. This chapter helps you learn to create trust and a lasting bond with your bird.

And baby makes three

Breeding parrots is not a great idea, for a variety of good reasons. First, there are way too many homeless parrots already, most in shelters or sanctuaries that are full to capacity. Second, breeding birds is a risky business — your veterinary bills will far exceed any money you make, and you put your parent birds in danger of illness and death, not to mention how delicate the babies are. And finally, the endeavor is one of the most time-consuming things you'll ever undertake.

That said, some of the smaller birds — such as budgies, lovebirds, and cockatiels — have a healthy following of hobbyists who do breed them for show (Figure 1-3). If you're interested in this, or you just want to find out how your parrot came to be, check out Chapter 17.

Figure 1-3:
Baby parrots are cute, but breeding them is best left to people who are experienced. Also, there's a shortage of good homes for parrots, so check out a local parrot rescue organization before you breed your birds.

Photo by Mary Jo Yarberry

A Caveat to the Wise

Hundreds of books about parrot care and behavior are on the market, and there are hundreds of Web sites. Everyone has a slightly different way of doing things and a slightly different parrot philosophy. There are different parrot *camps,* each with its own intense convictions. I try my best here to offer you a variety of viewpoints. Mainly, I focus on what has worked for me all these years working with parrots, both my own and those of my clients in my care and behavior practice.

You're not going to find absolutely *everything* you need to know about parrots in this book. This book is a great primer to get you started on the right foot, and even intermediate and advanced parrot people will find some valuable information here. In any case, you're going to run into situations that you may not know how to handle, and perhaps you'll remember something from this book that will help you deal with the problem or at least point you to a good reference where you can get some help.

Chapter 2

Expectations of a Companion Parrot

*T*he reason this chapter is not called "Expectations *from* a Companion Parrot" is because it's your job as the human to make your parrot's life great, not the other way around. I'd like people to be far more interested in what the parrot wants out of life than what the humans want from the parrot.

Yes, parrots do add a lot to their humans' lives — friendship, music, color, company, love — and though I don't want you to think of the relationship as one-sided, I do want to stress that the one with the opposable thumbs is pretty much accountable for the one with the feathers. This chapter discusses what your parrot expects from you and why those things are important to having a good relationship with your avian friend.

Defining a Companion Parrot

Parrots in the wild are *wild parrots,* and parrots living in a home are *companion parrots.* The problem with this definition is that all parrots, no matter where they live, are still wild and have the same needs, whether in a rainforest or a living room. So the definition needs to go a little further.

Parrots are not cows. Bear with me for a moment. Somewhere around 9000 B.C., people realized that they could get more from wild cows than just meat and began milking them. Eventually, through selective breeding, the cow became what it is today — a docile creature that man uses for meat, milk, and leather. There are over 1,000 different breeds of cattle. Some produce a lot of milk, and some are very lean, which lends a certain quality to the meat. This process is called *domestication*. The same was done with dogs, which is why the Chinese Pug and the German Shepherd look and behave so differently. Other animals — such as horses, cats, sheep, and pigs — have also gone through the domestication process.

The process of domestication, which takes many years, has not been done with parrots. They don't really "help" mankind the way cows and dogs do, so not a lot of effort has been put into making parrot species into breeds. The closest thing to a domesticated parrot is the English budgie. This large version of the native Australian budgie isn't found in the wild. It was bred to be large and have certain features. A budgie society in England sometime in the early 20th Century decided that being big was an asset, and so they bred big budgies to other big budgies, and eventually the English budgie became its own breed. Like the dog, it's different just because people encouraged it to be that way through breeding practices.

That exception aside, parrots aren't domesticated. They still have all their wild instincts intact. They don't rely on people for survival unless they're kept in captivity and have no choice. This is the companion parrot. Put this way, it sounds kind of sad, doesn't it? In a sense, it *is* sad. It's about as sad as keeping a whale in a backyard swimming pool. Sure, someone could feed the whale, clean the water, and love the animal, but it's still a wild animal with wild-animal needs, and its life isn't really going to be complete and healthy.

I'm not trying to make you feel guilty here. Remember, I've got parrots in my home too. I love them and feed them and clean their housing. But do they have everything they'd have in the wild? Nope. Not even close. It doesn't make me a bad parrot guardian — it just makes me . . . well, a parrot guardian. That's the situation companion parrots have been given. It's just too bad for them that they're so beautiful and intelligent. If they weren't, most people wouldn't want to have them, and they'd probably be better off. Check out Figure 2-1 to see a wild parrot in its element.

Figure 2-1:
This wild, green-winged macaw not only enjoys flying — it also *needs* to fly for survival. Flying is the healthiest activity for parrots.

Just Being Themselves

That said, there are some lovely ways to keep parrots that allow them to be themselves and get more of what they need in captivity. In the past few decades, zoos around the world have been exchanging their philosophy of small cages for natural habitats. It is clearly far better for any captive animal to have as much "wilderness" as possible. For parrots, this includes a safe place to fly.

The Shyne Foundation (of which I am a board member) is a parrot sanctuary in South Florida that illustrates what the average person can do to create a natural setting for parrots. You don't have to be a zoo to allow your birds to feel some measure of freedom. Bob and Liz Johnson, the founders and care-takers of the Shyne Foundation, have built a ¾-acre enclosed "rainforest" where 150 parrots, mostly rescues, can fly and cavort all day, rain or shine (see Figure 2-2).

"Someday, in a more enlightened age, the practice of confining any bird to a life limited to the synthetic environment of a cage will be viewed as morally and ethically unthinkable," says Liz Johnson, who believes that anyone can build a habitat for their birds, even in an apartment. Indeed, there is a new wave of thinking regarding parrots, how they're kept, and how people relate to them. I talk more about the Shyne Foundation and free flight in Chapter 12.

Before you throw up your hands and toss this book into your parrot's cage for use as a shredding toy, let me say that I have cages for my parrots. I am also an advocate for free flight and habitats. I'm realistic in that not everyone is going to create a habitat for their parrots, though it would be great if everyone could. And I'm not going to tell you not to get a parrot unless you can build one, because most people reading this book probably already have a parrot, if not several, as I do. I have a responsibility to tell you how to properly use both options. You'll find more about parrot housing in Chapter 5.

Figure 2-2: The parrots at the Shyne Foundation enjoy free flight, the weather, and one another.

Photo by Bob and Liz Johnson

The Joys of Parrot Guardianship

Whew! Now that we've gotten some of that heavy stuff out of the way, here's the good stuff: the joys of living with a parrot. There are some wonderful aspects to living with parrots. They are good companions, but they are nothing like dogs and cats. They don't have a pack hierarchy, as do dogs, and they don't consider themselves rulers of all they see, as do most cats.

Most parrots expect to be treated as equals. They don't like to be talked down to or shoved aside as just another thing in the house. That attitude is part of the joy of having a parrot in your home. You can truly be friends with a parrot. Here are some things that a parrot offers you:

- ✔ Parrots are relatively long-lived, depending on the species.
- ✔ Parrots offer some joyful noise to a household. Well, joyful to certain ears, in any case.
- ✔ Parrots talk. Depending on the species, you can carry on a simple conversation, even one based on clicks and whistles.
- ✔ Parrots are intelligent, allowing you to really have a friendly relationship based on being equals, not on a hierarchy.

Considerations before Buying

Becoming a friend to your parrot isn't difficult if you take its needs and its psychology into consideration. You can't expect the bird to do this for *you,* so you've got get into parrot mode to come to a mutual understanding. The workings of your parrot's birdy brains are different than yours. As predators, humans have reactions to certain stimuli that are much different than those of prey animals, such as birds, and so communicating with birds isn't intuitive. Most of the time it's counterintuitive, in fact, which means that you have to learn how to do it because the behavior doesn't come to you naturally. I talk more about this in Chapter 11. For the moment, this section discusses some things that make a regular human into a spectacular birdy pal.

Who's gettin' the parrot?

The first consideration before even thinking about getting a parrot is: Who's going to take full responsibility for its nutrition, veterinary care, housing, basic care, and attention? A parrot of any size shouldn't be bought on a whim. You have to really consider whether you're the right person for the particular bird. Do your homework, and look at the personality traits of each species.

For example, take two birds of relatively similar size: a sun conure and a caique. The conure is persistently noisier, and the caique is beakier (uses its beak to test out the world, which would include your fingers). They are both equally beautiful. Which one you'd choose has everything to do with what you can handle as a guardian.

Why a parrot?

Just because a parrot is easy to shove inside a cage and close the door on doesn't mean it's an easy companion. Sure, it doesn't need to be walked, but a parrot's care is actually a whole lot more complex than a dog's care. Speaking as someone who lives with, trains, and writes a lot about dogs, I can vouch for that. In the time it takes to make the food for the parrots every morning, I could walk the dogs, give both of them a bath, and play a hardy game of fetch. As it stands, the dogs just hang around in the kitchen waiting for some of the parrots' food to fall as I make it. Please see Chapter 8 for more information on feeding your parrot properly.

If you're getting a parrot because you can't have a cat or dog, please reconsider. A bird isn't a substitute companion. But if you really want a parrot, and you know that you can deal with whatever comes up in the relationship and that you can offer proper care, then you're on your way.

The parrot's personality

Parrots aren't hatched to be *sweet.* They are hatched with a full set of instincts that tell them to flee from predators and danger and to fight back if attacked. It's amazing, then, that they can adapt to the average human home. Just about everything humans do to parrots can be seen as threatening to a prey animal. Yet they accept people voluntarily if treated well and even come to think of some guardians as mates. As far as I know, marriages between human and parrot aren't legal yet, but don't tell that to the parrot in love.

But parrots require a lot of attention to remain as sweet as they are as babies. The wild-child part of a parrot's personality does emerge if the bird is neglected. Some parrots — lovebirds, for example — will revert (become mean and wild) if left alone for only a couple of weeks, and even the bite from a small parrot such as a lovebird can be nasty.

The reason why parrot sanctuaries are overflowing with birds is because parrot personalities can change, sometimes drastically and sometimes overnight. Hormones kick in, someone or something frightens the bird, or the bird is just a "little" neglected for just a "little" too long, and before you know it you've got a monster on your hands.

When the biting starts, guardians usually become afraid of the parrot. The more afraid they are, the less trust the parrot has in them, and the parrot becomes fearful, which can show itself either as aggression or fleeing behavior. The parrot gets neglected even more and may begin screaming and plucking.

At that point, many guardians decide to relegate the parrot to the basement or back room, give it away, or get it a mate, hoping that will help. The parrot gets shuffled from home to home, or it may land in a sanctuary. What could have been a great relationship wasn't even given a chance. And it's certainly not the parrot's fault. So just know what you're getting into with a parrot. The bottom line is this: If you meet *all* of the parrot's needs possible in captivity, its personality should be pretty constant (with the exception of breeding season, which I discuss in Chapter 17).

The parrot's home

If you don't have room for very large housing for a very large parrot, don't get one. Size down to what you do have room for. If you really want a macaw, but you don't have a lot of space, consider a mini-macaw or an even smaller bird. A small bird in the largest space you can provide will be a lot happier than a large bird in the same area.

Parrots are birds that are created to know only boundless space.

Going on vacation

Who's going to take care of the parrot when you're away? It's not like a cat or dog. Most pet sitters are used to cats and dogs and hamsters and the like. Birds don't show their illnesses until it's too late for someone unfamiliar with the bird to notice — usually, the bird is belly up in the cage by the time a pet sitter figures out that something's wrong. You, as the bird's guardian, will notice small changes in behavior or eating patterns that can indicate illness. You'll also be able to detect changes in feather quality and in the droppings. Someone else watching the bird may not.

Of course, you can always take the parrot with you. I give you some good travel tips in Chapter 21.

Parrot lifespan

Some smaller parrots, such as parakeets and lovebirds, live about 15 years with proper care. The medium-sized parrots tend to live 20 to 30 years or more. Greys are said to live about 50 years, and Amazons, more than 70. The larger birds, such as the large macaws and the cockatoos, have been known to live over 80 years. One blue and gold macaw named Charlie, once owned by Winston Churchill (who taught the bird some choice language that will not be repeated here), is said to be 104 years old.

Where will you be when your parrot is 15, 20, 50, or more? For a larger parrot, you're going to have to consider who's going to care for the bird when you can't anymore. Leaving a legal trust for parrots is becoming popular these days. You'll have to see a lawyer to draw up the necessary paperwork, and you'll have to designate a trustee — someone who knows and loves your bird — as well as a sum of money for the trustee to receive for caring for your bird. That's one other expense to think about when you're tallying up your *parrot total*.

Allergies

Before you get a parrot, make sure that no one in the household is allergic. Some parrots — like cockatoos, cockatiels, and African greys — emit copious "feather dust," which can trigger allergies in some people. However, these aren't the only birds that cause allergies.

If you are allergic, placing a Hepa filter near your parrot's housing can help, as can misting the parrot every other day or so with clean, warm water. Don't use an "ionic" filter near your bird, however, because these can cause respiratory problems (the same goes for humans).

Costs of parrot ownership

Speaking of the parrot total, parrots aren't cheep . . . er, cheap. After the cost of the parrot itself, housing is the next most expensive proposition on the list and can be more costly than the parrot. Here are some basic costs:

- **Parrot:** $15 to $30,000
- **Housing:** $150 to $3,000 to sky's the limit
- **Accessories:** Toys, perches, and so on can run $30 to $250 or more
- **Food:** $25 to $75 monthly — more if you buy organic
- **Supplements:** $50 to $150 monthly
- **Veterinary care:** $200 to $1,000 or more per year
- **Time off work to spend with your parrot:** Priceless

Responsibilities of parrot guardianship

There's no such thing as a low-maintenance parrot. That's what a lot of people ask for when they walk into a pet shop: "Which one is easy to take care of?" Well, I will admit that it's easier to take care of a pair of birds who love each other — for example, male and female parakeets, lovebirds, parrot-lets, cockatiels, and others (the small and small/medium birds). If these birds have the proper spacious housing and care, they don't need any human inter-action other than feeding, cleaning, and veterinary care. As for a "family parrot," the low-maintenance idea is out.

The sad fact is that many parrots, from the little parakeet to the large cocka-too, get shuffled to another home about every two to five years. Even sadder is that most parrots don't live even half of their lifespan. It's not so much that parrot parents are lazy about proper care; it's more that information about proper avian nutrition and medicine is just now getting to the general public. Birdkeepers have known for many years that you can't just feed parrots seed and water and expect them to thrive.

Even so, the majority of food seen in pet shops is still seed or seed based, but that's changing. As an alternative, manufacturers began to make *pellets,* claiming that they're a whole diet for birds, the way kibble is a whole diet for dogs. Neither an all-seed nor all-pellet diets is truly *whole.* Fortunately, people who have had birds a long time have come up with pretty good dietary regimens for parrots, though nothing's perfect. The "right" diet for a parrot takes a lot of effort — buying a multitude of the correct kinds of items, chopping, cooking, peeling, and so on. I talk more about diet in Chapter 8.

Time matters

Timewise, think dog, cat, hamster, turtle, and fish tank *combined.* Yes, creat-ing the proper diet takes time, as does cleaning, but more time goes, or should go, into interacting with the parrot — the fun stuff. The more time you can spend with your bird, the better. Even just being in the same room and watching television is good time spent.

You cannot expect to spend half an hour in the morning and half an hour at night with a parrot and expect it to be happy and thrive. That's when behav-ior problems arise. Parrots can also become ill due to neglect. The immune system becomes compromised because the bird is stressed. Remember, par-rots aren't used to being alone all the time.

Mess and more mess

There's no such thing as a nonmessy bird. There are only degrees of mess. Small birds will make smaller messes, and large birds make larger messes. Get ready for some heavy-duty cleaning. If you're not into having food all over the floor and walls, and can't deal with some poop here and there, then reconsider getting a parrot. Poop happens.

Noise (Sorry, I can't hear over my screaming parrot)

As with mess, noise comes in degrees. The smaller the parrot, the smaller the noise; the larger the parrot, the louder the noise, as with the blue and gold macaw in Figure 2-3. But this doesn't mean that small parrots aren't noisy — what they might lack in decibels, they make up for in persistence. All parrots make noise. Some just make less annoying noise.

Whether the noise bothers you depends largely on your own ears. Most parrot parents get so used to their parrot's noises that they don't even hear the bird anymore. People come over to my house and ask, "What did he just say?" when my African grey talks. I'm always surprised. "Oh, did he just say something?" I don't even hear him a lot of the time because I'm used to tuning him out. Well, certain noises I *always* hear, unfortunately, such as his version of police and fire-truck sirens, garbage trucks backing up, and a multitude of car alarms (can you tell that he's a New York City bird ?).

Figure 2-3:
When humans truly understand and respect parrots, a positive relationship often results.

Photo by Nikki Moustaki

What a Companion Parrot Expects

Okay, now we're down to the nitty-gritty of this chapter: what your parrot expects from you. As if all of the above isn't enough, there's more. Fortunately, this is all stuff that you probably already have, especially if you already live with a parrot.

Tolerance

Only the most tolerant of people will be able to coexist with a parrot, especially a medium to large parrot. Not only is there noise and mess, but there's also the occasional bite to field, mischief to handle, and fussiness to contend with. And you have to take it all in stride.

Empathy

Realize that a parrot isn't really meant to live in a home, though he can be quite happy if cared for properly. Don't get angry if your bird is demanding. He's just acting like a bird. Try to empathize. Imagine what it's like to be that parrot. Is he locked in a cage a lot of the day? Does he have the right things to eat? Does he have enough to play with? Try to look at life through his eyes.

Sense of humor

If you can't laugh, you'll end up crying. Parrots do all kinds of chaotic things, such as chew the piano legs, make holes in walls, and poop on your taxes. Turn your back for an instant, and you never know what your bird is getting into. But remember, *it's not your bird's fault*. It's yours. So have a laugh at the things your bird does. Parrots can be quite humbling.

Attentiveness

An attentive parrot guardian knows his or her parrot so well, it's obvious when there are any changes, either physical and behavioral. Once these signs become readily visible, it may be too late to help the bird. However, if you know your bird well, you'll know all of his little nuances.

Decisiveness and action

If you do happen to run into a birdy emergency, or you believe your parrot is ill, you can't sit around and wait for things to get better. A parrot needs a decisive guardian who will rush to the veterinarian when necessary.

Constant companionship

Parrots aren't fond of being alone and won't stand for neglect very long. Behavior problems result from loneliness, as do physical issues. If you have a lone parrot, or even a few parrots that all consider you their main squeeze, you'll have to set aside a considerable amount of time to interact and play.

A loyal friend

Above all, a parrot needs you to be a loyal friend who doesn't run at the first signs of trouble. Before you ditch the relationship for whatever reason, do yourself and your parrot a favor and consult an expert. Many good bird behaviorists and consultants are available to help you with issues that arise. No need to dump the bird, even if it seems like he might be dumping you. Behavior issues are often temporary or remedied with a simple plan of action.

Chapter 3

Choosing the Right Companion

Choosing the best species for you is the most important decision you'll make as a parrot guardian. Choose the wrong species, and you may wind up with an animal in your home that you don't like, don't want, are afraid of, don't have time for, and wish you had never gotten in the first place.

But how do you know which species is right for you? It's certainly not a matter of choosing the prettiest. I know you've heard this before, but it really is what's inside that counts. Many people end up with a beautiful parrot that they can't stand and eventually give away. This is because not all species are created equally. They all have their quirks, some of which are easier to deal with than others. This chapter helps you weigh your parrot options. For a bunch of great photos of different species, see the special color section of this book.

Considerations for Choosing a Species

Parrots are long-lived animals. Even a bird with a shorter lifespan, such as a budgie or a lovebird, can be a child's companion from kindergarten to college. Don't choose while standing in the pet store admiring that big macaw or a bouncy caique. Instead, consider the following when picking a parrot.

Parrots are individuals

I can tell you about general characteristics of different species, but there will always be individual parrots that don't fit. You can choose a parrot based on species, but you really have to spend a little time with an individual bird to know its habits, temperament, and companionability.

For example, Amazons are known to be feisty and aggressive, but some Amazons wouldn't bite a soul. African greys are known for their talking ability, though some don't talk much at all, preferring to whistle and mimic household sounds.

The chemistry between you

Not every person is going to get along with every parrot. You will find that you have a rapport with some parrots but not with others, even within the same species. The only way to find out if you have chemistry is to spend some time with several birds, the way you would with puppies — or other people, for that matter. There's more on what to look for in an individual parrot in Chapter 4.

Not all species are created equal

The reason why you can't just walk into the pet shop and choose the prettiest parrot is because each species has different needs and behaves in a unique manner. You have to know what you're getting into before you think about taking a bird home. For example:

- Poicephalus parrots like a dark area inside their housing where they can retreat from commotion.
- Amazons, conures, and macaws need a lot of chewing material, especially wood and paper.
- Cockatiels and budgies are lighter birds and need a more extensive wing clip than other birds (you'll find more about wing clipping in Chapter 9).
- Caiques tend to be beaky birds who use their hard beaks to explore the world, which can include a guardian's fingers.
- Cockatoos need lots of preening toys and rope toys.

Noise: deafening or extremely deafening

A big reason why some parrots get re-homed is noise. Parrots are demanding and can become quite vocal about their desires. They are also programmed to make a racket at sunup and sundown — and there's nothing you can do about that. What you can do is choose a parrot that isn't as offensive as some others.

Noise is directly proportional to the size of the parrot. The smaller the bird, the smaller the noise. This doesn't account for the amount of noise the bird creates, just the volume. The *volume* indicates loudness and tends to go up with the number of birds as well. The *amount* of noise indicates the time span in which noise is made — for example, some parrots only vocalize for a couple of hours a day, but others do it nearly all day long. One cockatiel's vocalizations are tolerable — a flock of them can be deafening because they're all competing with one another to be heard. But a racket is in the ear of the be-hearer, isn't it? One person's unbearable din is another person's sweet melody.

African species tend to be a little quieter than other birds, whereas South American species tend to be loud and raucous. For example, most poicephalus species aren't as persistently noisy or loud. Cockatoos, on the other hand, are ear-piercing and persistent, noise being one of the main reasons they are re-homed or given up to rescue organizations. Of course, this generalization changes with the number of birds housed together and the state in which they are kept. Unhappy birds may screech to get attention.

Space: bigger is better

All birds need space to move around — ideally, the space should be large enough to allow for flight. The long-tailed species — the keets, cockatiels, and macaws — need very large, tall housing, or their tails become ratty and they become unkempt in general.

You can't skimp on housing size for larger parrots. A cramped bird is very unhappy, and unhappy birds can develop some very nasty habits, such as screaming, biting, and feather plucking, to mention a few. Some parrot species are tiny, like the parrotlet and the lovebird, but even these need large housing to get the exercise they require.

Lifestyles of the neat and messy

All parrots are messy. They scatter seed, poop wherever they want, spray water all over the place when they bathe, shred paper, and can even destroy items in the house if allowed to roam. There are no species that are less messy than others. However, the smaller the bird, the easier it may be to contain mess. Birds known to be particularly messy include:

- ✔ **Eclectus:** This species is known for messy eating, spreading wet foods all over the walls and floor. Eclectus guardians often invest in a special acrylic cube where they offer wet foods.

- ✔ **Lories and lorikeets:** These are among the messiest of parrots. Because they eat soft and liquid food, they have soft and liquid waste, which they somehow manage to spray all over the outside of the cage. Twice-a-day cleaning, at least, is required.

- ✔ **Lovebirds:** These feisty parrots love to fling every seed out of the dish and onto the floor. They are also notorious for shredding paper.

> ✔ **Amazons:** These destructive birds will shred and chew just about any-thing, making them quite a handful to clean up after. Lots of supervision is required with many individuals.

From easily affordable to taking out a loan

The most inexpensive parrot is the American parakeet (budgie), from $7 to $14. The most expensive parrot commonly offered for sale is the hyacinth macaw — about $10,000 — and some of the rarer parrots cost even more. Somewhere in between are the rest, from the green Quaker parrot at between $100 and $200, to the Moluccan cockatoo at between $1,500 and $2,000. One thing is for sure: Parrots aren't *cheep.* Of course, prices change all the time depending on availability, as with anything else.

What are you prepared to spend for a parrot? Remember that no matter what you spend, the cost of veterinary and general care is the same. You're going to spend as much money caring for a $14 parakeet as you will for a $400 blue-mutation parrotlet.

Talking ability

Some parrots are well known for their talking ability, but others may never talk at all. Most will whistle or make other sounds common to your house-hold. You'll find more information on talking parrots in Chapter 16. The most famous chatterboxes include:

- ✔ Parakeets (budgies)
- ✔ African grey parrots
- ✔ Yellow-naped Amazons

Child-friendliness

There's one irrefutable rule in the bird world: If it has a beak, it can bite. Some individual parrots may never bite anyone; some will bite every time someone is unlucky enough to come near its beak. Though some species are less likely to bite than others, parents should realize that any parrot can give a child a good nip, which can be painful and scary to younger kids. Children may not understand that a bite isn't personal.

Species that may make good hands-on companions for children include:

✔ Budgies (parakeets)

✔ English budgies

✔ Cockatiels

✔ Pionus

✔ Rosellas

✔ Bourke's

✔ Pyrrhura conures

Though it seems logical that smaller birds would be more suitable for children, some small birds are actually pretty feisty and can be too nippy or temperamental for younger kids to handle. These include:

✔ Lovebirds

✔ Parrotlets

✔ Lories

✔ Caiques

Of course, you can always have a male/female pair of parrots for a child to care for — but not handle. Budgies (parakeets) and lovebirds are especially suitable if they're a compatible pair. They are colorful, chatty, enjoy each other's company, and can live upwards of 15 years if cared for properly.

One, two, or more

Some parrots enjoy each other's company, whereas others will fight to the death with their own species. There's no guarantee that buying two birds of the same species will result in fast friends. You may notice two parrots canoodling with each other in the same cage. This may be a *true pair,* a male and female who like each other. Same-sex birds can also bond and be good friends, and you won't have to worry about babies resulting from the pairing. Just be careful about how you introduce same-sex pairs (see Chapter 13 for more information on introductions).

The parrots most likely to get along, given enough space, are:

✔ Cockatiels

✔ Budgies

✔ Hanging parrots

✔ Conures

The parrots most likely to become aggressive and even kill each other in the wrong situation are:

- ✔ Cockatoos
- ✔ Caiques
- ✔ Lovebirds
- ✔ Some macaws
- ✔ Lories

If you want to house birds of different species together, buy two young parrots and raise them together, though you can't always be certain that they'll remain friends forever. You'll find more information about having more than one bird in Chapter 13.

Species Profiles

Here are profiles of the parrots most often kept as companions. Realize that there are always exceptions — some individuals will vary from the descriptions here. I have included the most common traits of each.

African grey parrots

African grey parrots are recognized in two distinct subspecies: the Congo African grey *(Psittacus erithacus erithacus)* and the Timneh African grey *(Psittacus erithacus timneh)*. The Congo African grey has a natural range wider than just the Congo, but it is the most common name for the red-tailed parrot of this species. Large Congos are sometimes incorrectly called Cameroons. Because the African grey's native range is so expansive, these birds tend to come in a variety of sizes and shades of grey, which can lead owners to believe that they have different subspecies. There is also *Psittacus erithacus princeps,* once thought a subspecies of the Congo, but that division is now considered false.

The Congo grey has prominently scalloped feathers, a black beak, and a tail that becomes scarlet at maturity. The Timneh is smaller, with a darker grey body and horn-colored beak, and its tail ranges in color from maroon to dark grey or black. Both parrots make similar companions, and one is not considered superior over the other.

The intelligence and sensitivity to outside influences of the African grey is unsurpassed among companion parrots, with the probable exception of the cockatoo. This sensitivity is part of the grey's charisma but can also lead to behavioral issues. Even a slight change in routine or environment can lead to plucking and fearfulness.

Not only do most African greys develop outstanding vocabularies, but they may even come to understand words in context. However, not all African greys learn to talk. Some learn a variety of other household sounds as well as specific whistles. These birds aren't loud and don't usually annoy sensitive neighbors. However, some individuals will learn some pretty loud and annoying sounds. For example, if you have a noisy cockatoo, the grey will learn to sound just like it. Even a cockatiel's voice will be amplified by a grey, the master of repetition. If you don't want to hear a sound or phrase a million times, don't let your grey hear it.

Intelligence is one of the main factors making this species one of the most popular companion parrots. Greys are also social animals that welcome a lot of attention from a human guardian but are not known to appreciate intense physical contact — though some don't mind snuggling and petting. They are not known to get along terrifically with other species, though cross-species friendships do happen. They can live upwards of 50 years in captivity.

Amazon parrots

There are 27 species of Amazon parrots, some of which are endangered or rare and aren't kept in captivity. They are found in Central and South America, and on some Caribbean islands. They are long-lived (80 years, with proper care), and most are companionable, although feisty. Some are unpredictable, especially in the spring, when breeding season commences. Amazons are hardy, exuberant birds, best for an experienced bird guardian. They tend toward obesity and require a nutritious diet and proper exercise. Here are short profiles of three popular species.

Lilac-crowned Amazon

Also known as the Finsch's Amazon, this 13- to 14-inch bird is as fearless and feisty as the other Amazons. It is originally from Mexico, and though breeders didn't concentrate on it in the past, it has become more popular recently. Not the noisiest of Amazons, it is inquisitive and affectionate. It can live upwards of 50 years with proper care.

Orange-winged Amazon

The orange-winged Amazon used to be an inexpensive bird, brought into the United States in large numbers before importation was made illegal. In the years since, its numbers have dwindled, and breeders are now making an effort to bring back the species. It's an affectionate bird, though sometimes temperamental. Talking ability is limited. It is often confused with the blue-fronted Amazon because of the blue on the face, but the markings are quite different — the orange-winged has a blue "mask" and a hint of orange on the wings.

Yellow-naped Amazon

The yellow-naped Amazon is one of the most popularly kept Amazons, probably because of its supreme talking ability and intelligence. It is a quirky bird, tends to be unpredictable in breeding season, and can become aggressive. These birds aren't noisy in general, but they aren't quiet parrots. The nominate bird (the color most often found in the wild) is stout and green with a yellow patch at the back of the neck (nape), but the blue mutation has a white spot on the nape instead of yellow and can cost $30,000 each.

Brotogeris

There are nine species of Brotogeris parrots. These little parrots have become more popular over the years, especially the grey-cheeked and the canary-winged species. They were once imported into the United States by the thousands, but they went out of vogue until a few years ago, when breeders realized that they were going to lose the species if they didn't start paying a lot more attention to them.

Brotogeris are all 7 to 9 inches long, primarily green in color, with a long, slender tail. Handfed babies make good companions and are not loud, though a flock of them will get raucous and very noisy. They are a hardy species and can live upwards of 30 years with the proper care.

Budgies (parakeets)

The budgie *(Melopsittacus undulatus)*, also known as the *American parakeet* and the *budgerigar,* originates in Australia and still exists there in large flocks. The wild budgie is comparable to the companion budgie, though it is smaller and only found in the nominate color, green. Budgies are about 6 to 7 inches long and are bred in a large assortment of colors and patterns, called *mutations* — there are more than 70 variations to date.

Budgies are *sexually dimorphic* — meaning there are visual differences between males and females — and it's easy to establish gender at about 6 to 8 months of age, when the birds mature. The adult male's *cere* (the flesh above the beak) is blue, whereas the hen's is pink or brown. You can't tell the gender of babies, so you have to just choose the birds you click with.

The budgie is the most popular species of parrot in the world. It is affectionate; easy to tame; isn't loud (though it is extremely chatty and does make noise just about all day); and is the best talking parrot of them all, able to learn hundreds of words and phrases. Lifespan is about 14 years with good care.

Girl or boy?

Some parrots are *dimorphic,* and some are *monomorphic.* With monomorphic parrots, the male and female look identical (to the untrained eye) and can't be easily distinguished from each other. In dimorphic parrots, there are obvious differences between male and female. For example, mature male budgies have a blue *cere* (fleshy spot above the beak), and females have a cere that ranges from pink to brown. In most mutations, the male cockatiel's face is brighter than the female's, but the female has a barring pattern on the underside of her tail, and the male doesn't. In black cockatoos, the male's beak is black, and the female's is horn- or light-colored. In red-bellied parrots (poicephalus), the male has a red belly; the female, green. The eclectus male is bright green; the female, red and violet. There are other dimorphic parrots as well, though most commonly kept parrots are monomorphic. Most people who breed parrots have their little tricks to try to determine the gender of their birds, but it's really a 50/50 guesstimate most of the time.

At nearly twice the size, the English show budgie is also a popular companion. The temperament of the two birds is similar, though the English may be more docile. The English budgie's lifespan is about 7 years, half that of the American parakeet.

Caiques

The caique (pronounced *kai-EKE*) is a medium-sized, stocky, blunt-tailed, colorful South American parrot that has become popular in recent years. The black-headed caique *(Pionites melanocephala)* and the white-bellied caique *(Pionites leucogaster)* are the two most common. The yellow-thighed caique, a subspecies of the white-bellied, is less common.

Caiques are known as clowns — they're bouncy and very active, full of antics, always rolling around and playing. They're also beaky, which basically equates to being nippy. They are not loud birds, but they aren't silent either. They don't have great talking ability, though some individuals do amass a decent vocabulary. They are known for bird-on-bird aggression and should be kept from other birds or at least properly supervised.

Cockatiels

The cockatiel *(Nymphicus hollandicus)* is second in popularity only to the budgie. It is lively, affectionate, and easy to tame. It is also very easy to breed, making it reasonably priced in most pet shops. Cockatiels are easygoing but not unintelligent. Females are said to make better hands-on companions than males, which have feistier personalities. These birds are excellent whistlers, and the males are decent talkers. Though not loud, they are persistent, calling and whistling for most of the day.

The cockatiel has a head crest that it displays when excited, delighted, or frightened. It comes in a variety of mutations, including lutino (yellow), white, grey, pearl, and pied, and either has a "rouge spot" on each cheek or a bright white face, as in the fancier mutations. Cockatiels are sexually dimorphic, so it's easy in most mutations to tell the sexes apart in mature birds. Males have brighter faces; females have horizontal bars on the underside of the tail, no matter the mutation (though they are very difficult to see in albinos).

These birds can be kept together peaceably and will even get along with budgies, finches, and canaries if given enough space. They can live more than 20 years with the proper care. Cockatiels have one particular quirk: They tend to have *night frights* — thrashing around the cage in the middle of the night, afraid of something in the dark. A nightlight often helps with this problem.

Cockatoos

There are 18 species of cockatoos and a great many more subspecies. They range in size from the small Galah (also called rose-breasted), at 14 inches, to the large palm cockatoo, which can get up to 28 inches in length. Cockatoos are popular, known for cuddliness and affection. What most parrot novices don't know is that cockatoos are also very demanding and can be quite aggressive. The cuddly baby soon turns into a belligerent adult that can be destructive and deafening.

Cockatoos are also a long-term commitment, with a lifespan up to 80 years or more. They are prone to self-mutilation and the infections that result from that abnormal behavior. Another serious consideration is the powder dust that cockatoos emit, which can irritate people with sensitive respiratory systems or allergies. Regular bathing with clear, warm water helps. Following are profiles of some popular cockatoos.

Moluccan cockatoo

The Moluccan cockatoo *(Cacatua moluccensis)* is originally from Indonesia. It is also called the salmon-crested cockatoo because of its salmon-pink head crest feathers. The Moluccan is a large bird that can out-yell most any other parrot. Because of this, they are given away or neglected more than any other species. It takes a very special household to be able to live with a Moluccan. They are not known to be great talkers, but they will mimic a few words.

Moluccans crave attention and love, and can become pesky because of it — they are not very good at playing alone and will constantly vie for your attention. Like most cockatoos, Moluccans are sensitive and become neurotic and upset when neglected. They also have powerful beaks and can be temperamental. I once heard a story of a man in Australia who had a portion of his finger bitten off when he got too close to a wild Moluccan in his backyard. I have also seen gruesome photos of Moluccan bites to the face.

Check out rescue organizations if you're dead set on a Moluccan — they seem to be overflowing with them and will often place them in dedicated, experienced homes.

Sulfur-crested cockatoo

The sulfur-crested cockatoo is the "generic" name for a variety of commonly kept cockatoo species and subspecies. These cockatoos are placed in two groups: The *lesser* sulfur-crested from Indonesia, New Guinea, and the surrounding areas, and the greater sulfur-crested from Australia. These two groups combined comprise ten distinct subspecies, though only five of those are commonly found in the companion bird trade. All the cockatoos in these species and subspecies are white with a yellow or orangy-colored crest, which is how they got their name. They range in size from 15 to 20 inches.

In general, the sulfur-crested cockatoos are intelligent, sensitive birds with the capacity to be either good household companions or a family's worst nightmare. Much of the companionability of this bird has to do with its upbringing, socialization, housing, nutrition, and daily care. When a cockatoo isn't getting its needs met, the results are often disastrous.

- **Greater sulfur-crested** *(Cacatua galerita)***:** This Australian native has four subspecies. The bird most commonly called the greater sulfur-crested is the largest of the cockatoos in this species at 20 inches, rivaling the Moluccan in size. Its distinctive characteristics, other than size, are the bare, white eye-ring; lemony-yellow crest feathers; slightly yellow coloring over the ear coverts; and yellow on the feathers beneath the tail and the underside of the wings. It is considered an amiable and sensitive companion.

- **Triton cockatoo** *(Cacatua galerita triton)***:** The triton cockatoo is a subspecies of the greater sulfur-crested and is one of the more commonly kept cockatoos, known for its antics on the television show *Baretta.* It is slightly smaller than the greater sulfur-crested at 18 inches, and its eye ring is a distinct blue that's hard to miss. The triton is known for its loud mouth and its extreme intelligence.

- **Elenora cockatoo** *(Cacatua galerita eleonora)***:** This subspecies of the greater sulfur-crested is the smallest in the group at 15 inches and is often called the *medium sulfur-crested,* but *Elenora* is the most common name. This popular bird has a lemony-yellow crest and a slight tinge of blue on the eye ring, but not as blue as the Triton.

 ✔ **Lesser sulfur-crested *(Cacatua sulphurea)*:** The lesser sulfur-crested (and its subspecies) is from Indonesia and the surrounding islands, not from Australia. The crest is yellow, as are the ear coverts, and it is 12 to 13 inches in length.

 ✔ **Citron-crested *(Cacatua sulphurea citrinocristata)*:** This subspecies of the lesser sulfur-crested is easily identified by its orange crest (the other sulfur-crested cockatoos have yellow crests). Their ear coverts have an orange tinge. It is a popular companion, amiable and intelligent, but requires a lot of hands-on time (as do all cockatoos).

Other subspecies can be found in captivity but are less well known. The subspecies in the greater sulfur-crested is *C.g.fitzroyi* from Northern Australia; the other subspecies in the lesser sulfur-crested are *C. s. abbotti* (becoming more common), *C. s. djampeana, C. s. occidentalis,* and *C. s. parvula.* Because of cross-breeding (hybridization) among the subspecies, some individuals may be difficult to identify.

Umbrella cockatoo

The umbrella cockatoo *(Cacatua alba)*, shown in Figure 3-1, also known as the white cockatoo or the great white-crested cockatoo, is well known in bird circles as one of the most affectionate and affable companion birds. An Indonesian native, the umbrella is slightly smaller than the Moluccan but bigger in personality and charm. This outgoing cockatoo is famous for its outlandish antics and for being clingy with its human companions.

The umbrella can be distinguished from other white cockatoos by its entirely white crest that raises like an umbrella when the bird is excited, agitated, or ready to play (or bite). It is prone to bouts of loud screaming, especially if it is isolated, locked in a cage, or doesn't get its way. It can learn quite a few words and may substitute them for screaming (if you're lucky).

What's up with the crest?

Some cockatoos, such as the sulfur-cresteds, have a *recursive* crest, and others have a *recumbent* crest, such as the umbrella cockatoo. The feathers of the recursive crest are curved, so when the crest is down the feather tips curve upward, making the crest a conspicuous characteristic in these birds. With the recumbent crest, the feathers are straight and lie flat against the head when the crest is lowered, such as in the Moluccan. Other cockatoos have a combination of the two, with only slight curving of the crest, or have a very short recumbent crest.

Hybridization

Many parrots of the same family will breed together (cross-breed) to create *hybrid* birds. For example, different species of macaws will breed together, as will different species of conures and different species of lovebirds. This hybridization taints the gene pool for future generations. Because most commonly kept parrots are endangered, rare, or threatened in the wild, most breeders make concerted efforts to keep the genes of these parrots as pure as possible.

Also, there's a limited supply of parrots in captivity, so keeping the genes of each species intact is important. To keep your birds from nesting, simply don't supply them with a place to do so, and separate them for most of the day in the spring and summer if they persist. You can also limit their daytime hours to under 12 if you have artificial lighting. Bird "pals" of different species are fine to interact, but try not to let them nest and raise chicks.

Figure 3-1: Umbrella cockatoos have large, all-white head crests.

Photo by Sandy Tubbs

Conures

There are 42 species of conures, all from South and Central America. Most are small to medium-sized stocky birds, 8 to 18 inches, ranging in color from lime green to bright yellow. They are notorious for their loud mouths and destructive behavior, though they are affectionate companions. Many do end up in shelters because of their raucous and persistent vocalization, so be sure that you can deal with that before you get one. They generally get along with other conures, no matter the species, but should not be allowed to cross-breed. Conures can live up to 30 years, perhaps more, with proper care. Following are profiles of three popular species.

Jenday

The Jenday conure *(Aratinga Jandaya)* is one of the favorite medium-sized conures, just below the sun conure in popularity but not in personality. The Jenday is a member of the genus *Aratinga,* which includes the sun, gold-capped, half-moon (orange-fronted), blue-crowned, and mitred conures — all charismatic, amiable, and attractive birds. The best attribute of these parrots is their intense affection for their human companions.

The Jenday's body is primarily green, with a bright orange and yellow head. The colorful head appears only in the mature bird — juvenile Jendays are mostly green with a mottled yellow head until they are about two years old. Like most conures, the Jenday is persistently noisy.

Pyrrhura

The maroon-bellied conure *(Pyrrhura frontalis)* and the green-cheeked conure *(Pyrrhura molinae)* are intelligent, energetic, playful parrots. They are similar in appearance and are often identified incorrectly. They are both about 10 inches long, but the green-cheeked is a bit brighter than the maroon-bellied and has grey barring on its chest, fading into a slightly reddish belly. The maroon-bellied has a golden barring on its chest and distinct, heart-shaped maroon shading on its belly. Their talking ability isn't renowned, but they will learn a few words. They are considered the *quiet* conures, if there can be such a thing — they are simply quieter than the others.

Sun conure

The sun conure *(Aratinga solstitalis)* is one of the more popular conures due to its stunning plumage, extraordinary disposition, and exceptional quality as a companion. The sunny is lively, vocal, and extremely playful. It is 12 inches long and most recognizable by bright orange and yellow coloring, often mottled with splotches of green. It has a black beak, white rings around its eyes, and a long tapering tail. Immature birds do not reach their full coloration for about two years.

There's no visual difference between the sexes, though males are said to be a bit brighter in coloration. Males are also said to have squarer, flatter heads, and females rounder, smaller heads, though only experienced breeders are good at eyeing the birds and making an educated guess. The sun conure is not known to be an extraordinary talker, but it can learn to say a few words. It will appreciate another conure as a friend and will not lose its companionability if the owners are attentive to both birds. Because it's in the *Aratinga* group, it can be paired with a jenday, mitred, nanday, gold-capped, blue-crowned, or another *Aratinga,* but *not for breeding purposes.* Some breeders create "Sundays" or "Jensuns," but this type of hybridization taints the limited gene pool.

Eclectus

Eclectus parrots *(Eclectus roratus)* have nine subspecies, including the grand eclectus, the vosmaeri, and the Solomon Island eclectus *(Eclectus roratus solomonensis)*. Be careful that you don't buy a hybrid eclectus, as some unscrupulous breeders breed different subspecies together. This does not affect the companion quality of the bird. However, though this practice may seem harmless, it's important that the gene pool of these birds remain pure.

Eclectus are dimorphic — the males are bright green and have a horn-colored beak, a splash of bright blue on the wing, and a bright red underwing. The females are red with deep violet bellies and black beaks. These birds were not bred successfully for many years because breeders put males with males and hens with hens. It wasn't until a few decades ago that someone realized that the green birds were male and the red ones female. The feathers on this species do not have a distinct outline like the feathers of other birds; instead, they look as if they're covered with a fine fur.

Eclectus are not prone to excessive noisiness, but they can be quite vocal and will develop an extensive vocabulary. They are intelligent, gentle birds if raised properly, though they will not tolerate frantic activity or constant disturbing household noise. A bored eclectus has the tendency to pluck its feathers. I have seen them naked as a result of self-mutilation. They tend to be hearty, messy eaters but will need to be encouraged early to eat a variety of healthy foods.

Hanging parrots

Hanging parrots are found in a wide geographical range, including Indonesia, India, the Philippines, Malaysia, Singapore, Borneo, Java, Bali, Sumatra, and other Asian countries. They live primarily in woodlands and orchards, and feed on fruit, flowers, nectar, insects, and some seeds, much as lories do. They get their name from their unusual sleeping habit: hanging upside-down. They also feed this way, stretching upside-down to dip the beak into an open flower. Hanging parrots are dimorphic, though you might have to look hard on some of the species to know which is which. In the blue-crowned hanging parrot *(Loriculus galgulus)*, a popular species, the male has a blue crown and a red spot on the throat, and the female doesn't. Immatures look like females.

The blue-crowned needs constant attention to maintain its companion quality. It is a lively bird but can become shy easily if not well socialized. These birds are not known talkers, but they will mimic whistles. They are less noisy than lories and can be kept peaceably in pairs or as a colony. Because of their endangered status in the wild, many hanging parrots are kept exclusively in breeding programs.

Hanging parrots eat a wet diet, which tends to attract bacteria. Keeping clean, fresh food available at all times is extremely important and challenging. Warmth is especially important for the hanging parrot, which succumbs to cold easily. But it is prone to infections due to the combination of warmth, wet food spoilage, and droppings in and around the cage. Vertical cages are not recommended for this species because the droppings tend to land in all directions. Thin sleeping perches also help to keep the droppings inside the cage.

Hawkheads

Hawkheaded parrots *(Deroptyus accipitrinus)* have large, colorful crests, wider than those of cockatoos, which they raise when threatened. This is their claim to fame. They are not widely known as companions, but they are becoming more popular as people are being exposed to them. They make decent companions, though they are extremely active, excitable, and can be unpredictable. Some people find them to be affectionate, easy birds, but they are best left to a more experienced keeper. At 14 inches in length, they are not very large, but that flashy crest can be intimidating.

Lories

Lories, like hanging parrots, need more care and attention than other common companion birds. They require a much different diet from that of other hook-bills because their less-powerful gizzards cannot crush seeds. They have a brushlike tongue that they use to pick up nectar and pollen, and though some lories will crack a few seeds, their main diet is fruit, such as bananas, oranges, melon, and apples; they also eat flowers, such as hibiscus. The staple diet in captivity is a nectar made from juice mixed with specially formulated lory diet powder. This liquid diet causes very loose droppings, which tend to get sprayed outside the cage. Someone living with a lory will spend a lot of time cleaning. There are dry diets specifically for lories that will make the droppings less soft, but this diet should only supplement the liquid diet. Lories are also partial to mealworms and grubs. There is a common myth that lories don't need water, which is untrue.

The lory personality is intense, bubbly, enthusiastic, playful, and constantly busy. Their antics are entertaining for most people, but they can become more than a handful. These active birds tend to be mischievous and destructive, and will get into trouble quicker than someone can save them from harm. They are also often nippy and will generally bite out of excitement or fear.

Most lories don't get along with other bird species and may become vicious even with birds of their own species. They are territorial and should never be left unsupervised with other birds.

For the record, lories have a blunter, more rounded tail, and lorikeets have a longer, more tapered tail. There are 120 recognized species and subspecies of lories and lorikeets.

Rainbow lorikeets

Originating from Australia, the 12-inch rainbow lorikeet has at least 22 subspecies and is one of the most beautiful companion birds available. Rainbow lories are hard to miss, with their bright reds and greens, vibrant blues and violets, and splotches of lemon yellow flowing into intense oranges. The rainbow is more than just bright on the outside. It is a highly intelligent bird, able to learn complex behaviors, such as escaping from the cage.

Lories can be noisy, and the rainbow is no exception. Their voice is high-pitched, with a squeaky-squawky repetitive bark. They are wonderful talkers and will learn to speak many words and phrases clearly and frequently, though the rainbow isn't the best talker of the lories.

Lories bathe exuberantly and often, and they have a penchant for sleeping lying upside-down on their backs, often rattling the nerves of their guardians, who occasionally think the birds are dead. Rainbow lories can live 20 to 30 years, but it is the lucky and unusual lory who lives that long.

Lovebirds

There are nine species of African lovebirds, but only three are commonly kept as companions in the United States: the peachfaced, the masked, and the Fischer's. The others are rare or are more difficult to breed in captivity. The popular species breed like bunnies, making them far more available.

Peachfaced

A lone peachfaced lovebird is an affectionate companion. Pairs are fun to watch but eventually will not appreciate human hands-on attention once they mature. If neglected, even for a couple of weeks, lovebirds tend to become snappish. They live about 15 years with proper care.

The peachie is 6 inches long and comes in an artist's-palette array of colors. The nominate bird is green with a shiny blue rump and rosy peach face. Other colors (mutations) range from creamy white to almost black and everything in between, all shades of green, blue, yellow, violet, and pied, with different colored faces as well, most notably orange and white.

Temperament differences are minimal among the mutations. Males tend to be smaller and thinner, and females are often noticeably larger. Males are generally sweet and reserved, whereas females are spunkier, tend to nip, and can be argumentative.

The peachfaced is not a noisy bird but is prone to bouts of chattering and whistling in the morning, evening, and when excited. Talking ability is slim, though there are reports of talking lovebirds — perhaps one in a thousand.

Fischer's and masked

The Fischer's and the masked lovebirds are second in popularity to the peachfaced but are just as strong in personality. These species come in a variety of color mutations, though not quite as many as the peachfaced. The primary difference between the peachfaced and these species is the prominent eye ring, a fleshy circle around the eye that makes them quite distinctive. These eye-ringed lovebirds are known to be nippy and temperamental if not handled every day.

Macaws

There are 17 species of macaws, all from South and Central America, ranging in size from 12–39 inches. These popular birds are known to be loud and destructive — but they're also affectionate, talkative, and intelligent.

Some popular types of hybrid macaws have parents of two different species. This is highly frowned upon in most of the bird community, though some breeders still produce these babies. The resulting birds are no less affectionate or beautiful than the purebred macaws. I'm not advocating hybridization, though if you come across a hybrid macaw, be aware that it shouldn't be viewed as less worthy of proper care than a purebred macaw.

Blue and gold macaw

The blue and gold macaw *(Ara ararauna)*, a native of South and Central America, is the most popular and widely found macaw in the United States. Before the ban on imported birds, the blue and gold macaw was brought into the United States in astounding numbers, allowing for many breeders to obtain good breeding stock and keeping the price relatively low. Like most macaws, the blue and golds are noisy and prone to bouts of screaming. They are apt talkers, able to repeat simple words and phrases. If a blue and gold remains healthy, it can live upwards of 70 years.

Greenwing macaw

At about 35 inches from its crimson head to the tip of its tapered tail, and weighing in at between 2½ to 3½ pounds, the greenwing macaw *(Ara chloroptera)* is one of the largest birds in the macaw family. This big Central and South American beauty hails from roughly the same area as the blue and gold macaw.

Many people mistake the greenwing for the scarlet macaw, but it's easy to tell the difference: The scarlet has bright yellow feathers on the wing, whereas the greenwing has green feathers; the greenwing has bands of small, red feathers lining the fleshy patch on its face, and the scarlet's face is naked. In most cases, the greenwing is also far larger.

This bird's huge beak can look intimidating, but the greenwing is actually the gentlest of the large macaws and is not known for biting and mood swings. The greenwing can talk but is not known as a chatterbox; instead, a guardian can expect loud, intermittent screeching. The greenwing's size alone is a deterrent for many bird owners, who don't have the room for such a large animal. A small cage will ruin its tail feathers and put it in a raggedy and miserable condition.

Hahn's macaw and the noble macaw

Originally from South America, these two closely related subspecies *(Ara nobilis nobilis* and *Ara nobilis cumanensis)* are compact and companionable. Though they are not as flashy as their larger cousins, the Hahn's and the noble macaws are highly prized for their "large macaw" personality in a mini macaw body. They are easier to find than some of the other macaw species, especially the Hahn's, which is a favorite of breeders.

The smallest of the miniature macaws, both the Hahn's and the noble are primarily green with a fleshy white face patch. The noble is slightly larger than the Hahn's, and although both birds are smaller than some of the larger conure species, they can easily be mistaken for a conure by a novice. These birds are between 12 and 14 inches long, making them a good apartment bird (but only if your neighbors are deaf). These are noisy birds, especially if you have more than one, and their voices are grating. They are wonderful talkers and are good whistlers, too, but may take to whistling over talking. These birds are reported to live for more than 40–50 years if cared for properly.

Hyacinth macaw

The hyacinth macaw *(Anodorhynchus hyacinthinus)* is the largest in the macaw family. Originally from Brazil, the hyacinth is the Great Dane of companion birds, with the mature male reaching more than 40 inches in length. Often called gentle giants, the hyacinth is indeed affectionate, but *gentle* it is not. Hyacinths play rough with other birds and with their person. The beak has over 200 pounds of pressure per square inch and can snap a broomstick in half with one crunch. Best left to very experienced bird owners.

In the wild, the hyacinth's diet consists almost wholly of palm nuts from the queen palm. This diet is high in fat, and you can substitute queen palm nuts with Brazil nuts, walnuts, almonds, macadamias, coconut, pistachios, and cashews. You will probably never see an obese hyacinth, as it seems to metabolize fat very easily.

Military macaw

The military macaw *(Ara militaris)* is a lively, energetic bird and is considered one of the larger macaws, though at 27–29 inches it's smaller than the blue and gold macaw. There are three subspecies of military macaw, though to the untrained eye they look quite similar, with just slight shades of green differentiating them. There's no difference in companion quality among the three subspecies. It is thought that the majority of military macaws sold in the United States are of the Mexican subspecies, a little larger than the other two. In the wild, the military can be found in regions of Central and South America, though it has all but disappeared in some of its natural habitat and is on the CITES (Convention on International Trade in Endangered Species of Wild Fauna and Flora) list of endangered species.

The military macaw is sometimes confused with the Buffon's macaw, but the Buffon's is much larger, and though the coloring is remarkably similar, the Buffon's has a much more prominent tuft of red feathers at the base of the upper mandible (upper beak). Both macaws have a rose-colored naked face patch that blushes bright red when the birds are excited.

The military macaw earns its title only though its "attire." It looks ready to march in a parade in full regalia. But its personality is less salty sailor than boisterous recruit. It is great at *buffaloing* its human friends — putting on a show of being aggressive when actually just bluffing. Most individuals can be socialized to be sweet and affectionate.

Scarlet macaw

There's nothing flashier than a scarlet macaw *(Ara macao)*. It's not unusual for someone to begin a birdkeeping habit with a scarlet, even though this 32–39-inch bird is not a great choice for a novice. Sassy and filled with energy and personality, the scarlet is highly intelligent and a capable escape artist. The beak is formidable and can pack a wallop of a bite. Even the tamest of these birds can become nippy to get its way.

The scarlet has an enormous natural range in Central and South America and is found in two subspecies: *Ara macao cyanoptera,* which hails from Central America, primarily Belize, Guatemala, Panama, Mexico, and Nicaragua; and *Ara macao macao,* found in South America, including Brazil, Colombia, Ecuador, French Guiana, Peru, Surinam, and Venezuela. The Central American scarlet is said to be larger and have more blue than green on its wings than the South American, which barely has any green at all.

Some scientists believe that these aren't true subspecies, but the final word isn't in yet, and many scientists hold rigorously to the distinct classifications. Others break the scarlets into three groups, based on size and coloration: Mexican, Central American, and South American. In general, the Mexican is smallest and has less yellow; the South American is a little larger and has a little more yellow on the wing; the Central American scarlet is the stunning prize of the three, a large bird with a wide band of yellow on the wing. It might happen that the scarlet you buy from a breeder who may not know better is a hybrid, which doesn't harm its beauty or quality as a companion, but serious aviculturists recommend against such pairings because they dilute the gene pool, and eventually the regional differences will be lost.

Other keets

There are hundreds of different kinds of *keets* (long-tailed parrots), far too many to list here, many of which have lovely and exotic names — for example, the turquoisine grass keet, the scarlet-chested keet, the rosy Bourke's, and the rock pebbler. Following are some commonly kept keets.

Psittacula parakeets

There are 11 species of psittacula parakeets. Because of the psittacula's long tail, it needs larger housing than another bird of the same relative size. Psittaculas are known to be noisy and loud, though their beauty makes up for the loud mouth.

The Indian ringnecked parakeet *(Psittacula Krameri manillensis)* has been kept as a pet for centuries and remains a favorite companion bird today. As its name suggests, it originates from India, where it is still found wild in great quantities, even in urban areas. This species is playful, exuberant, and has a remarkable talking ability. However, it can become nippy and is very loud for a bird of its size. It needs attention every single day or will lose its companionability.

This bird is 16 inches long and is available in a variety of mutations: blue, yellow, pied, albino, and others. The color of these birds seems almost airbrushed on, and you can barely distinguish individual feathers. The Indian ringnecked parakeet is dimorphic, the males having a distinguishing ring around the neck at maturity. They can live for more than 30 years.

The Afro-Asian Alexandrine parrot *(Psittacula eupatria)* is a bright, gentle, independent, medium-sized bird known to be hardy and relatively quiet compared to its ringnecked cousins. This bird is a favorite among fanciers and is becoming more popular due to growing popularity with breeders.

The nominate Alexandrine has green plumage and an immense beak. As with many of the ringnecked variety, color mutations are becoming more available, including lutino (yellow) and blue. The Alexandrine has five distinct subspecies, some slightly larger or smaller than the nominate bird.

What is mutation, what is nominate?

Some parrots come in colors not commonly found in the wild (or not occurring in the wild at all). These colors are called *mutations* and are completely natural. A bird that is the color most commonly found in the wild, such as a green budgie or a grey cockatiel, is called normal or *nominate*. So when someone says that they have a normal peachfaced lovebird, they mean that the bird is green — not that it doesn't need psychotherapy.

Lineolated parakeet

The South American lineolated parakeet *(Bolborhynchus lineola lineola)* is sexually dimorphic, about 6 to 7 inches long, quiet and generally docile, and can learn to say a few words and phrases. These little parrots will perform a variety of antics in an aviary setting and are quite companionable, though not as popular in the United States as many other keets. They come in a variety of color mutations, making them a favorite of bird fanciers who like to breed for color.

Neophemas

Neophemas are making surprising leaps in popularity — surprising even though they have been an aviary staple in Australia for many years. The neophemas include the popular Bourke's parakeet *(Neopsephotus bourkii)*, recently reclassified from *Neophema bourkii;* the elegant parakeet *(Neophema elegans)*; the orange-bellied parakeet *(Neophema crysogaster)*; the splendid parakeet *(Neophema splendida)*; the turquoisine (turquoise) parakeet *(Neophema pulchella)*; the rock parakeet *(Neophema petrophila)*; and the less frequently kept blue-winged parakeet *(Neophema chrysostoma)*.

These birds are known collectively as the *grass parakeets* of Australia, each of which occupies a relatively small natural region in that large country. They are called grass parakeets because they feed on wild grasses and grass seeds. Because they feed on the ground, these birds are naturally skittish and always on the lookout for predators.

Neophemas make excellent aviary birds but should not be housed with larger, more aggressive birds. Care should be taken that two different species of neophemas do not successfully nest and rear young. As a group, neophemas are dimorphic. Males are generally brighter in plumage and may have more colors than the females, though it is easy to tell the difference only in the splendid and the turquoisine.

The most popular and widely available bird in the group is the Bourke's parakeet, slightly larger than an English budgie at 8 inches in length. The Bourke's comes in a variety of mutations, including the Rosy Bourke, a bright pink version of the more muted nominate. The Bourke's can be a shy bird, but a diligent guardian can train it to be as affectionate as a budgie, though many owners keep them as watching-only pets.

The turquoisine and the splendid are the most visually stunning of the neophemas. The turquoisine comes in a variety of spectacular mutations, most notably the yellow mutation. The turquoisine can be more bird-aggressive than the others in this group.

Rosellas

There are 15 species of rosellas and many more subspecies, all hailing from Australia and the outer islands. The golden-mantled rosella *(Platycercus eximius)*, often called the eastern rosella or the white-cheeked rosella, is the most colorful and popular of the rosella family. It is 12 inches long and has a crimson head and chest, white cheeks, bright yellow belly, cobalt shoulders, flight, and tail feathers, a pale green underbelly, and a darker green back.

This species is not a consistently noisy bird and not a great talker, but it may pick up a few simple words and will learn to whistle well. Most individuals do not stand for much cuddling but are content to ride around on your shoulder. A very tame rosella is a good bird for a child who is mature enough to behave properly around it.

Parrotlets

There are seven species of the tiny parrotlet: green-rump, Pacific (celestial), Mexican, blue-wing, Sclater (also called the black-billed parrotlet), spectacle, and yellow-face. The Pacific and green-rump parrotlets are the most widely available. There are some stunning mutations available too, including lutino (yellow) and blue.

Pacific parrotlet

The Pacific parrotlet *(Forpus coelestis)* is fast becoming one of the most popular small birds and is the most common of the various parrotlet species. Originating in Mexico and Central and South America, this "pocket parrot" has caught on fast. Its personality is fearless and feisty, packing a lot of intelligence and vigor into a tiny package about 5 inches long.

Pacifics are dimorphic. Males are green with blue on the rump and part of the wings, with a blue streak on the face. Females are mainly different shades of green. Some recent color mutations have been developed, including blue, yellow, and a darker green, among others.

Pacific parrotlets are not noisy birds. They will repeat words and simple phrases but are not known to be the finest talkers of the parrotlet family. They can live for 20–25 years or more if cared for properly.

Pionus

The pionus isn't the most popular parrot — it's often outflashed, outcolored, outtalked, and outnumbered by many of the more commonly kept parrot species. The pionus isn't much like its South American cousin, the Amazon, though it is shaped like a smaller Amazon.

The pionus is the best-kept secret of the bird world. It's got all the good qualities of the popular companion species with few of the negative aspects. Of the eight species of pionus, five are regularly available in the bird trade, and each has subspecies, though many of those are not available in the United

States. The pionus family consists of the blue-headed *(Pionus menstruus)*, bronze-winged *(Pionus chalcopterus)*, dusky *(Pionus fuscus)*, Maximilian's or scaly-headed *(Pionus maximiliani)*, coral-billed or red-billed *(Pionus sordidus)*, plum-crowned *(Pionus tumultuosus)*, white-crowned or white-capped *(Pionus senilis)*, and white-headed *(Pionus seniloides)*. The five most available species are the Maximilian's, dusky, blue-headed, white-capped, and bronze-winged.

Pionus are all roughly between 10 and 12 inches in length and are basically the same shape, with a short, square tail like the Amazons; they all have a bare, fleshy eye ring circling the entire eye; and they all have red feathers at the vent (underneath the tail). Those are the only physical characteristics they share — they differ so vastly in color, experts often puzzle over why the field biologists put them all in the same species. They used to be called *red-vented parrots* before the name *pionus* came into vogue.

The pionus, in general, is affectionate (though not a love sponge), quieter than other parrots (though not silent), and attentive and sweet. As with all parrots, the way a pionus is raised by its human guardians makes the difference between a shy bird and a great companion. Pionus aren't known as the best talkers, but some individuals can garner an impressive vocabulary.

Poicephalus parrots

As a family, these stout African parrots are known for their good nature and relative quietness. They are affectionate and very companionable, and can live upwards of 30 years. Following are a couple of the more popular species.

Meyer's parrot

The Meyer's parrot *(Poicephalus meyeri)* is one of the favorites of the poicephalus group because of its outstanding companionability and calm nature. Primarily a muted grey-brown, it is often overlooked among flashier parrots — it takes a real bird fancier to fall in love with the Meyer's.

The Meyer's is a quiet bird in comparison to most other companion species. They cluck and click and will occasionally emit a piercing squeak — but not often. Meyer's have been known to repeat a few words as well. It is a calm bird, content to ride around on a guardian's shoulder and just hang out. The Meyer's is not known to be nippy but can be as capricious as any other parrot and can bite on a whim.

Senegal parrot

The Senegal parrot *(Poicephalus senegalus)* is the most common of the poicephalus and is fairly easy to find in pet shops. Senegals are good-natured and less expensive than their poicephalus cousins. They are about 9 inches long, mostly dark green and brownish-grey with an iridescent green throat, orange thighs, and yellow chest. The beak and feet are black, and the eye is a light yellow-orange, set off by the darker grey of the face. Some individuals can learn to talk quite well, but they tend more toward whistling and clucking. Senegals can be very sweet and tend to get very attached to their humans.

Quaker parakeets

The Quaker parakeet *(Myiopsitta monachus)*, a native of South America and also commonly referred to as the monk parrot, is one of the most popular parrots of its size due to its availability, low cost, and outstanding mimicking ability. The Quaker is reported to live more than 30 years with the proper care. This intelligent 12-inch bird is found in large, feral colonies from southern Florida to the Northeast and Midwest, and is a charming addition to the landscape of those areas, though many places consider them pests and have outlawed them. Because they are so prolific and destructive when they colonize in the wild, Quakers are illegal to sell or own in some states, so check state laws before you purchase one.

The nominate Quaker is primarily green in color. The distinguishing features are its grey face, neck, and chest. Quakers are often confused with conures because of their size and coloration. There have been some recent mutations of these birds in blue, yellow, and cinnamon (a lighter greenish-yellow), though they are very expensive.

Possibly the most distinctive behavioral feature of the Quaker parakeet comes from its namesake behavior: quaking and shaking. The young birds bob their heads and quake in a way that appears abnormal, but it is actually a natural behavior exclusive to this bird.

Someone with noise sensitivity should think twice about bringing home a Quaker. They are very noisy and persistent, though their affectionate nature wins over bird lovers who can overlook this irksome characteristic.

Vasa parrots

Vasa parrots are possibly the strangest of the parrot species, hailing from Madagascar and the surrounding islands. They look a little like crows and are much darker in color than the African greys. The vasa comes in seven subspecies, including the black or lesser vasa parrot *(Coracopsis nigra nigra)* and the greater vasa *(Coracopsis vasa)*. It isn't often kept as a companion, though it's worth mentioning here; the vasa is becoming sought-after by fanciers because it is one of the more different parrots. Handfed babies are affectionate, playful, and lively.

Chapter 4

Purchasing and Adopting a Parrot

. . . .

. . . .

*W*here to acquire a parrot can be as difficult a decision as what kind of parrot to get. This chapter shows you how to choose the correct place to find your parrot, what specs you'd like in a parrot, and how to know if it's healthy.

You can just walk into any pet shop and pick up the prettiest bird you see. But that's not an informed way to choose a companion that can be with you for 15 to 70 years. Of course, if you've already done that, you're not alone. Many people have chosen parrots in just this way, your lovely author included.

Your Parrot Options

You have a few options to choose among once you decide on a species:

✔ How old would you like the parrot to be?

✔ Does it have to be a baby, or would you rather have one that's a little more mature?

✔ How tame would you like the bird to be?

✔ What are your expectations for physical contact? Best friend or charming housemate?

✔ Finally, are you willing to adopt a bird that no longer has a home?

These are serious considerations. People often think longer about what kind of shoes to buy than they do about what kind of animal to bring home and whether or not the animal will be happy living there. Animals are often impulse purchases, especially birds. You don't even have to try them on. They *seem* easy, and they can be so sweet. There's no question they're beautiful. The larger parrots are also status symbols. No wonder so many parrots get dumped into shelters every year. But if you're reading this book, you're doing your homework, and that's great. You'll be able to tell the right parrot for you from a feathered nightmare.

Handfed versus parent-raised

A *handfed* parrot is one that has been taken from the nest at a young age and fed by hand by a human. Parrots are *altricial* birds, meaning they are totally dependent on their parents from the time they hatch until they completely *fledge* (leave) the nest. The contrast is the *precocial* birds, like ducks and chickens, who can leave the nest and begin eating on their own soon after hatching.

Handfed parrots are bonded to humans from the beginning and lose their immediate fear of being handled. Many handfed parrots even love humans so much that they prefer them to other parrots. Handfed parrots that are socialized properly are considered "tame" and make good companions as long as someone takes the time to continue handling them.

Parent-raised parrots are those that have been raised by their parents and have had no human contact. They will need to be tamed to be hands-on companions — no easy task, depending on the species.

People who breed parrots often allow parrots to raise their young if they want the young also to be breeders. There is evidence that parent-raised babies are better parents from the very first *clutch* (group of eggs), though handfed birds do get the hang of it and can be great from the beginning too. However, handfed breeders aren't scared of humans and will defend the nest far more viciously than parent-raised birds, who will be more likely to flee the nest when the breeder wants to inspect it.

Birds such as budgies and cockatiels are often *handled* without being handfed — the breeder holds and pets the babies while they're still in the nest so that they are semi-tame once they leave the nest, making them easier to tame.

Choosing an age

Because many parrots are long-lived, you have the opportunity to welcome a baby or a senior into your home. Yes, there's a difference between baby behavior and adult behavior, but even if you get a baby parrot you're going to experience its adult behavior sooner or later.

It's a myth that baby parrots bond more deeply to human families than adult parrots when placed in a new home. Parrots are very adaptable animals and appreciate people who are respectful of them — beside above-adequate housing, nutrition, proper lighting, and veterinary care, that's about all they ask of us.

An adult parrot in a new home can become very bonded to its new family. On the other hand, an adult bird with social problems may never become affectionate and may never even like its new guardians, but that has less to do with age than it does with how the parrot was raised and treated by its previous humans.

Baby parrots

Baby parrots are sweet and practically beg you to take them home. Unfortunately, baby behavior is not really an indication of adult behavior. Remember that the sweet baby is going to grow up, become an adult, and display all the adult behavior typical to its species.

Baby parrots go through five basic baby stages:

- **Neonate:** A *neonate* is any baby parrot that is not yet eating on its own and relies on its parents or a human to feed it. Typically, this term refers to very young babies with their eyes still closed, also called *hatchlings*. All neonates can also be called *chicks*.

- **Nestling:** When the baby gets a little older and its eyes are open, you can call it a *nestling*. It still relies on a parent or human for food.

- **Fledgling:** When a parrot begins to fly, it is considered to be *fledging* the nest and is called a *fledgling*. It may be eating some food on its own, but it still relies on the parents (or a human) for food.

- **Weanling:** A *weanling* is a baby parrot that is in the process of weaning (just starting to eat on its own).

- **Juvenile:** A *juvenile* is a baby that is *weaned* (independent of its parents and eating on its own) but isn't yet sexually mature.

The time from hatching to juvenile is different for every species. Budgies can be weaned in about six weeks. Hyacinth macaws can take nine months to wean.

Juvenile parrots are the same size as adult parrots. The only real way to tell age is by looking at the bird's closed leg band. If the bird doesn't have a band, you can often tell a juvenile parrot by the color of its eyes, which will often be darker or a different color. Plumage in some juvenile species is also different. For example, sun conure juveniles are greener than they are orange and yellow. These birds *feather out* into their mature colors after a year or two.

Never buy a parrot that is still dependent on handfeeding formula, especially if you're not experienced in handfeeding. Many highly-experienced parrot breeders have accidentally asphyxiated (choked) a baby bird to death. Handfeeding isn't an exact science and takes a lot of practice and patience. You can buy a baby when it's nearly weaned and still eating soft, warm, nearly solid food but not when it still has to be handfed with a syringe.

Mature parrots

A mature parrot is one that can breed and produce young. It has passed the juvenile stage, and its personality is already formed. Don't rule out a mature parrot as a companion. If a lovebird is three years old, it's in the first fifth of its lifespan. If a blue and gold macaw is 10 years old, it is in the prime of its life, with 70 more years to go if cared for properly.

In the wild, baby parrots wean and then leave their parents to find mates. In captivity, many handfed parrots "turn" on their handfeeders, preferring instead someone else in the household. It makes sense to the bird to leave its genetic family, so a mature bird may actually appreciate bonding to someone beside the human parent who raised it.

Older parrots

An older parrot is in the last third of its lifespan — for example, a lovebird that's 10 or an African grey that's about 35 years old. Unfortunately, most parrots don't even make it to an age where they can be considered older. It's the lucky parrot whose guardians are conscientious enough to keep it alive and happy into its golden years.

There's no reason why you shouldn't welcome an older bird into your home. Yes, its personality is pretty much formed by the time the bird is well into its adulthood, but if you can accept the bird for who it is as an individual, then you may find a good friend, even if you had nothing to do with its upbringing.

About tameness

Most people want their parrots to be hands-on companions. It's much easier to have that situation when you acquire a parrot that's already tame. What I really mean by tameness is *allowing physical contact* and *how often you're going to get bitten.* The first thought most people have when it comes to acquiring a parrot is whether the bird is going to bite them. The second is whether the bird is going to be friendly.

One important thing to remember is that *most parrots do bite* at one time or another. Your parrot might not bite you, but it will probably bite someone if the situation demands it. Friendliness is relative. There are levels of tameness, of course:

✔ **The cuddler:** This bird wants nothing more than to be in your presence, preferably somewhere attached to you. This bird loves petting and *scritches* (that's parrot-ese for scratching affectionately). The cockatoo is known as a cuddlebug — most would like to be sewn to their humans. Of course, it's up to the individual bird and how it was raised. Some birds begin life as cuddlers and then become more aloof when they hit sexual maturity.

✔ **Hand-tamed:** The *hand-tamed* parrot is content to sit on your hand and will stand for some petting but won't really want any intense contact. This bird may never bite — it just may not want an abundance of physical affection and may become afraid (or bite) if you push it. The African grey parrot is a good example of this — some individuals do like to cuddle, but for the most part they don't love being manhandled.

✔ **Semi-tamed handfed:** The *semi-tamed handfed* parrot was taken from the nest as a baby and fed by a human but hasn't been handled a lot since weaning. Because this bird was handfed, it's not *really* afraid of humans. But because it's not used to human contact anymore, it is liable to bite when someone gets too close. It will react to fear by biting far more often than it will react by trying to flee. This is perhaps the worst combination of circumstances and is why it's important to keep handfed birds socialized if they are ever to find good homes.

✔ **The bronco:** The *bronco* bird is absolutely untamed. It was not handfed, was perhaps wild-caught, and has never really been handled by humans. Just because a bird is a bronco should not put it out of the running as a good companion. Some birds tame down easily — for example, the budgie, the cockatiel, and even the hyacinth macaw. Others, like Amazons and lovebirds, are more difficult. The bronco's main defense is flight, though most will not hesitate to bite if they feel threatened and trapped, and your finger is conveniently close.

✔ **Breeders or pairs:** *Breeder* birds and *pairs* aren't really interested in human contact. They are less likely to pick up human words and sounds (though sometimes they do) and are more difficult to tame, regardless if they were handfed or not. They make good hands-off companions.

✔ **The "sometimes" biter:** Most parrots fall into this category. Like people, most parrots are friendly sometimes, cranky sometimes, and sometimes give their human companions a well-placed bite. Hopefully, your human friends aren't biting you, at least if you don't want them to. There's not much you can do to determine whether or not the parrot at the pet shop will end up being a biter. Most of what determines that is how much handling you offer the bird and how you care for it. But even the finest-bred and most socialized parrots bite sometimes.

Secondhand parrots and adoptions

The larger cockatoos are very often abandoned to sanctuaries, as are Amazons (Figure 4-1) and the larger macaws, though any parrot can become "inconvenient" to people unprepared to care for it. As parrots mature, they can get noisy and destructive, and may turn into chronic pluckers or biters if they don't have the proper housing, nutrition, and social contact. Some of the larger cockatoos have been known to bite so viciously, the bite-ee has to visit a plastic surgeon to repair the damage.

This is not to say that you shouldn't consider a secondhand bird. Just make sure that you know what you're getting into and that you can handle the problems that may come with it. Many secondhand birds become loving, joyous companions when they're allowed to be themselves and blossom into the parrots they were meant to be.

The talker in the bunch

If you want a talking parrot, your best bet is to get one that's already talking, or you can try one of the species that is well-known to talk, such as:

- African grey parrots
- Amazon parrots, particularly the yellow-naped, the double-yellow headed, and the blue-fronted
- Budgies (parakeets)
- Indian ringnecks (and other ringnecked parakeets)
- Macaws, particularly the blue and gold and the scarlet

But how do you choose the parrot in the bunch that will be the most vocal when you get it home? It's difficult to tell just by watching the birds for a short period of time. Certainly, if you're watching a group of parrots, the one that's creating a racket is a vocal bird and will probably be the most interested in mimicking the voices and the noises in the world around it.

However, you might be watching the birds after a long day of playing, and the most vocal bird in the group might be sleepy and quiet. If you're buying the parrot from an experienced breeder, he or she should have a good idea of which one of the babies is most apt to talk. After a while, breeders come to know their babies, and a good breeder will tell you whether or not a particular bird might grow into a feathered chatterbox. Just realize that no one can really predict if and when a bird will talk.

Photo by James Parsons

Finding the Perfect Parrot

Now that you've noted the specs you might like in a parrot, you just have to find that parrot. Walking into your local pet shop may not be the best idea for a number of reasons, depending on the quality of the store. It may seem like a great idea to find a breeder, but how? Read on.

Pet shops

A general pet shop may have some bird stock. Depending on the type and quality of the store, the birds may or may not be in good condition. Here are some things to look for in a pet shop:

- ✔ **Cleanliness:** The water dishes should be spotless, the cages clean, the floor clean, and the birds themselves should be in a generally clean condition. If you notice a foul odor (no pun intended), don't buy from that store.

- ✔ **Food:** Do the birds have enough food? Are they being offered more than just seed or pellets? The birds should have a variety of foods available.

- ✔ **Toys:** Do the birds have anything to play with? They should have an abundance of toys available.

- ✔ **Perches:** The birds should have perches of varying size and diameter. If there are no perches in the cage, complain to the store's manager.

- ✔ **Employees:** Do the employees know anything at all about birds? Do they know where the birds in the store come from? Are they paying any attention to the birds? If they don't know anything about birds, you aren't going to get any help from them after your purchase.

- ✔ **Conditions:** Are they crowded together in small cages? If so, leave immediately. Disease is more likely spread in crowded conditions.

- ✔ **Illness:** You'll find a list of the signs of illness and signs of health later in this chapter. Make sure all of the birds in the pet shop at least *look* healthy to you. A lot of diseases don't have very visible outward signs, especially in the beginning stages, so even if the birds look healthy, that's no guarantee.

- ✔ **Large parrots:** Do the larger birds have enough space to move around, flap their wings, and play? If not, the store isn't properly caring for the birds.

All-bird shops

The employees in an all-bird shop usually know a lot more about birds than those in the general pet shop, and they'll give you more help after your purchase if you have a problem. There's also better choice in an all-bird shop — different species, ages, and so on.

Bird shops are generally pretty obsessive about preventing disease, and rightfully so. If the shop asks you to wash your hands with special soap or to disinfect your shoes before you walk into a room with their babies, you're probably in a decent place.

Newspaper classifieds

The classified section of the newspaper often has ads for birds. These ads could be placed by a breeder, a bird shop, or a *bird broker* — someone who buys birds from breeders and marks up the price. Or someone could just be tired of their bird or can't keep it anymore and is choosing to sell it through the classifieds.

What I'm trying to get at here is that you don't really know who's on the other end of the line when you respond to an ad from the newspaper. You could be getting the most reputable breeder in your area on the phone or someone who just stole a bunch of birds and is looking to unload them quickly.

✔ It's a good sign if you hear a lot of birds in the background when you call.

✔ It's a good sign if the person seems to love talking about birds and gives you a nice slice of time on the phone.

✔ It's a bad sign when the price of the birds is way too low. Beware of a "good" deal.

✔ It's a yellow flag when the person wants to meet you in a parking lot to show you the birds. Then again, some people are wary of having strangers come to their home these days, and I can't blame them.

Reputable breeders

A reputable breeder is one who comes with references, is very involved in the parrot *fancy* (a dedicated hobbyist), is a member of parrot clubs, and is a responsible parrot guardian. This person should be willing to chat with you on the phone and help you choose the right bird for you. Don't be put off if they refuse to sell you a type of bird or a particular bird — this is common practice with breeders who really care for their parrots' lives after they leave the nest.

Going to a breeder's home is a real treat. You get to meet your bird's parents and see the way the breeder keeps his or her birds. You'll have a chance to get a "vibe" from the breeder. Is this someone you want to have a long-term birdy relationship with? Remember, you'll probably be calling the breeder from time to time to ask questions.

A good breeder:

✔ Does not breed a pair of parrots more than two or three times per year, depending on the species. Birds need to rest for a few months a year. Babies of overtaxed parents can be weak and more susceptible to disease.

✔ Feeds a healthy, varied diet.

✔ Provides regular veterinary care. Find out who the avian doctor is.

✔ Doesn't say things like "I just do this for the money."

✔ Takes the time to answer your questions with patience and kindness and respect.

✔ Does not send you home with a bird that's not right for your lifestyle.

✔ Makes you wash up before handling any babies and wants to know if you have been near any other birds — you can carry disease into an aviary on your clothes and shoes.

 ✔ Makes sure that the babies are fully weaned before they go home with new guardians.

 ✔ Does not keep aggressive mates together. Some species are known for mate-on-mate violence.

 ✔ Is nice to the birds and seems to genuinely care for and respect them.

Flea markets

Some flea markets allow the sale of live animals, and it isn't unusual for there to be a couple of bird vendors there. These birds may be perfectly fine. However, what if you have a problem when you get home? Whom will you call? Will the vendor be at the flea market the next week? Be careful in this situation.

Bird shows or expos

Bird shows, expos, or marts are generally held by local bird clubs once or twice a year. There are usually birds for sale at these shows. Fortunately, most of the vendors are club members and are held to some sort of standard, though there's no real way to ensure that everyone at the show is legitimate.

Unfortunately, bird shows are a great way to spread disease, especially if there are unweaned babies present. You never know when you're going to get a diseased bird from a show or expo. You can go to ten great shows and then get stung on the eleventh. Your best bet is to get names and phone numbers of the vendors and then call the next day about the birds you're interested in seeing again.

Gift parrots

Many people give smaller parrots, like the budgie or the cockatiel, as gifts, especially to children. This is fine if the child has chosen the bird. If the bird is a surprise, the child may be disappointed, having wanted a puppy or kitten instead. A bird isn't an "instead" kind of companion. It's not a great idea to give *any* living thing as a gift.

Gift-giving holidays are terrible times to bring a new bird into the home. There is generally a lot of commotion during holidays, and the parrot might get lost in the shuffle. Holiday time can include a lot of scary things too, such as balloons, Christmas trees with all the decorations, and scary noises like fireworks. Your best bet is to bring the bird home (or to someone else's home) during a quiet time. This way, the bird can adjust without having to settle down in a new place and deal with a lot of hullabaloo.

Looking for a Healthy Parrot

Buying a healthy parrot is extremely important. This may seem obvious, but you have no idea how many people make a pity purchase when they see a sick bird. I've done it myself more times than I care to admit.

You'll discover more about parrot health in Chapter 10. For now, look for the following obvious signs of physical condition that should be easy to see when you visit the pet shop or the breeder's home.

Bright eyes

A parrot's eyes should be shiny, bright, and alert. If you notice any growths on the eyes or any crust or discharge, there's definitely a problem. Don't worry if the irises of the bird's eye are *pinning* (going from small to big and back again). That is normal in many species and does not indicate a health problem.

Clear nose and nares

A parrot's "nose" consists of two nostrils on the *nare,* the area just above the beak. On some birds, the nare is fleshy and very obvious, and on others, it is covered with feathers. The nostrils should be dry and clean. Worry if you see any kind of discharge from the nostrils.

Beak

The *beak* consists of the upper and lower mandibles. Both should be intact. Mites can attack the beak in some species, causing it to become crusty and overgrown. Malnutrition can also cause the beak to become distorted and overgrown, as can illness.

Sometimes a beak is misaligned — this is actually not a big deal and can be fixed gradually by a veterinarian. If part of the beak is missing, a veterinarian can bond it. In an African grey or a cockatoo, a healthy beak is powdery, not shiny. A shiny beak in these species can indicate the fatal virus called Beak and Feather disease.

Shiny feathers

Feathers should be shiny and tight in most species. In African greys, cockatoos, and mealy Amazons, feathers should be tight and powdery-looking. Ringnecks and eclectus have feathers that seem painted on.

There should be no obvious signs of missing feathers, which is an indication of disease, self-mutilation, or mutilation by another bird in the same cage. Cockatoos and cockatiels sometimes have a bald spot beneath the *crest* (feathers on the top of the head of some species that can be raised and lowered), which is completely normal.

A healthy bird has very clean feathers. A bird that's ill may not have the energy to preen itself and may let vomited food and defecation crust on its feathers.

Young birds tend to play and clamber around a lot, making their feathers ratty, especially the tail. Birds housed in too small a space may also look ratty, especially those with long tails. This is normal and should clear up after a few baths and the bird's first *molt* (a periodic general loss of feathers and regrowth of new ones) at home.

Feet

Feet should be clean and should grasp the perch tightly. Swelling, lameness, and crustiness are all signs of unhealthy feet.

Vent

The parrot's *vent* is where the waste and eggs come from and is on the bird's underside where the tail meets the body. The vent should be clean. If you notice crustiness or discharge, the bird is probably ill.

Attitude and stance

A healthy bird should show an attitude of health. It should be active, vocal, and interactive with the world around it. A fearful bird may not show the best attitude, so you'll have to use the preceding factors to decide whether the bird is simply afraid or if it's ill.

A bird that's puffy and sleeping on the bottom of the cage may be ill as well. It is trying to retain heat and energy. Of course, birds that are being picked on by other birds may exhibit the same behavior, especially if there's a bully parrot that won't let the other bird onto a perch. Parrots sleeping on two feet may be ill as well — healthy parrots pull one foot up close to the body when they sleep.

Getting a Guarantee

Wherever you decide to get your bird, you've got to request a health guarantee. Don't take the bird home without one. At the minimum, you should insist on a 48-hour return privilege — hopefully, you can get one that's at least 72 hours. This gives you time to take the bird to an avian veterinarian for a battery of health tests.

Of course, most people don't return the bird if the tests show an illness that can be taken care of easily. Once you've had the bird in your care for a couple of days, it's tough to take it back, especially when you know that the place it lived before is responsible for allowing it to get ill in the first place.

If the tests come back showing a fatal or incurable illness, it's a judgment call whether or not to take the bird back. Many do. I personally couldn't do it, because I'm a softie. I fall in love with the birds in my care, if even for a few days, and I go above and beyond to help them become healthy again (yes, it has happened to me). But it's totally within your right to ask for your money back, and you should if it's important to you. If you have other birds, and the illness is contagious, it is definitely important to get the ill bird out of your home.

Sometimes a bird will die within a couple of days of your bringing it home. In this case, your health guarantee will come in handy. Of course, you'll need to get a *necropsy* (a bird autopsy) performed by an avian veterinarian so that you know for sure what killed the bird. Sometimes something in the new environment kills the bird, and the guardian unwittingly blames the breeder or pet shop.

What to Ask Before You Buy

Before you buy any parrot, there are things you'll want to know about it and its background. The place where you're buying the bird should have adequate answers for you, or you shouldn't buy from there. Here are some potential questions:

✔ **How old is the bird?** You should be able to confirm the bird's age by examining the closed band around the bird's leg, which has the year of hatching imprinted on it.

✔ **When did the bird become fully weaned?** Make sure the baby is eating fully on its own before you take it home. Nobody should sell unweaned babies to inexperienced people. If someone offers to sell you an unweaned baby, turn it down.

✔ **How do you handfeed your birds?** Some breeders feed slowly with a syringe or a bent spoon. Some *tube feed,* shoving a flexible tube down the throat into the baby's crop (first stomach) and then pumping in the food. This method doesn't give the baby any individual time with the breeder and doesn't allow for natural feeding behaviors.

✔ **What has this bird been eating?** You'll want to continue with the same diet for a while, gradually adding lots of other healthy foods.

✔ **How much time is spent playing with the birds here?** Some places that sell birds don't play with them at all, which is very sad for these social creatures.

✔ **How long is your health guarantee, and what does it cover?** You'll want at least 72 hours to be able to take the bird to the avian veterinarian.

✔ **Can I call here if I have a problem? Who will help me? How much does this person know about birds?** You'll want to know that there's someone reliable to call if you run into a problem.

✔ **Is this bird vaccinated against the polyomavirus?** This virus is deadly in young birds and is extremely contagious. Most parrots today are vaccinated against it. There are also vaccines for Pacheco's disease, avian pox, and Newcastle's disease. Your bird may already come with one or more of these vaccines. Discuss these with your veterinarian, who will recommend whether or not your particular bird needs any of these.

Part II
Bringing Home Your New Parrot

The 5th Wave   By Rich Tennant

"I really don't think there's anything funny about teaching the parrot to sing the theme song from 'Mission Impossible' every time I use my Ab—Cruncher."

In this part . . .

Okay, you've got your parrot — now where are you going to keep him? This part is all about housing, accessories, and keeping a parrot safely in your home. Chapter 5 helps you choose the best cage, aviary, or habitat for your parrot. Chapter 6 is for the shopaholics out there — you know who you are. You'll find out what kinds of perches, toys, cups, and other accessories are appropriate for your new companion. Finally, Chapter 7 is a primer on parrot proofing your home and family introductions.

Chapter 5

A House to Call Home: Choosing Proper Housing

*I*t's not safe to allow a parrot to have free rein in any household. There are too many hazards for a curious parrot to find. A bird needs proper, safe, roomy, easily cleaned housing of its own.

Unfortunately, the words *bird* and *cage* have been associated for so long, most people think that parrots belong in cages. That's like saying whales belong in fish tanks. But as any parrot guardian will tell you, a parrot needs physical boundaries. So what's the solution?

The answer is to give the parrot the absolute largest and best cage possible. Ideally, the parrot should be able to actually fly around inside the cage. At the very minimum, the bird should be able to stretch both of its wings freely and be able to flap for exercise. Remember, a cage isn't a prison — it's a home.

Matching the Housing to the Species

Don't think about housing size in terms of the size of the bird. A lovebird will be well off in a cage of the same dimensions as a cage for a large macaw. The difference is in how the cages are built. I wish I could give you an idea of the exact dimensions of housing for each species, but that's impossible. In short, bigger is always better. Remember, parrots in the wild fly for miles a day to find food and water. That doesn't compare at all to the few feet of space that most captive parrots have. Those little pastel cages found in most pet stores and labeled for "budgies" aren't acceptable for any bird. Think big.

The cage bars should be spaced such that the bird can't stick its head through. If the bars aren't close enough together, the head can become stuck, and the bird can panic and break its neck. Smaller birds should have bar spacing no more than ½-inch wide.

The size of the bars is also important, depending on the species. Larger birds need thicker bars because they are powerful animals and can break thin bars — which can be extremely dangerous.

The "Right" Cage

There's no real "right" cage for a parrot. There are just better cages than others. The most important factor, other than size, is safety. A cage should be made of safe materials and contain no safety hazards. Ideally, parrots should be housed in a space large enough for flight, so keep that in mind.

Because parrots like to climb, a cage should have both horizontal and vertical bars. Horizontal bars give the parrot something to hang onto. Some cages today are made of acrylic, which doesn't offer any climbing area because of the smooth sides. With an acrylic cage, provide the bird with plenty of branches and safe rope for climbing.

Shape

Basically rectangular cages are best, shaped horizontally rather than vertically. Most parrots don't really use the bottom part of the cage much (except for those that like to *ground-forage,* like African greys and cockatiels) and will prefer to remain in the top third. Most of the activity is done in the higher area. A square cage is also okay, as long as it's large enough. A "dome" top or a top shaped like a house is okay as well.

Avoid round cages and cages shaped like pagodas or other complicated structures. The bars are often "tapered" as they reach the pinnacle of the cage, and a bird can get its neck or foot trapped in the small spaces. Imagine that the bird may stick its head through the bars in a larger spot and then climb up, wedging its neck in the smaller space between the bars — this can cause panic, which can cause injury. Also, decorative cages tend to be built more for the human than the bird and can contain scrollwork and other flourishes that can hurt the bird.

Sturdiness and material

A flimsy cage or a cage built for a small bird isn't safe for a large parrot. Some of the larger parrots can exert over 500 pounds per square inch of pressure with their beaks. The large hyacinth macaw is said to be able to exert 1,200 pounds per square inch. Such a bird can easily break out of a flimsy cage and harm itself on the broken, sharp metal rods.

The best material for caging is metal, preferably stainless steel, or regular steel coated with durable, nontoxic paint (see Figure 5-1) or powder coating (paint that's sprayed on as a powder and then baked onto the cage at high temperatures). Make sure that the cage you buy is from a reputable company, preferably one with a "brand name." Check out the company's Web site or brochure. Most good companies will have copious safety information. Beware cheaper no-name cages. Some cages may look safe, but the decorative parts or locks may contain lead and other toxic metals that can kill your bird pretty quickly. Also, the paint can chip on inferior cages, which is part of the reason why uncoated, medical-grade stainless steel cages are becoming so popular, even though they are more expensive, sometimes more than twice the price of a powder-coated cage, though powder-coated cages are a fine substitute and are what most people use.

Figure 5-1:
Stainless steel is thought to be the premium caging material. It's sturdy and easy to clean, and there's no danger of paint chipping off.

Photo by Carol Frank, Avian Adventures

Never put a parrot of any kind in an all-wood cage. It *will* chew its way out. Even if the bird doesn't chew the cage to bits, wood becomes damp and harbors bacteria, which can make a parrot ill. Wood can also harbor mites that infest birds. Also, beware of the cages that incorporate wood with acrylic or glass. These are lovely and look like a beautiful piece of furniture, but they are a nightmare to clean, and I've heard of parrots becoming very ill due to living in them.

Acrylic cages are becoming very popular these days and are great for people with allergies — they keep much of the mess inside, and some offer a ventilation system. Acrylic cages are very expensive, more than three or four times the price of a powder-coated metal cage, but are a nice alternative to cages with bars.

Cage bottom

The bottom of the cage should have wire grating. Some parrots, like African greys, who are ground-foragers like to play around in the bottom of the cage, and if there's no grate, they will play in their waste, which isn't sanitary at all and can lead to illness. In the wild, adult birds are never in contact with their own waste.

The cage should have a tray that pulls out so that you can easily change the newspaper. The bottom can be metal or plastic and must be washed and disinfected weekly.

Door types

The best doors fold downward (like a drawbridge over a moat) or open to the side, like your front door. The worst doors are "guillotine style," sliding up and down. These are very dangerous for mischievous parrots who try to escape, only to find the door slammed down on their neck. If your cage does have guillotine doors, be sure to clip them shut with a safe clip, like a stainless steel quick link. You can find these oval-shaped links at any hardware store, but make sure they're stainless steel, not another metal.

Most larger parrots need locks on their cage doors. Many cage manufacturers have come up with some ingenious locks that can withstand even the cleverest feathered Houdini. Don't use a padlock, though. You may need to reach your bird in an emergency, and it will take longer to remove. Also, some padlocks are made of dangerous metals. Of course, some birds absolutely do need a padlock because they keep escaping. In this case, find a stainless steel lock, and keep the key on a peg near the cage.

Cage dangers

Some metals, such as lead and zinc, are highly toxic to birds. Metal wire or mesh that you find at the hardware store is often *galvanized,* meaning that it's covered with zinc to withstand the weather without rusting. Galvanized wire isn't good for bird housing — unless you manage to get the zinc off, which I discuss in the next section.

Beware of cages that have a sliding plastic component to the doors. The plastic doesn't slide up and down easily, and your parrot's head can become caught. Also, beware of any spaces in the cage that your bird can fit its head into — a stuck bird tends to panic and injure itself.

Building your own cage

Some people build their own bird cages, which can be a nice alternative to store-bought cages. However, if you try it, you have to make sure that you build a safe cage. You can use a wooden structure, but the wood must be untreated, and every bit of wood should be covered completely with wire, or the parrots will chew it.

Galvanized wire can be made safe by spraying it a few times with pure white vinegar and scrubbing it roughly with a stiff wire brush. Then rinse it well and leave it out in the weather for about a month (preferably in rain and sun). It should be safe after that, but your best bet is to try to find nongalvanized wire to begin with.

If the cage is outside, it should have adequate shelter from the weather and the sun. If you're in a cold climate (where temperatures get below 55 degrees Fahrenheit), it should have a solid shelter area made of untreated wood with wire on the inside so that the birds can't chew it too much. The wire also must be doubled — one layer of wire placed over another, with about an inch between layers. Predators like raccoons, opossums, and rats lurking outside can pull a bird (or part of a bird) through even the smallest space in the wire. This double-wired cage is like a cage inside a cage — imagine the area where your birds will live encased by another cage that is only about an inch or two larger all the way around.

Cage Placement for Comfortable Living

Place the cage in a part of the house that gets a lot of traffic, but not so much traffic that the bird won't get any rest. A busy hallway is not a good idea. The best spot is a family room or the room where everyone watches television. Don't place the cage in a bathroom, garage, or the kitchen, as these rooms have too many temperature fluctuations and fumes.

Place the cage against a wall, preferably in a corner, where the bird will feel secure, and not too out in the open. Don't place the cage against a window, because the view may stress your bird if there are predators outside or cars going by. If the bird can see outside through the window, that's great, but it shouldn't be the bird's only option.

The Bedtime Cage

Some birds enjoy sleeping in a smaller, covered cage, especially if they live in a very large cage or aviary. A dark room and a small cage can make a parrot comfortable if the daytime cage is in a room that gets too much morning light or that becomes noisy early when someone is getting ready for work.

Your parrot should never, ever sleep in the bed with you. Many parrots have been killed by a sleeping guardian rolling over onto them. Your parrot should sleep in its cage or in a separate bedtime cage.

Cleaning the Cage

Clean the bottom papers in the cage every day or at least every other day. Clean perches at least twice weekly, as well as the bottom grating. Scrape the dried poop; then wash everything thoroughly with water. Clean the rest of the cage once a week or so, using only water. Allowing the cage to become damp and filthy is a good way to make your bird ill. Dampness allows mold and other fungi to thrive, which can give your bird a respiratory infection. Dried fecal matter can become airborne and infect the lungs, including yours.

Disinfecting the cage and toys is easy. A solution of 10 percent bleach and 90 percent water will kill most germs. Be sure to rinse and dry everything thoroughly. Bleach fumes are toxic for your parrot.

Don't use any commercial household cleaning products in or near the cage, as most of them are dangerous and can even be deadly. If you need to scrub with something abrasive, use baking soda and a stiff brush. If you need to disinfect, use plain vinegar mixed with water. Rinse thoroughly with water. Grapefruit seed extract (GSE) makes an excellent, nontoxic disinfectant, and all you need is one drop per ounce of water.

The Aviary

An *aviary* is an enclosed space where birds can fly free without being hampered by bars. Flying is great exercise — indeed, parrots were meant to fly, and it's the most natural thing they do. An aviary is usually located outside the home, but some larger homes may be able to have one inside.

The flight cage

A *flight cage* isn't quite an aviary, but it's considered larger than an regular cage. The idea is that the birds inside are able to fly, and the cage is small enough that it can fit inside a home. Be wary of so-called "flight cages" that seem too small for your birds to actually take flight.

The habitat

A *habitat* is an aviary on a grand scale, one that attempts to mimic a parrot's natural environment (Figure 5-2). Building a habitat is easier than you might think. A small aviary can be fitted with nontoxic trees and branches and a small waterfall. Voila! — a habitat that will stimulate your parrots physically and psychologically. Eventually, this will be the way most people house their birds. You can even build a small habitat in an apartment if you've got an extra room.

For a list of unsafe plants and trees for parrots, see the Web sites www.liparrotsociety.org/non-toxi.htm and www.cockatielcottage.net/houseplants.html.

Figure 5-2: The guardians of these macaws have built them a very large habitat so that they can fly and enjoy the weather.

Photo by Bob and Liz Johnson

Chapter 6

Let's Go Shopping! Avian Supplies and Accessories

. . . .

In This Chapter

▶ Furnishing the cage

▶ Finding the best toys

▶ Using nighttime accessories properly

▶ Cleaning . . . and more cleaning

. . . .

*W*hen you go to the bird section of the pet shop or your favorite e-commerce retailer, the multitudes of products to choose among can be dizzying. Which ones does your bird need? Which are useful, effective, and safe? Don't worry — you're in good hands here with an expert bird-shopper. Come along and discover the wonderful world of *bird stuff.*

Once you have your cage set up and placed in the appropriate spot, you need to furnish it with all the supplies that your parrot needs to remain contented and healthy. Read on to discover the essential accessories.

Perches

Your parrot will spend most of its life standing — parrots don't lie down to sleep — so you'll have to pay special attention to the health of its feet. Birds that stand on only one size and texture of perch can develop sore feet. Imagine wearing one pair of not-so-comfortable shoes day in and day out. Not a happy prospect.

Don't think of perches as permanent additions to the cage. Think of them as something for your parrot to chew and for you to replace. Many perches even come with toys attached as a bonus.

Fortunately for you and your parrot, many types of perches are available today. There's no one "miracle" perch on the market — to maintain foot health, you'll have to include various perches in various widths and materials.

Wooden perches

The cage you bought probably came with smooth, straight pine dowel perches. These are okay, but they certainly lack creativity. Better are twisty manzanita wood perches, holey cholla wood perches, hard cow wood, and other natural branchlike perches. Perches with various widths and textures promote foot health, and soft woods are great for chewing. So that pine perch is fine, just not as the only perch your parrot has. A voracious chewer is going to make toothpicks of it quickly anyway.

If the plain pine dowel is too large for your smaller bird, and he seems to be losing footing, use a very rough sandpaper to give the perch some texture. Then score the perch every half-inch or so, using a razor blade. That should make it easier for your bird to hang on.

You can even make your own wooden perches from trees you have in your yard. Just make sure that the tree is nontoxic (see Chapter 10) and has not been sprayed with pesticides or fertilizers — wash anything before putting it in your bird's cage. Nontoxic, fresh branches with leaves attached are especially fun and enrich the bird's environment.

Concrete and cement perches

These perches are rough and come in many sizes, shapes, and colors. The concrete perch helps with nail trimming, and your bird will also use it to file its beak. Make sure to clean these types of perches weekly.

Some people are stuck on the practice of slipping those little sandpaper sheaths over their bird's perches, thinking that they help with nail trimming. Actually, those sheathes hold moisture and can cause foot problems. Stick with the concrete perch that you can clean and disinfect easily.

Rope perches

Rope perches offer something else in the cage to tear apart and/or "preen." Make certain that you cut off any fraying threads as they appear. Rope threads can wrap around your parrot's neck or feet and can cause injury and death. If you notice that your parrot is ingesting the pieces of rope that it tears from the perch, take the perch away, and replace it with something less dangerous.

Heated perches

I recently invested in heated perches for my parrots. These plastic perches are plugged into a wall socket and maintain a low-grade heat. I didn't know how the birds would like these new-fangled things, but they absolutely love them.

There is a concern that the birds might chew the cord (which is reinforced to prevent just that), but a properly supervised parrot shouldn't be able to get into that kind of mischief.

Plastic perches

Plastic is easy to clean, but it doesn't promote great foot health. One plastic perch is fine for a parrot's cage, as long as the bird has many other types to choose among.

Coop Cups

The *coop cups* that come with a cage are usually plastic and too small, and you probably got only two — one for food and one for water. Your parrot should have at least three dishes, one each for:

- ✔ Basic diet (seeds or pellets)
- ✔ Water
- ✔ Fresh foods

You might even want two dishes for fresh foods. Don't ever mix fresh or cooked foods inside the seed or pellet dish. Seed and pellets tend to mold when damp.

Replace all your plastic dishes with stainless steel or ceramic dishes. Stainless steel is easy to clean and durable. Ceramic is nice because it's heavy and easy to clean, though it may break or chip, and if it does, you must replace it. Stainless is best because it doesn't scratch. Even tiny scratches in plastic or ceramic can harbor bacteria.

Buy two sets of dishes for your parrot — six dishes total. Make sure that the dish holders are compatible or that the bowls have their own bolts. Each morning, remove the old, soiled dishes, and replace them with new, freshly filled dishes. You can then thoroughly clean and dry the first set for next morning's feeding. This saves time and ensures that your bird's dishes remain clean, an important factor in keeping your parrot healthy.

TIP

For a messy bird that likes to fling seed everywhere, buy a covered crock or dish that has an opening in front for feeding. A covered dish is also protected from being soiled by waste or water. Just make sure that the opening in the cup is large enough for the bird to get its head in and out of easily.

Toys

Toys are extremely important to your parrot's mental and emotional health. Yes, birds have feelings, and though their feelings may be different from ours in some ways, they do have the capacity to become very unhappy, which can lead to neurotic and self-mutilating behaviors. Toys may not prevent or solve these problems, but they will help keep your parrot busy, which is a start.

Not all toys are created equal. Hanging a few indiscriminate toys in your parrot's cage won't necessarily make it content. Different types of toys offer different types of stimulation for your parrot (see Figure 6-1). The purpose of a toy is to allow your bird to expend energy. Remember, parrots in the wild fly many miles a day in search of food. They also engage in nesting activity and spend time raising their young. Your bird probably doesn't do these things. Toys simulate natural behaviors and may prevent your parrot from turning its pent-up energy on itself — or you.

Figure 6-1:
Many parrots love playing with elaborate toys such as this rope geodome.

Photo by Vicki Johnson

REMEMBER

Invest in more toys than will actually hang in your parrot's cage at any one time. Rotating toys in and out of the cage weekly keeps them new and entertaining. If your parrot has a particular favorite, keep that toy always in the cage, and rotate the others. This gives you a chance to clean and maintain the toys before you put them back into the cage at a later time.

Safety

Make sure that the toys you buy for your parrot are safe for it to use while unsupervised. Following are some tips for making sure a toy doesn't end up hurting your bird:

- ✔ Avoid toys that have "jingle bells" on them, which can easily catch a toe or beak.
- ✔ Avoid flimsy plastic toys.
- ✔ Avoid toys with very small parts, such as the clapper in a small bell (remove the clapper).
- ✔ Supervise any playtime with whiffleballs. Smaller birds can get their beak or toes caught in the holes, and larger birds may break the balls and ingest the little pieces.
- ✔ Parrots can catch a toe in chain links that aren't closed properly, so inspect all toys that have chains.
- ✔ Toys with unnatural materials that can be torn apart and ingested — such as stuffed animals or toys made from PVC plastic — are inappropriate for your parrot and will be effective dirt holders as well.
- ✔ Plush and fabric huts are okay, though *not inside the cage* — these are fine around the *playgym* (a freestanding playstand for parrots — may also be on top of the cage) and should be used only with supervision. If you notice the bird chewing holes in it or fraying it, remove it immediately, as this poses a strangling hazard.

A determined parrot can certainly break a toy designed for a much smaller bird. Make sure that any toy you buy is appropriately sized. Rings of any kind are especially dangerous if the toy and the parrot are mismatched. Many a parrot has stuck its head through a ring and been unable to get it out. Many of these cases result in death.

The rings and links that attach toys to the cage bars are huge offenders, injuring and killing many parrots each year. The only type of link you should use anywhere on the cage is a *stainless steel quick link*. You can find these at any hardware store. Never use snaphooks or key rings, as these can cause injury and death.

Eliminating unsafe toys does not limit your bird's toy selection. There are many types of safe toys to choose among.

Wooden toys

All *hookbills* love to chew on wood, and your parrot is a hookbill, so it naturally follows that you've got to invest in some wooden toys. Wooden toys usually come as chunks of colored wood strung on a thin rope, chain, or metal rod that you hang in the cage. Often, leather, treats, or other materials are strung along with the wood. Make sure that colored wood has been dyed in a natural dye, and look for any places in the toy where a toenail could potentially catch and break.

Preening toys

Some toys come with what looks like a little brush on the end and give a lone parrot the opportunity to *preen* (groom) something other than itself. Toys with intentionally frayed rope serve the same purpose, but watch these for strings that get too long, because they can become wrapped around a neck or foot.

Acrylic toys

Acrylic toys are virtually indestructible. Your parrot might own a single acrylic toy for its entire life. Just keep in mind that as pretty and fun as they are, acrylic toys do not allow for chewing and destroying, so they can't be the only type of toy you offer.

Puzzle toys

Toys with treats hidden or embedded in them are a great way to keep your parrot entertained. Your bird will have to work to get the treat and will expend energy doing so. These kinds of toys are often made for larger birds, so you might have to shop around to find one for a smaller parrot.

Making your own toys

Making your own toys is an inexpensive way to keep your bird entertained. Many household items can make safe, fun toys for your bird. Be sure, however, to *always* supervise playtime with homemade toys.

Save your Popsicle sticks, and tie them together with sisal twine into fun shapes — ladders, swings, and so on (sisal twine is made from natural fibers and is biodegradable; you can find it at the hardware or craft store). These are entertaining, safe to chew, and won't cost you much (though you'll have to eat a lot of Popsicles). Supervise, supervise, supervise!

Buy some small brown paper bags, and fill them with nuts, popcorn, cereal, plastic bottle caps, and other dry goodies. Then tie the end with a small piece of sisal twine, and offer the "lunch" to the parrot. You can also wrap up goodies in white tissue paper and tie with a snippet of twine. Never use twist ties. Clean brown boxes are fun to chew as well and can be filled with goodies.

Swings and ladders

Swings and ladders are also important accessories (see Figure 6-2). I haven't met a bird yet that didn't like its swing, as long as the swing is appropriately sized. Just be sure to change whatever link the swing came with to a safe quick link.

Ladders offer birds a little more exercise in the cage and are great chewing fodder as well. Don't place the ladder underneath a perch, because it will become soiled quickly.

Figure 6-2:
Swings and ladders can be as simple or elaborate as you like. This one is a combo and is made of soft wood that these poicephalus parrots can chew.

Photo by Ashley Lynn

Setting Up the Cage

Because birds have a natural tendency to want to be in the highest space in their cage, you have to take a few things into consideration when placing all the accessories inside.

Water and food dishes should be easy to get to. Often, the manufacturer places the cup holders toward the bottom of the cage, which isn't convenient. Use coop cups that can be attached higher in the cage.

Placing perches over food and water dishes will cause contamination. Don't crowd the cage or aviary with perches and toys — allow for some free space for flying, flapping, or clambering. Perches should be placed high in the cage, but not so high that your parrot has to crouch. Don't place perches under other perches, where they'll become natural poop catchers. Make the cage easy to clean by allowing room for your hand to enter it easily. Blocking the door with perches and toys is a bad idea.

Once you put your bird in the cage, watch to see if it's comfortable. Does it have to navigate too many objects to get to the water dish? Does it constantly bang into its perches and toys? You might have to do some rearranging.

Playgyms and Stands

The *playgym* or *playstand* is a play station made of wood, metal, or plastic that has perches attached (see Figure 6-3). A playgym allows your bird to play outside of the cage. You can place a playgym on top of your parrot's cage and have another, simpler stand that you can tote around the house. Many playgyms come with ladders, swings, and hanging toys. The more elaborate the playgym, the more your parrot will be able to do there.

Some parrots naturally learn to stay put on the playgym, whereas others flutter off the second you turn your back. Be sure to supervise all playgym activity.

Figure 6-3:
This playgym is stocked with lots of toys, giving these parrots something to do with their time out of the cage.

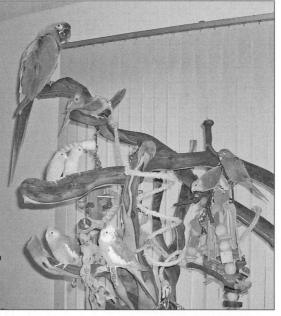

Photo by Carolyn Woodburn

Litter and Cage Bedding

The best bedding for the cage tray is and always has been newspaper. Printed newspaper has the additional bonus of having antibacterial properties. However, the ink isn't great for your bird if it likes to tear the paper. Unprinted newspaper is great, as are white paper towels and brown craft paper. Most absorbent paper is fine.

Kitty litter, corncobs, ground nut shells, pine and cedar shavings, and other such materials are absolutely not appropriate for your parrot's cage. These things cause illness when ingested, and cedar shavings cause respiratory distress.

Because the bottom of the cage must be cleaned daily, cut paper to the size of the cage, and put seven layers in the tray. Remove a layer each day, and at the end of the week, you'll know when it's time to remove the entire tray for a wash-down.

Bird Lighting

If you live in a northern climate, or if your birds never venture outside to get direct sunlight, you need to invest in *bird lighting.* Special wide-spectrum bulbs offer birds the degree of light that they need to remain healthy. Why? When sunlight hits the feathers, a certain oil on them becomes activated and changes to Vitamin D, which the parrot then ingests during preening (more details on this in Chapter 10), and bird lighting mimics sunlight in the Vitamin D–producing department. A few parrots — Amazons, for example — lack the gland that produces the oil, but regardless, all parrots should have bird lighting.

If you can't find the special bird bulbs, reptile bulbs will do. Place the lighting fixture about a foot away from the cage. If the parrot plays on the outside of its cage, place the light where the bird can't reach it. These bulbs get very hot.

Nighttime Cage Covers

Some people house their parrots in one cage or aviary during the day and place them in a smaller cage for the nighttime hours. Your parrot may feel more secure in a smaller cage at night. Birds don't see well in the dark and can become frightened, thinking that a predator is lurking (when the "predator" might just be someone in the kitchen making a midnight snack).

Mite protectors

Many people buy over-the-counter *mite protectors*, fearing that their parrot may succumb to an infestation of mites. These protectors come in the form of a small metal container with holes poked on one side and a chemical inside that is supposed to ward off mites. In fact, most indoor parrots do not get mites, and in the rare circumstance that they do, you will simply take your bird to the veterinarian. Mite protectors contain a pesticide that is actually harmful to your bird. Do your bird a favor, and forget the mite protector.

Some parrots, such as cockatiels and ringnecks, tend to have night frights — thrashing around the cage in the darkness. Night frights are very dangerous and can lead to serious injury. A smaller cage, along with a nightlight in the room and no cage cover, should help.

Covering your bird's cage keeps out nighttime drafts and can help keep the inside of the cage warm in a chilly home. The cover also enables your parrot to enjoy a certain amount of darkness in a room that may otherwise have a light on all night, such as a computer screen. Moreover, your schedule may allow you to sleep late, and you may want to use the cover as a sleep aid to ensure that your bird doesn't start whistling and chattering at the break of dawn.

Some birds enjoy having their cages covered. It allows them to settle down and gives them a sense of security. Some birds, however, are scared of the dark. If you want to cover a scaredy-cat bird, leave a small flap of the cover open so that some light comes through.

A custom, fitted cover is nice, because your bird will probably not be able to get to it and chew holes in it. Holes in a cage cover can cause the material to shred and the strings to get caught around your parrot's feet or neck. Any cage cover that becomes frayed or tattered should be tossed and replaced with a new one immediately.

Preventing Mess

Now that you've gotten your parrot plenty of accessories, think about yourself and your home for a moment. Parrots, as wonderful as they are, are messy. Flinging seed and soft food is their second-favorite hobby, right behind getting poop everywhere. There's nothing you can do to eliminate mess, but you can work to keep it to a minimum (see Figure 6-4).

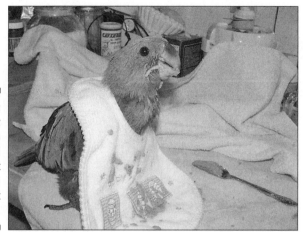

Figure 6-4:
This baby
eclectus's
owner had
to get
creative to
prevent
mess.

Photo by Roseanna Launstein

Mess accessories

Cage bloomers and other wrap-around devices that keep seed inside the cage
are great for finches, canaries, parakeets, and other smaller birds but are not
for larger parrots. Larger birds may become entangled in the bloomer. Cages
these days come with their own metal skirts that are great for containing mess.

You need something on the floor underneath the cage, especially if you have
carpeting. A plastic desk chair mat from the office-supply store works nicely
and is easy to clean. Of course, newspaper is a great old standby, and you can
toss it each day when it gets messy.

Air filters

Because some parrots are *dusty* birds — particularly cockatoos, cockatiels,
and African greys — meaning that they produce more feather dust than other
companion birds, you might want to invest in an air filter. I have two Hepa fil-
ters running 24 hours a day in my home, and I couldn't do without them. An
air filter is especially good for a person living in close quarters with their birds
or for someone with allergies. It's also good for the bird to breathe the cleanest air possible.

Cleaning solutions and supplies

Most household soaps and cleansers are not safe to use around your bird.
They can be toxic and may leave a residue, even if you thought you rinsed
well. Plenty of nontoxic materials are often around the house that clean just as

well as, if not better than, commercial cleansers. For example, baking soda is a great substitute for an abrasive cleanser. A vinegar solution (¼ cup vinegar per 1 cup of water) is a wonderful disinfectant and can be sprayed on just about everything. A 10 percent bleach solution (10 percent bleach, 90 percent water) is safe to use too, as long as you rinse *very* well (though the fumes aren't good for you or your bird, so be sure to ventilate well when you use bleach). Rinse everything three times; then rinse again, even if you're sure everything has washed away.

A wonderful and safe disinfectant can be found at every health food store these days: grapefruit seed extract (GSE). This bitter-tasting stuff kills fungi, bacteria, and viruses, and does a better job than alcohol or bleach. It's also nontoxic and is actually healthy to ingest. Use one drop GSE per ounce of water, and spray on everything. You can soak your bird's dishes in this product, too, and you should even include a few drops in the drinking water to prevent the growth of bacteria. Always dilute this product with water. This is my cleaner of choice, and I use it on everything.

Cleaning the cage

Replace your bird's soiled cage papers with clean papers every day, and thoroughly clean the cage once a week, including bars and perches. Soak everything in a 10-percent bleach, vinegar, or GSE solution, and scrub to remove debris. Don't let poop build up anywhere on the cage — that's just asking for health problems.

Your parrot's coop cups should be clean enough that you would eat and drink from them. Perches and toys should be scrubbed and disinfected at least once a week.

Chapter 7

Bringing Home Birdy: Introductions and Parrot-Proofing Your Home

The first few days — even the first few weeks — of a bird's life in a new home can be quite disconcerting for him. Give him the time and space to adjust to his new location and his new family, rather than expect him to be a part of everything right away. You'll probably adore your new bird from the first moment you see him, but he might be thinking, "What the heck am I doing *here?*"

Bringing a parrot into your home takes some forethought and preparation. Like puppies, parrots are curious. They are known to get into all kinds of mischief, which can often be deadly for them. Before you bring your new bird home, or very shortly thereafter, you should parrot proof any areas where your bird might roam. This chapter gives you tips for the first night, family introductions, and parrot proofing.

The First Night

Some baby parrots will settle in right away and want to be cuddled or at least played with on the first day at home. But others are more cautious and may be afraid of various household residents, such as the family dog, and will need some time to adjust to the new environment.

Don't force interaction right away. It's easy to get disappointed with a new parrot that behaved friendlier in the pet shop or breeder's home. It's not that the bird doesn't like you. He just doesn't know you yet.

If the parrot is fearful, give him a few days before you try to fish him out of the cage. Have the family talk to him and give him treats. If it seems that he really wants to come out, you can take him out and play. Ideally, the parrot's only job at this point should be to get used to his new housing and environment. The good news is that most handfed and well-socialized birds are pretty good about adjusting quickly. Wild-caught and parent-raised birds take more time.

Naming Your Bird

Give your new parrot a name right away, and start using it every time you play with her or pass her cage. Make your voice as soothing as possible, and repeat the same phrases every time you service her cage, such as "Roxy, want some fresh water?" and "Roxy, want to come out and play?"

The best names for birds are one or two syllables and generally have a "hard" sound somewhere in them, like k, p, t, x, d, q, and the like. This is only because these sounds are easy for a parrot to pick up and repeat more quickly than other sounds. Of course, no one's going to stop you from naming your parrot Supercalifragilisticexpialidocious. But don't expect her to repeat that back to you.

Thriving on Routine

In the wild, the parrot agenda revolves around the sun and the seasons. They eat at a certain time, roost at a certain time, and nest at a certain time. Your companion parrot is the same bird with the same programming, but his life is far different from the lives of his wild cousins. Your parrot lives in a world where lights go on and off at random times, where the temperature is basically constant, and where the same type of food is plentiful all year long. Cushy life? Actually, the lack of natural cycles can be stressful on your bird, who will want to sleep when the sun goes down and rise when it comes up.

A solid routine is a must for your parrot. Get into the habit of waking him up at a regular hour and covering him or darkening his room at a certain hour, starting with day one.

Using an automatic timer connected to a lamp near your parrot is a great idea.

Feed the same things at the same time each day, and stick to a cleaning schedule. This way, your parrot will come to expect certain things and become comfortable with his environment. Remember, in the wild the sun does not choose to come up at a radically different time each day.

To ensure that you and your family stick to a routine, buy a calendar or a dry-erase board, write down everything that needs to be done on a daily basis, and cross off the tasks as you do them. That way, you'll always know that your parrot has been cared for each day.

Parrot as Member of the Family

The parrot is a family companion and, like a person, will develop a different relationship with each member of the household. Part of the reason for this is because certain parrots are attracted to certain people and are afraid of or don't like others. No one really knows why parrots prefer one person over another. It may have to do with hair color, hair style, height, or other physical characteristics. It may have to do with body language. In some cases, it has to do with who raised the bird or the types of people who were or weren't nice to it in a prior home.

You won't know ahead of time how the bird is going to react to everyone in the household as she becomes comfortable and gets to know the family. This is why it's important to know how to behave around a parrot so that you don't *teach* her unwanted behaviors from the start.

Be unafraid; be very unafraid

It's important that none of the members of the family is afraid of the parrot. Parrots don't necessarily sense fear the way dogs can, but they do pick up on body language. Of course, some people can't help being afraid, and that's normal. The beak is formidable on most parrots, and one bite can turn a wary person into someone who never goes near a parrot again. Even someone who is afraid of the parrot can have a relationship with it, though the relationship doesn't necessarily have to be hands-on. That family member can feed and talk to the bird and perhaps can develop a mutual trust over time.

There's a problem with the scaredy-cat member of the family, however. Many parrots like to play psychological games with their humans, and the most fun person to play with is the fearful person. Here's an example of how this happens: The fearful person tries to give the parrot a nut, and the bird reaches for it, of course. The fearful person becomes afraid, pulls his or her hand away quickly, and perhaps even makes a noise indicating fear. "Ah," the parrot thinks. "That was kind of fun. Let me try that again." Now, when the fearful person approaches, the parrot lunges a little, getting a reaction from the person, of course. This continues until the parrot is out-and-out diving at the fearful person, often with no intention of biting but merely to get the fearful reaction. Because this is *so* fun, the bird may start lunging at other members of the family, scaring them, too, until the bird has no friends in the household at all. Meanwhile, he can't understand why he's being left alone — he's just playing, after all. Eventually, because no one handles him, he becomes wild or neurotic, and his life in the family goes downhill. He gets sent to another home and eventually winds up in a shelter or, worse, in the basement or closet.

Another scenario is the person who holds his or her hand out to the parrot to have him climb on. Just as the parrot is about to do so, or perhaps has already stepped a foot onto the hand, the person becomes afraid and jerks the hand away. The parrot learns that this person isn't to be trusted and views him or her suspiciously. When the person goes to pick up the bird again, the bird is likely to bite or climb away from them. Then the person gets insulted. "The parrot doesn't like me! To the basement with that bird!"

You see, being afraid is one thing — *behaving* afraid is another. When you behave afraid around a parrot, you either teach it to become fearful or aggressive. Often, the aggression is just an act, but not many people stick around long enough to find out. Imagine that there's someone in your life who's deathly afraid of you and behaves that way when they're with you. Wouldn't you begin to view that person with deep suspicion? It's not exactly the same thing with parrots and people, but it's always a good idea to try to see the world from your parrot's perspective. I discuss unwanted behaviors in Chapter 14.

In the meantime, here are some things to think about. The ideal parrot family:

- Isn't afraid of the bird at all and sees parrot games for what they are most of the time: just bluffing.
- Approaches the bird with confidence and respect, and knows when the bird is buffaloing and when it means business.
- Doesn't get insulted or have a bruised ego when the parrot bites or behaves coldly. Biting and giving the cold shoulder don't mean the relationship is over and don't mean the parrot has gone bad. There's always a reason for aggression.
- Handles bites with calmness and grace.

Introducing people

Everyone in the family should meet the bird when the household is calm and quiet. If the bird is a baby or very friendly, sit on the floor with him, and allow him to approach whomever he likes. If the bird keeps going back to his housing, try another room. Pass the bird around gently, and talk to him in a soothing tone.

Most smaller parrots love millet spray, and larger parrots love nuts, such as almonds, so have some of these on hand.

If the bird is from a shelter, it may behave differently in the first week than it will later. Some birds are fearful but calm down as they get to know the household. Others parrots have an aggressive streak that they hide well in those first few days but then begin antagonizing the household once they are comfortable there. Don't let those first few days set the tone for the rest of the relationship. Watch for any changes in behavior, good or bad, and reward good behaviors with verbal praise and treats. Ignore bad behaviors as best you can. I discuss more about this in Chapter 14.

Introducing pets

If you have other pets or want to acquire some in the future, this section is going to be important for you. There are plenty of stories of parrots getting along with other pets, but for every success story, there is another story with a tragic ending. Parrots are delicate and can be injured or killed with the barest scratch of a tooth or nail. Even if Fido *is* just playing, your parrot can be killed in an instant. Don't let this happen!

I can't caution you enough to keep your parrot and your other pets far from one another. Please, if you take no other advice from this book, take this: Keep dogs and cats well away from your bird (see Figure 7-1).

Dogs and cats are predators, and parrots are prey. This is fundamental to understanding the relationship between them. Dogs and cats have eyes in the front of their heads (like we do — we're also predators). Parrots have eyes on the sides, so they can see far more of the world around them. This is one way of telling predator animals apart from prey animals.

Cats are mesmerized by small, moving objects, including small parrots. Cats have a type of bacteria in their mouth called *Pasteurella bacteria* that is deadly to birds. If your cat even grazes your parrot with a tooth and breaks the skin, the bird is doomed unless you get him to the veterinarian's office *right away,* and even that doesn't guarantee that he will live. Most die within 24 hours. Don't think that just because Feathers and Meowsy are amicable when you're home means that they get along when you're gone. Surely you've seen the cartoons about this hidden drama in the household. Never, ever, *ever* (did I say ever?) allow your cat access to your parrot at any time.

Figure 7-1:
Kitties and parrots — not a good mix. For one thing, cats have bacteria in their mouth that is deadly to birds. This kitten looks like it has met its match!

Photo by Robin Miller

Some dogs, such as terriers and sighthounds, are bred to chase small, swift, moving objects. Other dogs — like spaniels, poodles, and retrievers — have been bred to specifically hunt and retrieve *birds.* Other breeds are content to not think of your parrot as a meal, but as more of a toy, which is not a good circumstance either (see Figure 7-2).

Figure 7-2:
Dogs are the natural enemies of birds, but there's a slight chance that some dogs and some parrots can get along reasonably well — *supervised* only!

Photo by Denise Bell

Other pets in the household can also pose a threat to your parrot. Snakes are a natural enemy of birds, and a snake is smart enough to figure out how to weasel inside your parrot's cage and eat him whole. Imagine waking up in the morning to find your snake curled up in your parrot's cage with a big lump in his body. Bye, bye birdie. It happens more often than you'd think. Never let your snake loose around your bird. A related issue is that birds are so programmed to be fearful of snakes, even a shushing sound that you might make to calm your parrot can frighten him because it sounds like snakes hissing. Instead of shushing, speak in a calm, relaxed voice.

Ferrets and rats are quite dangerous to birds as well. Both are predators, and both will be attracted to the movement and smells coming from your bird's cage. Though a well-fed rat may not attack your bird (it will more likely want the fruit at the bottom of the cage), a ferret is a voracious predator and won't hesitate to pounce on your parrot.

Fish also pose a danger to your parrot, believe it or not, or at least their tanks and bowls do. Drowning is a major cause of death in birds, so be sure to keep your fish tank tightly covered, and double your precautions if you keep piranha!

Introducing other birds

People often keep parrots in mixed aviaries. Indeed, some parrots have a docile and amiable nature, and can live well in a large enough space with other birds. But some parrots can be quite fierce and treacherous to other birds. Lovebirds, for example, will not accept any other birds of similar size in their area and will even kill a much larger bird. Unless birds show signs of deep affection for one another, such as feeding and mutual preening, it's best to keep them apart. Also, larger birds should never be housed with much smaller birds, and playtime between "Laurel and Hardy" should always be supervised. See Chapter 13 for more information on introducing parrots.

Quarantine

Before you bring another bird home to the birds you already have, you should set up a place where you can quarantine the new bird. This spot should be well away from your other birds, preferably with a separate ventilation system. Care for the new bird *after* you've cared for the established birds, and wash thoroughly after each interaction. Quarantine traditionally lasts 40 days, though some people quarantine for only 30 days, whereas others do for 3 to 6 months.

Take your new bird to an avian veterinarian during this time to run the full gamut of tests to make sure your new addition is healthy and not carrying any diseases that are contagious to your existing feathered pals.

Parrots and Children

Parrots can teach children about accountability, empathy, and camaraderie, and can provide a child a valuable, hands-on lesson that will last well into adulthood: how to love, care for, respect, and maintain another being. When a child cares for a bird, the relationship lasts longer than the life of the pet. Becoming guardian to a parrot also teaches an important lesson everyone has to learn: Nothing lives forever.

If you buy a parrot for a child, expect that you will be the one caring for the bird for the long term. Because parrots live for 15 to 80 years or more, your child may grow out of this companion and move on to bigger and better things, such as college and marriage. The bird is often left behind.

Unfortunately, small birds that belong to children are often housed in tiny cages that fit the size and décor of the child's room. These unfortunate birds are subject to the whimsies of the child, whether that means too much stimulation or none. A child's room might be too dark and quiet while the child is at school, and the parrot might sit alone and languish, too sad to even play with his toys. Even though the parrot is the child's bird, place the cage in a room where it will get attention from the whole family. Explain to the child that the bird will be lonely in his or her room, because he or she is away most of the day.

Many parents and relatives with good intentions give birds as gifts to children. This is not a wonderful idea. What if the child doesn't want the bird? Also, holidays are not a great time to give any living creature to a child. There's too much commotion during holiday or birthday time, and a new parrot's needs may get forgotten. A better gift is an IOU for a parrot, along with a parrot book. Then you can take your child with you to pick out his or her own bird. This is also a good way to determine whether or not your child actually wants a parrot (see Figure 7-3). Little Johnny may become more entranced with the turtles.

You probably have ground rules for many things in your home when it comes to your children, and your parrot should not be exempt. Younger children can be unintentionally rough, and older children might be absentminded or inattentive. Creating rules from the start can help transition your bird peacefully into the family.

All interaction between bird and child should be closely supervised. I have heard horror stories that I won't repeat here, but I'll just repeat my warning: Supervision is essential.

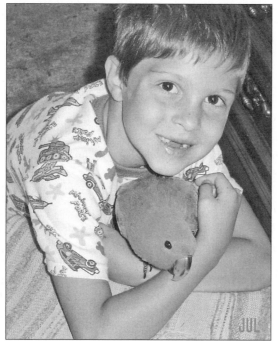

Figure 7-3:
Kids and birds can have a great relationship as long as there's adult supervision.

Photo by Debbie Collier

Some basic ground rules are important for a child/bird relationship. Share these rules with your children when you first bring your parrot into your home:

- ✔ **Move slowly.** Birds are frightened by rapid movements. The child may be afraid of the parrot and may jerk his or her arm away, flinging the parrot to the floor. Explain to the child that your parrot will not hurt him or her (not badly, anyway) and that it's important to remain calm around a bird, no matter what happens.

- ✔ **Speak softly.** A screaming child, even if he or she is screaming with delight, is terrifying to a new parrot. Teach your child to use a soft, soothing voice when talking to the bird.

- ✔ **Don't fear the parrot.** Teach your child not to be afraid of the parrot. Fear of the new companion will lead to an unhappy and neglected bird.

- ✔ **Never shake, hit, or rattle the cage.** Your parrot is just being a bird and is only going to be as amusing as he can be. Your child may not understand that and try to get the bird to do something more exciting. Explain to your child that the bird will become terrified if his whole home is rattled.

- ✔ **Your parrot needs playtime, just like you do.** Parrots need out-of-cage time every day. Children have busy lives and may forget that their bird relies on them for interaction. Perhaps your parrot can sit on the child's shoulder while he or she does homework, watches television, or practices piano.

- ✔ **Your parrot thrives on routine.** Birds like to know what will happen and when it will happen, every day. Create a routine including your bird and your child, and make sure that he or she sticks with it.

- ✔ **Birds need "time out" too.** Parrots can get overstimulated and tired if handled by an active child for hours on end. The poor parrot will want nothing more than a drink of water, a snack, and a nap! Make sure that your child knows that the bird needs a break every now and then. After a few minutes of refreshing himself, your parrot may be ready to play again. A tired bird becomes cranky and may get nervous and agitated. This is a good time to put your bird back into his housing and let him recover.

- ✔ **Never take your parrot outside without a carrier.** Your child may want to show off the bird to friends, but there are a lot of dangers lurking outside, including having your bird take off into the wild blue yonder. If your child just *has* to show your bird to her friends, make sure that you supervise the introductions and that your parrot is safely stowed away in a carrying cage. The "chain around the leg" isn't used anymore as a result of too many broken legs. Today, you can find flight suits and harnesses that go around the bird's body and are attached to a leash, but not all birds will allow such a contraption, and you'll only lose your bird's trust if you force the issue. Your best bet is a safe carrier when the bird goes to show-and-tell.

- ✔ **Don't squeeze the bird.** Birds are not able to breathe if they are held around the chest, even if held lightly, because they have a different breathing system than we do. Tell the child not to carry the bird around, but instead let the bird perch on a hand or shoulder and be carried that way. It is best that your child not try to *hold* the parrot. Your child should never be in the position of restraining the bird. That is reserved for wing clipping, toenail clipping, and veterinary examinations.

It depends on the kid

Gauge the maturity level of your child. Is he or she able to be responsible, at least partially, for a companion as fragile and complicated as a parrot? A child between the ages of eight and ten can probably take care of a parrot, with supervision. A younger child might become panicked if the parrot bites or scratches, and in doing so, the child could possibly injure or kill the bird.

Here's a good, practical tip: Place a long strip of masking tape a few feet in front of your parrot's cage. The space between the masking tape and the cage is considered the Quiet Zone, where everyone moves slowly and speaks softly. This will help your children remember some of the rules.

Houseguests

Strangers often find birds fascinating, especially if they don't have one themselves, and they may ask to hold or interact with your parrot. Sometimes they don't ask at all but just approach the cage. If you are certain that your parrot won't mind the attention from a stranger, you can allow the interaction. Take the bird out of the cage yourself, and place him on the guest's hand. Always supervise interaction between your guest and the bird. Your guest might not be used to handling birds and may become alarmed by something the bird does, which can result in an injury to either party.

If the guest owns birds of their own, make sure they wash their hands before handling your parrot. Don't take the chance of possible disease transmission.

Don't *ever* let your guests smoke around your parrot. Your bird's respiratory system is very sensitive, and he can become quite ill from smoke. Also, nicotine residue from a smoker's hands will get onto the bird and can cause plucking behaviors. If your guest insists, suggest that he or she go outside or into another room, or smoke out the window far from the bird, and that all hands are washed before touching the parrot.

Houseguests should follow the same ground rules with your parrot that the rest of the family does. Don't be afraid to enforce these rules. Your parrot can become distressed by a stranger. Often, it's not even the stranger that's the problem, but the stranger's watch, jewelry, hairstyle, hat, glasses, or anything else the bird isn't used to. Have the guest remove anything obtrusive that you feel might scare the bird.

You might want to have some excuses on hand for not allowing a houseguest to play with your bird:

- ✔ The bird bites and will draw blood. He goes for the jugular.
- ✔ The parrot doesn't like (color of guest's shirt) and will attack it.
- ✔ Okay, you can hold the bird, but he'll poop all over you. Is that okay?
- ✔ The parrot is afraid of people with (guest eye color, hair color, nail color, and so on).

Polly does not want a cracker, especially from you

I might as well mention something that drives me crazy about guests. When people come over to my home, they inevitably start talking to my parrots in "parrot speak" — that obnoxious, whiny, shrill, "Polly wanna cracker? Rrraaawk!" cliché parrot voice. I cringe every time I hear it. I tell my guests that they should speak to the parrots in a normal voice so that the parrots learn to speak that way, too. The main problem, really, is my African grey, who is likely to pick up the "Rrraaawk!" part of the phrase and repeat it over and over until I have no hair left to pull out. See Chapter 14 for advice on extinguishing unwanted words and sounds.

Parrot Proofing Your Home

Yes, you have to parrot proof your home, just like you'd toddler proof it, only twice as much. Usually, it's enough to lock doors and put things out of a toddler's reach. With parrots, everything from the ground up is fair game.

Here's a parrot proofing protocol designed to keep your bird safe:

1. **Give away all toxic houseplants.** (See Chapter 10 for tips on plants.)

2. **Get rid of all cookware that has polytetrafluoroethylene (PTFE).** That's nonstick cookware, a coating that comes on anything from pans to cookie sheets. I know, scrubbing pots is a pain. But it's worse to have to rush a dying bird to the veterinarian. When PTFE is heated, it emits an odorless fume that's deadly for birds. I use stainless steel, glass, and ceramic, and I love it all.

3. **Get rid of everything *else* that has PTFE in it.** That means space heaters, hair dryers, breadmakers, clothing irons, and many other items that are heated. If you do use these things, make sure the room is extremely well ventilated when you do. By the way, the fumes that PTFE emits aren't good for you, either, and can cause you to feel flu-ish.

4. **Cover *all* standing water.** This includes the dog's bowl, a fish tank or bowl, the toilet (put the lid down), fountains, pools, and even glasses of water.

5. **Sticker all mirrors and glass, and/or leave them very dirty.** Birds often fly right into glass, thinking it's open space — a good way to break a neck.

6. **Screen all windows.** Make sure all windows in the house have intact screens.

7. **Remove or cover *all* lamps, especially those with halogen bulbs.**
Those lamps are very hot, and if a bird lands on one, especially a small bird, injury will definitely result.

8. **Remove all lead objects from where the parrot can reach them.** I'm talking about stained glass, fishing weights, curtain weights, pottery, and anything else containing lead. It has to go. Some jewelry also contains lead. Get rid of all old lead paint on your walls — you should do this for your own health as well.

9. **Hide or remove all exposed electric wires.** These are irresistible for chewing. Dangerous!

10. **Remove anything scented from the room.** That includes those plug-in scent warmers, scented candles (all candles, really), and anything else that emits an odor that's supposed to cover up another odor, because they will harm your bird's respiratory system. Also, those wax pellets that burn like candles are especially problematic, because they seem like a treat — yet they're deadly. The same goes for any aerosol sprays or scented sprays. Even if you spray something on an item, don't bring the item into the bird's area until it is completely dry, and ventilate the area anyway, just in case.

11. **Put away all household chemicals.** Stow everything away in cabinets.

12. **Get rid of sticky fly traps or any kind of mousetrap.** If your bird does get stuck in the sticky stuff, dust a generous amount of flour on the bird and sticky item, and work the item off gently. See Chapter 10 for more advice on how to get sticky stuff and oil off a bird's feathers.

13. **Make the laundry room off limits.** Curious birds can get into the dirty clothes pile and suffocate or get washed accidentally.

14. **Remove ceiling fans.** If that's too drastic, at least put a warning sign on the wall switch: *If fan is ON, make sure bird is IN.* A ceiling fan is an effective birdie blender. Ouch.

15. **Scrape all chipping paint, and repaint.** Curious parrots might find the chips tasty, and many old paints contain lead. Ventilate well if you paint while your bird is in the house.

16. **Make all beds, all the time.** This is a great way to get your kids to make the bed. Curious birds can wriggle under the covers while you're not watching and either suffocate or be crushed when you lie down.

17. **Change your flooring.** Okay, this is pretty extreme, but it's fairly dangerous to have a parrot that's the same basic color as your carpet or floor. Many a camouflaged parrot has been the victim of a misplaced shoe.

Part III
Caring for Your Parrot

The 5th Wave   By Rich Tennant

©RICHTENNANT

"The bird's diet is regulated pretty carefully, except when Doug falls asleep after dinner with his mouth open."

In this part . . .

*E*ating, pooping, flinging seed — yep, sounds like a parrot. This part gives you the lowdown on the best diet for your feathered friend. Seed and water isn't going to cut it. Chapter 8 tells you all about nutritious foods and why keeping your parrot fit is so important. Chapter 9 is all about grooming, from the beak to the toesies. Chapter 10 is about illness and health and gives you the info you need to be able to tell if your parrot is ill. You also get info on how to choose an avian veterinarian, your bird's best friend aside from yourself.

Chapter 8

Eating Like a Bird: Proper Parrot Nutrition

A good, balanced diet is one of the most important factors in keeping your parrot healthy. A lifetime of poor nutrition can mean a life cut in half, or worse — a very short life filled with illness and pain. A parrot that "lives" on an inadequate diet is prone to many nutritional disorders, liver problems, feather disorders, and respiratory diseases, among other issues.

Most people think that seed and water is the proper diet for a parrot. Seed has been considered the standard parrot diet for so long that many people still believe that seed and water are enough to sustain a companion parrot. This is hardly the case. Research in recent years shows that birds need far more than just seeds to thrive. Sure, your parrot may survive for a while on seed and water, but it would be like a human being consuming only white bread and water. This chapter helps you discover the best diet for your parrot and shows you how easy it is to make sure that your bird is getting what he needs.

First Things First: Water

Any discussion of diet has to begin with water, which is essential to all life. Clean, fresh water is crucial to your parrot's health. Many parrots live in very wet regions where water is plentiful, though others live in places where there is drought for a few months of the year. But don't think that just because a wild parrot deals with drought that your companion bird should. A small parrot drinks approximately two to three teaspoons of water a day — barely a sip for an adult person — but it's that sip that keeps your bird alive.

Tap water isn't great for your birds because it contains all kinds of contaminants, depending on where you live. At the very least, most tap water contains chlorine, which isn't good for your bird's bodily system. Use only bottled or filtered tap water. I wouldn't ever give my birds unfiltered tap water (or drink it myself — I use a filter attached to my tap).

Clean and refresh your parrot's water dish at least twice a day, once in the morning and once in the late afternoon. Clean it any time you notice that the water is becoming murky or soiled. Parrots tend to toss things in their water, and there's always the potential for the dish to be spoiled by droppings. This charming mixture is often affectionately called *poop soup*. Pretty gross, huh? You wouldn't want to drink it, and your parrot shouldn't have to either. Soiled water breeds bacteria that can be very harmful for your bird if ingested. Keep water dishes out from under the perches, and try to hang them higher in the cage rather than on the cage floor.

Your bird's water dishes should be clean enough that you would drink out of them. That means a daily disinfecting of the dishes. A 10-percent bleach solution does the trick, but it's not good for the birds and can leave a residue. Instead, use Grapefruit Seed Extract (GSE), which you can buy from any health food store. GSE has a lot of other uses, too, which I discuss throughout this book. GSE has been found 100-percent effective as an external disinfectant, as opposed to alcohol, which has only 72-percent effectiveness. Even surgical soap, which doctors use to clean their hands before going into the operating room, has only 98-percent effectiveness in killing all germs. Add 20–30 drops of GSE to a sink full of water, and let the dishes soak for a half-hour. The GSE is nontoxic even in large doses and can be used for a variety of external and internal purposes. Having two sets of dishes is really helpful with keeping the water dishes clean — one can soak while you refill the other. You can also rinse all of your produce in GSE to remove or kill any germs or debris.

Some people like to give their birds water from a bottle or tube. I'm not a fan of this practice. The bottle can get clogged, and the water in the tube can become stale and filled with bacteria if it's not changed often enough. When people use these types of waterers, they tend to change the water less frequently, leading to yucky water that's not fit to drink. Better to change the water more often than deal with a bird that's getting ill from his water. However, some people do like using the bottles. Avian veterinarian Dr. Gregory Burkett, DVM, owner of The Birdie Boutique in Durham, North Carolina, recommends that his clients use water bottles because the bacteria in a water dish doubles every 2–3 hours, but the water in the bottles can't become contaminated like bowls in open air. He recommends checking the bottle twice a day to make sure it's not clogged and changing it once every 24 hours.

For my money, stainless steel is the best material for water dishes. It doesn't scratch, and it's easy to clean. Plastic tends to scratch with scrubbing, and bacteria will make nice little homes in the small grooves in the dish. As the months go by, a plastic dish becomes impossible to disinfect. Ceramic is a good material as well, but the glaze can crack, and bacteria will set up shop in the fissures. Better to begin with stainless steel, a dish that might even outlast your bird.

When you go to the pet store, you will notice various water-soluble-vitamin supplements available. These supplements are supposed to give your parrot the extra vitamins she needs to stay healthy. The supplements that you can buy in the pet shop are not regulated or set to any standards the way human vitamins are, so you can't really be sure what you're buying. I know many bird guardians (myself included) who use human-grade multivitamins and minerals in their birds' water. Also, some bird companies are now manufacturing avian supplements to human-grade standards. Some birds, such as African grey parrots, seem to need extra calcium, as do breeding birds, so a mineral supplement is a good idea.

If you do choose to supplement your parrot's water, put two or three drops of GSE and two or three drops of organic apple cider vinegar in the water as well. Both of these items retard the growth of bacteria. Just don't think more is better with either of these products. The GSE is very bitter, and the apple cider vinegar is stinky, though both are very healthful for your bird, both inside and out.

Anything else that you add to your bird's water should be cleared first through your avian veterinarian or an avian expert that you trust. Birds that have nutritional disorders, illnesses, behavior problems, and other issues may need other types of supplements in their water (and food), which I discuss a little later in this chapter.

A Parrot's Dietary Requirements

Most of what veterinarians know about bird nutrition comes from research on poultry. The fact is, there are so many varieties of parrot species living all over the world, it would take many decades of research to discover all of their individual needs. The parrot has been the subject of dietary research for a fraction of the time that poultry has.

When you go to the pet shop you will probably see foods labeled *Finch* or *Parakeet* or *Parrot*. Think about this: Some birds come from Australia, and some from Africa. So is one food right for both kinds of birds? Well, yes and no. Because little research has been done on parrot nutrition relative to the research done on poultry, there's no *perfect* diet formulated for any parrot-type bird. The best anyone can hope for is an *approximation* of the correct diet for any given species. The good news is that many breeders, hobbyists, and parrot guardians have had wonderful success with an approximated diet. Success here is defined as raising and keeping healthy, productive, long-lived parrots.

The digestive system

Before I launch into what to feed your parrot, I'd like to take a look at how the food works once it's inside the bird. Your bird's digestive system is far different from your own (see Figure 8-1). First of all, your parrot's digestive system is equipped to handle far more food on a food-to-body-weight ratio than yours can. You'd have to eat 20 to 40 pounds of food a day, depending on your weight, to equal the dietary needs of a parrot, who will eat 20 percent or more of his body weight daily. Imagine if you had to eat ten pounds of chocolate cake a day just to stay at your current weight (a girl can dream, can't she?). The next time someone accuses you of stuffing yourself, say you're eating like a bird. Birds have to eat a lot more than we do because their body temperature is higher and their metabolism is faster — lucky ducks!

Unlike your moist mouth, your parrot's mouth is relatively dry. It crushes food with its hard beak and swallows it down the esophagus, where the food is moistened before entering an organ called the *crop,* a sac located at the breast where the food is softened before moving on to the stomach. The crop is an interesting organ — it expands a great deal to allow a bird to pig out on something and still allows the bird to make a swift getaway to a safer place to digest the food. Many of a wild parrot's favorite foods are at ground level, which is not a safe place.

The stomach is divided into two parts: the *proventriculus* and the *gizzard.* From the stomach, the food is broken down and nourishes the body before being carted off to the *cloaca,* which is kind of like our large intestine. After that . . . well, you know what happens. You have probably cleaned up enough of it not to need a more detailed explanation.

Birds poop more frequently than we do for an important reason: A heavy bird expends more energy during flight than a light bird, and poop has weight. That's why there's so little space in a bird's cloaca. Okay, enough on poop — next topic!

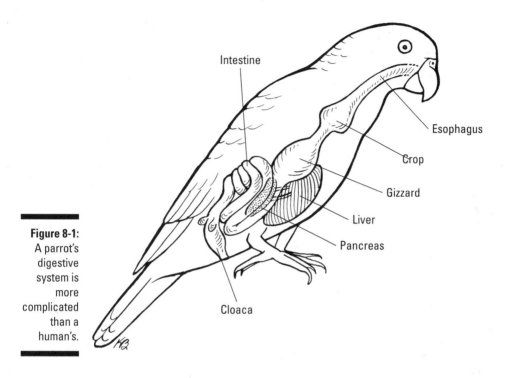

Parrot Digestive System

Intestine

Esophagus

Crop

Gizzard

Liver

Pancreas

Cloaca

Figure 8-1:
A parrot's
digestive
system is
more
complicated
than a
human's.

Eating in the wild

A wild parrot eats the foods that are available during a particular season. For example, at some times of the year young grass seeds are available, and a wild cockatiel will feast on them. At other times that species will eat grasses, fruits, and berries. The wild parrot has no choice but to vary its diet according to the time of year. Seeds do occur in the wild, but only for part of the year. Parrots are programmed to view seeds as food to be eaten in large quantities, as quickly as possible. This is because fresh, young, living seed is nutritious and high in calories that a flying, nesting, breeding parrot needs to survive. However, your companion parrot does not know the difference between the seed you feed him and seasonal seed. He thinks, "Look at this bounty! I'd better eat all I can before it goes away." The problem is, in most situations, the seed never goes away, and this leads to nutritional disorders.

Because parrots are programmed to eat a lot of seed when it's available, your parrot may ignore any other nutritious foods you give him and choose the seeds as his favorite. This is nature at work, after all. It follows that a healthy parrot needs a variety of foods, because that's what he would get in the wild, even though seeds are part of the wild parrot's diet. Offering a parrot a wide variety of healthy foods, with seeds as only about 20 percent of her weekly intake, will help keep her fit. Yes, feeding seeds is easy, but feeding a nutritious diet is not all that difficult.

Another thing to consider is that many wild parrots eat approximately twice a day: once just after dawn and once a few hours before the sun goes down. These are the times when the temperature affords foraging and when the bird is hungriest. Now, think about your companion parrot. He has a cushy life, doesn't he? The seed dish is always full, and so is he. If you feed healthier foods at the times that he's programmed to eat, and supplement with a couple of tablespoons of seed in the middle of the day, then he'll eat more of the better stuff. Well, that's the idea, in any case.

Nutrition-Related Disorders

There are literally hundreds of vitamins and minerals that I could mention here that your parrot needs to remain healthy. But it's not important that you know all the names of all the nutrients. What *is* important is that you take the advice of this chapter and feed the widest variety of healthy foods possible, and that a lot of those fresh foods be *green.* Keep reading to get to the nitty-gritty of proper parrot nutrition.

Vitamin A deficiency

The most prominent nutritional problem with companion parrots is vitamin A deficiency. Neither seed nor pellets have enough vitamin A. Leafy greens, dark green veggies, and most orange fruits and veggies are high in vitamin A and other nutrients, and can help solve this problem if you can get your bird to eat them. Egg yolk is another good source of vitamin A. Egg whites are a good source of protein, which is needed for vitamin A to be properly used in the body.

A bird with vitamin A deficiency has skin, foot, and feather problems, and is susceptible to fungi, bacteria, and viruses. Basically, lack of enough vitamin A compromises the immune system, which opens the bird up to illness. In most cases, the respiratory system is severely affected, causing labored breathing, ulcers, and infection. Unless you take drastic measures, it's tough to bring a bird back from such a degraded state.

Feeding an ailing parrot

An ill or convalescing parrot may not have the appetite that he had when he was healthy. Feed this parrot the foods that he's most likely to eat, and don't worry about excessive calories unless your avian veterinarian warns you about that.

An ill and recovering bird needs more calories than a healthy bird to keep his energy level up. Sprouted seeds and beans are particularly good for ill birds because they are easy to digest and have a high nutritive value.

Fortunately, putting your bird on a good diet *today* can help reverse the deficiency, but that doesn't mean buy vitamins. Vitamin A in supplement form can be overdosed and cause toxicity. Unless your parrot is suffering from severe malnutrition, it's better to load the bird up with greens, orange veggies, and fruits — the form of vitamin A in these isn't toxic.

Calcium deficiency

Calcium deficiency is next on the list. Low calcium levels can cause seizures and feather picking, as well as lowered immunity. Seed and pellets don't have enough calcium. Feed your parrot calcium-rich foods, such as almonds, carrots, kale, and watercress. You can also use a liquid calcium supplement in the water a few times a week for a deficient bird, but don't use it unless the bird's blood calcium levels have been tested by an avian veterinarian and were seen to be low. Also, for smaller birds, a cuttlebone and mineral block will offer some usable calcium.

Seeds versus Pellets: The Big Debate

Your parrot needs a wide variety of nutrients to survive, and you won't find all of them in seeds. Seeds — especially dry seeds that you'd buy in the pet shop — are high in fat and low in calcium; Vitamins A, D, and B-12; iron; and selenium, among many other nutrients your bird needs to remain healthy. So where is your bird going to get these important dietary components? From other things that you feed him, naturally.

In recent years the *pelleted diet* has come into fashion as the "real deal" in avian nutrition. The pelleted diet consists of a variety of nutrients cooked and mashed together and then extruded through a machine to form various shapes or crumbles. Pellets come in a variety of shapes and sizes — globe shapes; chip shapes; and small, pretty shapes like stars and fruit.

Switching your parrot to a pelleted diet

If you're going to feed your birds pellets on the advice of your avian veterinarian or another avian expert, buy organic pellets that are dye- and fragrance-free. These are the only pellets safe enough for your bird.

If your parrot is not already eating pellets, you will have to make the switch, and that isn't always easy. You can't let your bird go cold turkey (pardon the pun) from what he was eating, because he won't immediately recognize the pellets as food and might starve or become ill before he does.

Your best bet is to make the switch a month-long task. Begin by mixing the regular seed mix with pellets, at about a 60-40 ratio. Gradually increase

the pellets until, by the end of the month, the parrot is eating the pellets. Any faster than this, and you risk harming your bird. Of course, there are those birds that take to pellets easily, so keep an eye out for what your bird is eating.

The safest way to make the switch is to buy a gram scale and weigh your bird every day to make sure that he's not losing weight during the switch. Changing a bird's diet can be stressful, and you don't want to risk making your bird ill. Of course, you will also be feeding many other foods at this time, so your bird won't get too hungry during the switch and may even fill up on healthier foods. Don't let your bird exist on pellets alone!

Pellets became all the rage very quickly. For starters, many avian experts and veterinarians began to tout them — *and manufacture them.* The primary argument the experts used for touting these pellets is that there was complete nutrition in each and every bite. So the pellet made for the Australian cockatiel can be fed, in a larger pellet, to the African grey, and both birds would supposedly get the same, perfect nutrition *for their species* in every bite. But that doesn't add up. Sure, their dietary requirements are similar, but they're not exactly the same.

Furthermore, there's evidence that long-term use of pellets *only* can cause liver and kidney problems, feather disorders, and many other terrible ailments. A great deal of these so-called complete diets include artificial coloring and fragrances. If the bag of pellets smells fruity enough that you'd want to eat it, it probably has fragrance added. Dyes are easy to see — the unnatural blues and reds and other vivid colors are generally synthetic. Parrots can develop allergies to these additives and begin to have behavior issues and pluck their feathers. Fortunately, there are some pellets that don't use any additives and use only organic ingredients.

Imagine someone coming to you claiming to have developed a pellet that had every nutrient you ever needed in it and that this pellet was all you would eat for the rest of your life. First, you probably would be skeptical, and with good reason. Second, you'd get bored out of your mind eating nothing but a few of these pellets a day. Imagine how a parrot feels.

Pellets are designed to give your bird all the nutrients he is *known to need.* But nutritional research is still inconclusive in the realm of avian nutrition, so a claim for a pellet with *all the nutrients your bird needs* and in the *correct quantities* is quite premature.

I'm not a veterinarian or an avian-nutrition expert. What I am is a passionate bird hobbyist with many years of experience raising — and feeding — many types of birds. I happen to know scores of breeders, numerous bird-rescue-league organizers, and a great number of bird guardians, and not one of them feeds their birds solely pellets or solely seeds. As for my birds, I do feed both pellets and seeds — as a small *part* of their weekly diet. I regularly use high-quality pellets in my birdy cooking — in the bread, pasta, and egg dishes that I make for my birds. Some seed blends actually come with pellets included, and my birds happen to like them.

As a disclaimer, I will advise you to feed your parrot as your avian veterinarian or trusted avian expert advises. Your avian veterinarian knows your individual bird, and I don't. But I will say this — if you take the time to give your parrot a balanced diet, including *some* pellets and *some* seeds and lots of *other* much more nutritious foods, you will do much better than if you choose one thing to the exclusion of everything else.

The Cooked Base Diet

The *cooked base diet* consists of a cooked mixture of beans (black, lima, kidney, black-eyed, garbanzo , and so on), brown or whole-grain rice, quinoa, amaranth, couscous, and other grains, along with whole-grain pasta, some seeds and nuts, perhaps even some pellets. Mix in some dried veggies, fruit, supplements, and herbs, and it's a pretty good base diet.

If it sounds like quite a task to create this diet, that's because it is. But the good news is that there are great commercially made versions of it on the market today. You can make a pot of this diet each week, freeze it in baggies, and heat one up each day for use. Though this diet is much better than seed, it's still not complete and should be supplemented with fresh fruits and vegetables, as well as any other supplements that your avian veterinarian or avian expert recommends.

The only real problem with the cooked base diet is that it spoils in warm weather. This diet should be left in the cage for only a few hours at a time, especially if you live in a warm climate. Use your best judgment in terms of how much you feed and how long you leave it in the bowl. Personally, I offer a cooked diet every day, and my birds love it.

Purchasing and Storing

The fresher the seed, pellets, and cooked diet, the more nutrients they contain. You can test the freshness of seeds by sprouting a teaspoon of them between two damp paper towels. If most of the seeds in your mixture sprout within a couple of days, you know you've got a pretty good batch. If only some of them sprout, consider replacing them. If none of them sprouts, begin buying seeds from another store.

Some stores sell seeds and pellets in large, open bins as an option to the more expensive bagged food items. It's not a great idea to buy from these bins. Other bird owners and store employees may have run their hands through the seed and contaminated it, or it may have been picked at by rodents. Seed stored and sold in an airtight plastic container or bag is a better choice.

You will notice that the more expensive seed mixes are "fortified" with vitamins in the form of various-colored seed hulls. The fact is, these vitamins are spread over the *outside* of the seed, but your bird eats the *inside*. Parrots peel and discard every single husk and eat *only* the inside of the seeds. A lot of work, right? Your bird's mouth is not moist enough to remove enough of the vitamins on the husk to make it worth your money. Buy the plain seed, a bag of organic pellets, and some finely chopped dried fruit — voila, a fancy seed blend!

Keep your parrot's base diet (seeds or pellets) in the refrigerator in an airtight plastic container. This will prevent it from growing mold and attracting pests and vermin, such as seed flies and mice. If you notice *seed moths* or webby stuff in the seed, freeze the package. You can still feed webby seed to your bird, but never feed moldy or foul-smelling seed. If you do get an infestation of seed moths (also called *flour moths*), you can purchase special sticky traps online or at your local feed store that attract the moths. Put all seed, flour, cereal, rice, and other grains into airtight plastic containers or seal-tight bags.

Never scoop the food from the container or bag with your parrot's food dish, which can be contaminated with feces or other material. Instead, use a clean scooper. A measuring cup with a handle does nicely. I use a plain disposable plastic cup that works just fine.

Sprouting seeds

Sprouted seeds and beans are wonderfully nutritious and have far more vitamins and minerals in them than their dry counterparts. If you're lucky, you may be able to find a health food store near you that sells already-sprouted beans and broccoli. If not, you can buy a cheap seed sprouter and sprout your own.

Mold and bacteria are very harmful to your parrot, so don't take any chances feeding her

even slightly old spouts. Even the sprouted beans from the market last only about three days. If you notice a funky smell or the sprouts become slimy, toss them out. Use a few drops of GSE in the water you use to sprout the seeds, and wash any sprouts (or veggies, for that matter) in a GSE wash — one drop per ounce of water makes a great disinfectant.

Vegetables

I hope I've convinced you so far that variety is the key to a good parrot diet. As you know by now, the wild parrot eats a wide variety of vegetation. Your companion parrot should likewise consume a variety of fruits and vegetables. If he doesn't eat veggies, keep offering them in various forms until he does. The more variety of foods you can get your bird to eat, the more vitamins and minerals he will be getting into his system. Table 8-1 lists some vegetables that are healthy for your parrot.

Table 8-1		Vegetables to Feed Your Parrot		
Here's Just a Partial List of Veggies You Can Offer				
Yams	Spinach	Broccoli Leaves	Kale	Collard greens
Broccoli	Winter squash	Artichoke	Cauliflower	Brussels sprouts
Cucumber	Tomato	Hot pepper	Asparagus	Peas
Celery	Jalapeños	Green pepper	Red pepper	Yellow pepper
Beet tops	Pumpkin	Zucchini	Corn	Green beans
Endive	Dandelion	Carrots	Yellow squash	
Watercress	Greens	Chard		

Dark green or orange veggies (and fruits) are full of Vitamin A, an important nutrient for your parrot's respiratory system and overall health, and a nutrient that's sorely lacking in seed. Feed as many and as much of the veggies listed in Table 8-1 as you can on a daily basis. Don't worry about your parrot overeating this kind of produce. The more you can get into your bird, the better.

If you're running late or have run out of fresh veggies just when you need them, keep a stock of frozen mixed veggies on hand, just in case. My birds like the defrosted veggies, though they tend to go straight for the fatty lima beans. Frozen isn't supernutritious, but it will do in a pinch. Just don't use frozen veggies in the place of fresh stuff on a regular basis.

Spinach, chard, parsley, and some other veggies contain a substance called oxalic acid that makes your parrot unable to use the calcium that the greens contain (it does the same to your body, too). I feed greens almost every day, but I make sure to also feed other calcium-rich foods, such as almonds and carrots. Regardless of the calcium-binding oxalic acid, greens offer a ton of other good nutrients, like Vitamin A.

Fruit

Fruit, like veggies, is a rich source of vitamins, minerals, and fiber. If your bird is chunky, feed more of the tarter fruits that contain less natural sugar. If you can, always feed organic produce. See Table 8-2 for a list of good fruits.

Table 8-2		Fruit to Feed Your Parrot		
Here's a Partial List of Nutritious Fruit				
Figs	Apples	Apricots	Watermelon	Grapes
Cantaloupe	Bananas	Cherries	Oranges	Peaches
Plums	Papaya	Mango	Kiwi	Honeydew
Berries (various)	Grapefruit	Pineapple	Persimmon	Cranberries

Fruit can attract little pests called *fruit flies.* These little guys buzz dizzyingly around your bird's cage, and though they are not particularly harmful, they're quite annoying. You can avoid them by removing fruit from your parrot's cage after a few hours and by keeping the cage clean — remove all dropped fruit and soft foods from the tray. If you have a fruit-fly infestation, don't serve fruit for a week (nonsweet veggies are okay) and keep the cage very clean and dry, and they should go away. You can also fill a long-necked bottle with a few ounces of wine or orange juice mixed with sugar, and the flies will be able to get into the bottle but not out again.

If your bird has been diagnosed with *candida,* or yeast, hold back on feeding sweet fruits for a while until the condition gets better. Instead, feed lots of green veggies.

Pesticides

Now that I've told you to stuff your parrot full of fruit and veggies, I've got to give you the bad news: Unless you purchase organic produce, there are a lot of pesticides, fungicides, and other chemicals on it. Some of the most healthful produce, unfortunately, has a lot of potentially deadly stuff on it.

High-pesticide fruits and vegetables

Carolyn Swicegood, an avian expert and enthusiast who does a lot of research and practical application on avian nutrition, says that the following produce comes with an unacceptable amount of chemicals:

1. **Strawberries:** The Food and Drug Administration (FDA) detected 30 different pesticides on strawberries, second only to apples, with 36. Swicegood recommends never feeding nonorganic strawberries to parrots. Offer other fruits with far lower pesticide residues, such as blueberries, raspberries, oranges, grapefruit, watermelon, and kiwis.

2. **Bell peppers (green and red):** Bell peppers are more heavily contaminated with neurotoxic insecticides than all other crops analyzed. Substitute broccoli, romaine lettuce, green peas, asparagus, Brussels sprouts, and carrots.

3. **Spinach:** Spinach contains DDT, permethrin, chlorthalonil, and other carcinogenic pesticides. Substitute broccoli, Brussels sprouts, asparagus, and romaine lettuce.

4. **U.S.-grown cherries:** Cherries from the United States are three times more contaminated with pesticides than their imported counterparts. Except for their marginal amounts of Vitamin C and their value as a treatment for gout, they are not as nutritious as many other fruits, though it is worthwhile to seek out imported cherries. Substitute oranges, watermelon, blueberries, raspberries, and kiwi.

5. **Peaches:** Peaches are heavily contaminated with cancer-causing fungicides and neurotoxic pesticides. Peaches contain low amounts of Vitamins A and C, but many other less contaminated fruits provide as many or more nutritional benefits. Substitute nectarines, watermelon, tangerines, grapefruits, oranges, and kiwis.

6. **Mexican-grown cantaloupe:** Cantaloupes from Mexico tested positive for 2 or more pesticides in 48 percent of the samples, more than any other crop analyzed. Avoid offering it to parrots during January through April, when Mexican imports are at their peak. Substitute U.S. cantaloupe in season, papaya, nectarines, and watermelon.

7. **Celery:** Eighty-one percent of samples contained detectable residues of pesticides. Considering the minimal amount of nutrition in celery, it is not worth the risk. Substitute carrots, romaine lettuce, broccoli, and radishes.

8. **Apples:** Apples contain 36 different pesticides, more than any other fruit or vegetable, according to FDA data. Substitute pears, U.S. cantaloupe, kiwi, watermelon, nectarines, bananas, or citrus fruit.

9. **Apricots:** Apricots contain high levels of pesticides. Substitute nectarines, tangerines, U.S. cantaloupes, watermelon, oranges, and grapefruit.

10. **Green beans:** Green beans are a major source of carcinogenic fungicides, neurotoxins, and endocrine disruptors. Substitute green peas, broccoli, cauliflower, Brussels sprouts, asparagus, and potatoes.

11. **Chilean-grown grapes:** Grapes from Chile contain cancer-causing and endocrine-disrupting fungicides. From January through April, 90 percent of the grapes sold in the United States are from Chile, where growers use less sophisticated pest-control techniques than U.S. growers. Substitute domestic grapes in season.

12. **Cucumbers:** Cucumbers contain unacceptable levels of an extremely carcinogenic pesticide that was banned in the United States over 20 years ago. Unfortunately, it is persistent in the soil and is absorbed by cucumbers. One of every 14 cucumber samples from across the United States and Mexico contained this highly toxic compound. Substitute carrots, romaine lettuce, broccoli, or radishes.

Swicegood says that the preceding list contains the most toxic conventionally grown fruits and vegetables, according to the not-for-profit Environmental Working Group.

Low-pesticide fruits and vegetables

Here's a list of the safest fruits and veggies for your parrot — the ones with the least pesticide residue, according to the Environmental Working Group.

1. **Corn**

2. **Sweet potatoes**

3. **Cauliflower**

4. **Brussels sprouts**

5. **Grapes (U.S.)**

6. **Bananas**

7. **Plums**

8. **Watermelon**

9. **Broccoli**

Three of the cleanest foods were left off the preceding list because they are unacceptable for parrots (though good for you): avocado, onion, and green onion. Do not feed these items to your parrot.

Parrots, like people, can become sensitive (or allergic) to properties in foods or pesticides and additives. Rotate a wide variety of foods in and out of your bird's diet to help prevent sensitivity from building up. Food sensitivities can lead to feather plucking, agitation, behavioral issues, or worse.

Snacks

Snacks are additions to your parrot's diet. Store-bought snacks are often high in calories for little nutritional reward, though you can find healthy alternatives. Here are some common parrot snacks:

- **Millet spray:** This snack looks like a little branch filled with tiny golden jewels, and it's a favorite of many smaller hookbills, such as budgies, cockatiels, lovebirds, and parrotlets. Offer millet spray twice a week in the late afternoon once your bird has eaten other, more nutritious foods. Millet is a fun food because it comes in its natural form. Thread millet through the cage bars so that the bird can work at eating it. Don't buy a spiral millet holder, because items like this have been involved in bird injuries and deaths.

- **Popcorn:** Air-popped popcorn is a fun, low-calorie snack. Offer it once or twice a week late in the day. You can drizzle olive oil over it and then sprinkle on some nutritional yeast, spirulina (greenfood), garlic powder (without the salt), probiotics, and no-salt herb mix to make Parrot Popcorn. It is delicious! I make a big batch and share it with my birds whenever I make it (I eat most of it, I'll admit). Nutritional yeast sounds gross, but it actually tastes very cheesy, and it's packed with B vitamins and iron. The popcorn itself isn't very nutritive, but all the stuff on it is.

- **Seed sticks:** Store-bought seed sticks are like candy for a parrot. You can offer one a month if your bird likes them. Beware, however, of how the stick is hung in the cage — some birds have been injured by sharp metal hangers.

- **Crackers and almond or cashew butter:** A healthy, no-salt, whole-wheat cracker or whole-wheat bread thinly spread with a natural (no sugar, no salt) almond or cashew butter makes a nutritious treat. Remember, nut butter is high in calories, so stay away from it for a while if your veterinarian has suggested that your parrot is porky.

- **Nuts:** Almonds contain lots of calcium. Nuts contain essential fatty acids and lots of protein. But don't feed peanuts or peanut butter. Peanuts contain *aflatoxins* that are harmful to birds, and fungus can grow inside the shell, making your bird ill when exposed to it. You're better off with raw tree nuts. You can feed them roasted if you're eating them that way, but they lose some of their nutritive properties in the roasting process. Feed a few nuts as a snack every day if your parrots like them.

Table Foods

Table foods, the foods you eat every day, can be a great addition to your parrot's daily diet. He can eat *just* about everything that you eat — but not quite everything. Keep in mind that some foods that we like to eat are toxic for birds, and that salty and sugary foods are unhealthy for them (for us too, for that matter). Don't feed your parrot junk food.

Feel free to share your meals with your parrot, but make sure to cool the food you offer first, and remove it about an hour after you offer it. Some foods spoil quickly.

Protein is essential for the processing of other nutrients. Yes, your birds can eat meat, even that of other birds. It may sound like a horror movie, but parrots do enjoy chicken and chicken bones, along with beef and eggs. Try to feed only organic and hormone-free animal meats and eggs. When you're feeding any kind of animal meat or eggs, especially fowl, *overcook* it. No ten-minute eggs for your parrot. Eggs should be boiled for at least half an hour, and scrambled eggs should be very dry.

Parrots aren't built to process dairy well, but you can feed it in very small amounts. Some lowfat or nonfat organic yogurt and a small bit of cheese are quite nutritious. Don't feed milk, and don't overdo dairy in general. Remember that dairy isn't part of a wild parrot's natural diet — parrots aren't biologically predisposed to digest it the way most humans are.

Toxic Foods

There are a few foods that you may eat that you shouldn't share with your birds. These include:

- ✔ Avocado
- ✔ Rhubarb
- ✔ Chocolate
- ✔ Raw onion
- ✔ Salty and sugary foods (chips, pretzels, and so on)
- ✔ Alcohol

These foods are toxic or deadly, or can simply make your bird ill.

Avoid feeding your parrot fatty or sugary snacks. It might be funny to watch your parrot eat a cheese doodle, but think of all of the other, more nutritious things she could be eating instead. Also, parrots tend to become porky if they eat too many fatty calories and don't get enough exercise. Better to stick with the healthier stuff. Too much salt can actually be deadly for a parrot, so no chips and pretzels.

Parrot-type birds *do not need* grit in their diet, despite the myth. Do not feed your parrot grit. It can cause crop impaction, and he'll be unable to digest his food properly. Excess grit in the gut can lead to death.

Nutritional Supplements

Some people think that feeding their parrot a nutritional supplement along with a bowl of seeds will take care of nutritional deficiencies. Nothing could be further from the truth. Imagine living on a diet of white bread, water, and vitamin pills — eventually, you'd become ill. Some vitamins and minerals need the presence of other vitamins and minerals to absorb into your body, and the same goes for your parrot.

Not only do nutritional supplements not make up for a poor diet, but they can actually cause other problems. Some nutrients, such as Vitamin A, are toxic at high doses. If you're not consulting your avian veterinarian or avian expert on supplements, it's best to leave them alone and opt for a better diet. Yes, offering a balanced diet takes more time and expense, but it's worth it.

Here is a list of supplements that round out the diet or help heal ailments:

- **Aloe vera:** Put aloe juice into the water to help digestion and improve health in general. One product, Aloe Detox by Naturade, also contains other herbs and has been known to have healing effects on ill birds. Aloe products that you get from the health food store are nontoxic, so you can't really overdose. You can also put the gel on cuts and scrapes.

- **Cayenne:** Parrots love hot and spicy foods, and cayenne is great for the digestion and helps with arthritis. Sprinkle on food or cook with it.

- **Cinnamon:** Great for digestion and blood sugar. Sprinkle over soft foods or cook with it.

- **Cuttlebone and mineral block:** Both of these items can be found in the pet shop and add valuable calcium to your parrot's diet. Be sure to include one or the other (or both), especially for breeding pairs or female parrots laying eggs.

- **Essential fatty acids (EFAs):** Birds need EFAs for skin health and feather production. Nuts are a good source of EFA. Or you can sprinkle flax seed oil on some bread or cooked food. Don't put oil on seeds, and don't heat the flax oil in the cooked food.

- **Garlic:** Garlic is a natural antibiotic and has other healthful properties. Use an extract from the health food store, or juice some carrots and garlic cloves together and offer it to your bird.

- **Grapefruit seed extract (GSE):** This item has incredible antibiotic, antiviral, and antifungal properties. Put one drop per ounce in water to disinfect countertops, water dishes, and fruit and veggies. It's nontoxic, so you can't overdose it. Put a couple of drops into your bird's water, but not too much — it's very bitter.

- **Greenfood:** Spirulina and other "super" greenfoods are wonderful for any parrot (and for you).

- **MSM** (methylsulfonylmethane): Birds that pluck tend to do better with some MSM mixed into the water. Birds with poor feather production in general could benefit from MSM, as can most captive parrots. MSM is nontoxic, so you can't overdose it.

- **Nutritional yeast:** Contains lots of B vitamins. Sprinkle on soft foods.

- **Probiotics:** This product is great for the digestion and health in general. It's a live microbial culture, the same stuff found in yogurt, including lactobacillus and bifadophilus.

- **Vitamin C:** Birds synthesize their own Vitamin C, but when they're ill or stressed, a pinch of powdered Vitamin C in the water is a good idea. Otherwise, your best bet is to serve citrus fruits, berries, and other items high in Vitamin C.

Even though the preceding supplements, and a great many others, are healthful and can have healing effects on ill birds, there has been no research done on parrots and supplements. All the benefits recorded on these products are anecdotal; however, this amateur research has shown very positive results.

Your best bet with all of these items, and others you may find, is to rotate them in and out of your bird's diet. For example, if you put Vitamin C into your bird's water for seven days, don't put it in for the next seven. The same goes for all of these supplements. Unless you're trying to boost your bird's immune system because it has had an illness, don't overdo it.

Getting a Parrot to Eat

Now that I've discussed nutritious options for your parrot, how are you going to get him to eat them all? First and foremost, begin offering these foods at a young age — even on the first day you bring your bird home. A parrot is often wary of things that are "different" and may not even recognize some of these items as food, so it's important that you start offering them early.

Patience is the key to getting your bird to eat new things. Many owners offer a food for a few days and then discontinue it, claiming that their parrot doesn't like it. In fact, it may take two weeks or longer for a bird to nibble at something new. Keep offering the foods, and eventually your bird will take a taste.

Use separate dishes for each type of food, but if you're having a difficult time getting your bird to eat, say, bananas, put a chunk of banana in the dish of the food he likes best (usually the seed dish). This way, he'll have no choice but to go near the offending food item. Note that mixing the wet and dry foods is not a good idea in the long term, because the wet foods will cause the dry foods to spoil. This is a short-term option only.

Many healthful veggies and fruits can be prepared in various ways that may be appealing for your parrot. For example, yams and carrots can be offered whole, shredded, cut into chunks, cooked in chunks, mashed, baked into bread, or mixed into a grain-and-bean concoction.

Try a wide variety of greens to see which your parrot likes best. Weave them in and out of the cage bars to get her interested. A dish of very wet greens at the bottom of the cage is a fun treat, and some birds will even bathe in it.

Easy Recipes

Cooking for your bird? You may think I've gone off the deep end here, but you'd be surprised how many people actually cook for their birds. I cook for mine a couple of times a week, at least. Remember, it's hard enough to get a parrot to eat nutritious foods, so the more you can offer, the better. Here are some fun, flexible recipes to get you started.

Parrot muffins and bread

One easy recipe that I use all the time uses a corn-muffin-mix base with lots of goodies added. Simply buy a box of corn-muffin mix, and follow the directions for the batter. If you can find a mix from the health food store, use that instead of the supermarket brand.

WARNING!

If your bird has candida (yeast), skip this recipe until he gets over it, or make sure that the bread mix you use doesn't include sugar.

TIP

Prepare the batter, using the directions on the box (if it calls for an egg, smash the shell in there with the rest of it), and then add several different healthy items: fruits, veggies, dried fruits, pellets, bits of cuttlebone, whatever you think your bird will love. Then bake according to the directions on the box — except double the baking time, or check a few times to make sure it's done. The added water in the fruits and veggies will add minutes to the baking time. Once cooled, cut into squares and freeze. Each day, thaw a chunk and offer it to your parrot. This bread is fun because you can vary it each time you make it.

Parrot mac and cheese

This recipe is also easy and can be varied. Begin with a high-quality whole-wheat pasta prepared as suggested on the box (parrots need the whole wheat for the added nutrition). Then shred soy cheese (nondairy cheese, because parrots don't digest dairy very well) over the hot pasta. Once that's melted, add dried fruit, chopped veggies, pellets, crumbled hard-boiled egg, or whatever else you want. Spread the concoction into a shallow pan, and cut into squares when it cools. Freeze for daily use.

Parrot eggs

No, I'm not talking about cooking your parrot's own eggs. Chicken eggs are a good source of protein, vitamins, and minerals. Make scrambled eggs just as you would for yourself, but scramble the shell with them (for calcium), and add pellets, veggies, and whatever else you think your bird will relish. Again, you can make a batch of this and freeze it in small portions for later use.

Whenever you use chicken eggs, make sure they're cooked very well. Chicken eggs can potentially carry diseases that can pass to your bird. Scrambled eggs should be very dry, and boiled eggs should be cooked for over half an hour.

Parrot juice

Fresh-pressed juice is full of a lot of vitamins and minerals that are essential for your bird's good health. If you have a juicer, press carrots, beets, apples, melon, garlic, kale, and any other fruits and veggies your parrot likes. Don't place the juice in his cage, but offer it to him during playtime. Juice can spoil very easily.

Parrot flapjacks

This recipe is like the parrot bread but uses whole-wheat pancake mix instead. Make the batter as directed on the box, and then add fruit, veggies, egg, pellets, and anything healthful you have in the house. Cook well and cool before offering. Freeze and offer one thawed flapjack a day along with other foods.

Parrot grain

Personally, I use a commercial grain mix that I cook every week, but if you're a cook and you want to get inventive, you can make up a batch of this every week and have a nutritious warm food for your feathered pal. I've done this before, and my birds really like it.

Using the directions on the boxes, make a serving each of quinoa, amaranth, brown rice, whole oats, and whole-wheat couscous. Mix them all together once they're cooked separately.

Next, soak and cook a few types of beans — lentils, red beans, black beans, garbanzo beans, and so on. Or if you're in a hurry most of the time, you can open a few cans of beans, rinse them, and then add them to the grain mixture. For a really nutritious treat, sprout the beans before you cook them.

Finally, fold in shredded carrots, yams, chopped jalapeno peppers, peas, broccoli, kale, soybeans, and anything else you have in the house. Toss in a handful of almonds, walnuts, organic pellets, and anything else that seems like it belongs in the mix. Add cinnamon, calcium powder, and any other dry supplements that you have on hand. Freeze in small baggies. Heat and serve one baggie a day.

What I Feed My Birds

I get asked all the time: What do *you* feed your birds? Of course, I can give you nutrition advice all day long, but if I didn't put it into practice, I'd be a hypocrite. So I'll give you the breakdown of what I feed my own birds on a weekly basis:

1. Once a week, I cook up a batch of a prepared cooked diet that I use as their base diet (Beak Appetit). I separate the batch into seven little baggies and freeze them. Every day I heat up one of the baggies and put that in the dish. I tried to make my own cooked diet for a while, but they prefer the commercial stuff, which is just as well, because it's nutritious and easier to make. I make sure the mixture is warm, but not hot, when I serve it.

2. Once a week or so, I make my version of parrot bread or something similar and freeze it in portions. I defrost some of it and put it in the dish with the cooked diet.

3. I defrost a handful of soybeans and put them in the dish, too.

4. I toss a bunch of veggies in the electric chopper: carrots, broccoli, kale, other greens, watercress, yams — whatever I have in the house. I put the chopped stuff in the dish with the other stuff.

5. I toss chunks of fruit in the dish — whatever I have in the house, generally melon, grapes, berries, cranberries (in season), oranges (they love the oranges cut in half), persimmon, and kiwi. Generally, I serve three fruits a day.

6. I sprinkle nutritional yeast, spirulina (greenfood), and probiotics over everything in the dish. Then it's ready to offer.

7. Along with the dish of food, the larger birds get whole carrots, an apple, and a well-washed bunch of some sort of greens hung all around the cage and at the bottom. It's fun for parrots to play around with a bunch of greens.

8. Two or three times a week, I make parrot scrambled eggs or hard-boiled eggs; smash them up, shell and all; and offer them along with the cooked diet. I also make the vegan parrot mac and cheese about once every couple of weeks (see recipe earlier in this chapter).

9. When I can find them very fresh in my local market, I buy sprouted mung beans, lentils, garbanzo beans, and broccoli sprouts, and offer those, which the birds love. I used to spout my own beans and seeds, but it's a good deal of work, and it's easier for me to buy them. I try to offer these a couple of days a week. I offer the sprouts and nothing else for the first part of the day. This way, the hungry birds eat them early (and they *love* these sprouts), and then later I offer all of the other goodies.

10. My birds get healthy table food nearly every day, whatever I'm having for a meal or a snack. My African grey likes to drink out of my cereal bowl every morning — soy milk, of course. He also gets fresh veggie/fruit juice a few times a week, and he gets first dibs on drinking out of my cup — he goes nuts for fresh juice. Remember, if you're feeding your bird all fresh, healthy stuff, it's impossible to overfeed.

11. About three times a week, I fill another dish with a seed mix (that has pellets in it, too) — about a cup or so of seeds does the trick. I consider the other stuff the base diet and the seeds a treat. If my birds were flying around all the time (like they would be in the wild or in a habitat), I would probably offer a seed mix every day. But they get to fly only short distances, so they don't need the extra calories.

12. A couple of times a week, I offer human-grade nuts in or out of the shell, generally almonds, walnuts, and cashews. *Never peanuts.*

13. When I can get them to eat it, I like to offer plain yogurt (but I've noticed that it's an in-the-mood kind of thing for them). A couple of times a week, they get a very small piece of cheese, generally when I'm eating it.

14. In the water, I put a couple of drops of GSE and a couple of drops of organic apple cider vinegar. A couple of times a week. I put an aloe-and-herb product into the water. A couple of times a week. I also add a powdered vitamin supplement and a liquid calcium supplement. Often, when I get around to it, I'll also mix in some herbal tea, generally chamomile, pao d'arco, and echinacea for immune-system health. About once a week, I just give plain, filtered water with nothing in it. I'm not recommending that you do any of these things, just telling you what I do with my own birds. Here and there, as I learn new things, I'll add a human-grade supplement to the food and water for a while, and then try something else, rotating different healthy supplements in and out of the diet. With any supplementation, it's important to give the body a rest, so if you offer a supplement for ten days, for example, don't offer it for the next ten days. You can overdo supplements, so use your own judgment, and always err on the side of caution.

As you can see, I go through a pretty good effort to offer my birds the best I can, and it still probably falls short of *everything* they need. A *total diet* can only really be found in the wild. I should probably be feeding only organic foods every day, but I admit I don't always do that. I wish *I* would eat only organic foods all the time. There are also a lot more supplements and foods I could be feeding, but I tend to add things gradually, and I tend to feed things that I eat, too. So just do your best, and feed as wide a variety of healthy foods as possible.

Chapter 9

Pretty Bird! Grooming Your Companion

*1*t might seem that grooming should be left to poodles and Himalayan cats, but believe it or not, your parrot needs some attentive grooming as well. The grooming of a bird does not involve brushing and combing, nor does it require shampoo. Grooming your parrot is far simpler than that.

A healthy parrot has a keen sense of cleanliness. He will preen his feathers to make sure there's no debris on them. *Preening* is when a bird moves its beak through its feathers, making them neat, clean, and tight. A filthy bird has far more trouble flying than a clean bird does, which is just one of the reasons why birds are so fastidious. Preening may look to you like your parrot is bothering his feathers, but this is a normal behavior for a healthy bird and should be encouraged by regular bathing.

Feathers are a bird's source of protection from water, cold, and heat. Finely preened and groomed feathers are better able to resist moisture and extreme temperatures. Birds have a normally high body temperature, and the feathers help keep them warm. Feathers are also used to attract the opposite sex and to indicate sexual maturity. No wonder your parrot spends so much time preening. Feathers are crucial.

Feathers

Before we get into a discussion of grooming, I'd like to take a moment to discuss feathers. Feathers are akin to hair in mammals. Feathers began millions of years ago (at least 130 million years, give or take) on the dinosaur *Sinosauropteryx prima.* This remarkable development in evolution was discovered in a fossil in 1995 and was confirmed in the summer of 2001 with a fossil in China. This "first bird" was flightless and is suspected to be closely related to the *Velociraptor* (the savvy, meat-eating dinosaur in the movie *Jurassic Park*). Today, birds are the only creatures on earth with feathers, making them truly unique.

Feathers are made of *keratin,* the same material that comprises their beaks (as well as our fingernails and other animals' horns), and are over 90 percent protein. Several types of feathers are found on your parrot. Here's a quick run-down:

- **Contour feathers:** These are the feathers that cover your parrot's body and include the flight feathers and the tail feathers.
- **Flight feathers:** The wing is composed of 20 flight feathers: ten primary flight feathers (the long feathers at the end of the wing) and ten secondary flight feathers (closer to the body). Also called *remiges.*
- **Tail feathers:** Also called *retrices.*
- **Semiplume:** The semiplume feathers occur underneath the contour feathers and help with insulation.
- **Filoplume:** These hairlike feathers have a long shaft with a few *barbs* at the end (see next section for a definition of *barb*). They are "sensory" feathers used to help the bird feel the positions of its other feathers.
- **Bristles:** The stiff, tiny feathers around your parrot's beak, nares (nostrils), and eyes.
- **Down:** The undercoat of fluffy feathers beneath the contour feathers are called the down feathers. These help a great deal with insulation.
- **Powder down:** The powder down feather is closest to the skin and crumbles during preening, resulting in a white, powdery substance that spreads throughout the feathers and helps with insulation, waterproofing, and keeping the feathers clean. This powder is why many people with allergies may choose not to have a parrot (or at least choose to buy an air filter).

The feather itself is fascinating. It is made up of four basic components:

- **Quill:** The hollow end of the feather (where it enters the skin follicle). Also called the *calimus.*
- **Shaft:** What looks like the feather's long stem. Also called the *rachis.*

- ✔ **Barb:** The thin strands emanating from the shaft.

- ✔ **Barbules:** Very tiny structures emanating from the barbs. Down feathers do not have barbules and therefore aren't neatly "zipped" like the contour feathers.

- ✔ **Barbicels:** Miniscule hooks attached to the barbules that keep the barbs together to form the feather. There are about 30 million barbicels on one feather!

(See Figure 10-1 in the next chapter for more on feather anatomy.)

When your bird sheds a contour feather, pull the little strands (barbs) gently apart; then try to push them together again by sliding your thumb and index finger along their length. If you do it right, the barbs will zip together again. This is part of what your parrot does when he is preening.

The barbicels that keep the feather zipped aren't incredibly strong, but because there are so many of them, the feather manages to stay together and is remarkably strong. The overall, combined effect of the feathers creates a very powerful structure, the wing, which creates enough force to defy gravity.

Healthy feathers are generally shiny, except in cockatoos, African greys, and some Amazon parrots. One thing to look out for are *stress bars* in feathers: dark or discolored lines that grow into new feathers when a bird is ill or going through a period of stress, malnutrition, or a round of antibiotics. If you see these lines, it's time for a trip to your avian veterinarian. Another sign of illness or malnutrition is a significant change in feather color that's not due to maturing.

Birds of a feather

You might be surprised to find out that parrots aren't really green or blue or many of the striking colors that they seem to wear. The only pigments that parrots really have are red and yellow. Parrots also have melanin in their feathers, which creates what we perceive as *light* and *dark*. The combination of the yellow, red, and the amount of melanin in the feathers creates patterns on the feather, which are then refracted by light, much like a prism. When light hits the feathers, some of the pigments absorb it, and some reflect it — humans see the reflected light as different colors, depending on the wavelengths of light. So like the ocean and the sky, the colors of birds have everything to do with how light reacts to the human eye.

Wing Clipping

Now that I've told you how amazing feathers are, we have to have a chat about clipping them. *Clipping* is when the primary wing feathers (only the *first half* of each feather) on both of a bird's wings are cut off so that he is unable to fly very high or very far.

Clipping feathers is kind of like getting a haircut, except you don't rely on your hair for mobility. It doesn't hurt the parrot, and the feathers grow back. Parrots are extremely skilled flyers, and many a parrot guardian has been surprised by a "clipped" parrot's taking off into the wild blue yonder, never to be seen again. Most parrots are light, streamlined, and designed to fly for long distances with little effort. This is why some people advocate clipping not only the primary flight feathers, but most or all of the secondary flight feathers in the lighter birds (such as budgies and cockatiels) as well.

To clip or not to clip

A parrot can live its whole life with its wing feathers clipped. There's little or no effect on insulation. A clipped parrot gets less exercise than a flighted one, but beyond that, there's not much that clipping does to adversely affect a bird's physiological health. Nevertheless, and predictably, there is a controversy about wing clipping — for and against. Both sides have valid points. Ultimately, whether to clip your bird's wing feathers is your personal decision. Here are some of the arguments that may help you make it:

- ✔ A clipped parrot is less likely to get away from you, whereas a flighted parrot may soar through an open window or door one day.

- ✔ A home is a very dangerous place for a flighted parrot, who may fly into glass, a mirror, or wall.

- ✔ A flighted parrot will be able to get to dangerous items in the home, such as toxic metals, the toilet bowl, or a hot stove (though a clipped parrot can often get to these things as well).

- ✔ A clipped parrot is easier to handle because he can't fly away from you (though he shouldn't want to if he's tamed and well socialized).

- ✔ A bird is meant to fly. That's why it has wings and feathers, hollow bones, and a muscular frame.

- ✔ It is believed that breathing and flight are directly correlated, and that a bird which is allowed to fly has a stronger respiratory system.

- ✔ A clipped bird has its best defense taken away from him; he is no longer able to get away from the family dog or cat or other danger.

- ✔ Bad wing-clips can lead to plucking, and extreme wing-clips can lead to injuries due to falling.

> ✔ Birds that are allowed to fly have stronger psychological well-being and are healthier due to the exercise they receive from flight. A flighted parrot is more autonomous and is happier in general.

Flight's effect on parrot behavior

It is common for people in the United States to clip a parrot's wings, but bird-keepers in Europe would consider this animal abuse. The practice is not done there and is seen as barbaric. This attitude is just now reaching American birdkeepers. It has long been believed in Europe that clipping a bird's wings greatly affects its behavior.

Flighted birds allowed to fly are highly self-directed creatures, able to make their own decisions about where they're going and what they're doing (see Figure 9-1). They can defend themselves by flying away from something they fear. They expend a lot of energy while flying — energy that will then *not* be spent plucking, screaming, and trying to figure out a way out of a cage. A clipped bird does not have the benefit of any of these aspects of *birdness* and so must change its personality to compensate for what it lacks.

Clipping a bird's wings takes away a large part of what it is meant to be as an individual. A clipped bird can become abnormally fearful, aggressive, neurotic, or depressed. This same bird, unclipped, may be more confident. Most responsible bird breeders advocate that all baby birds be allowed to fly at least until they are ready for their new homes.

Figure 9-1:
This poicephalus parrot enjoys supervised flight.

Photo by Ashley Lynn

Options in between

Wing clipping is a touchy subject among bird fanciers, bird-rescue organizations, avian veterinarians, breeders, and guardians, each of whom has a different opinion. Each side's argument is solid. Personally, I'm in the flight camp, so I can't tell you which option to choose because I have a definite bias. I know that it's dangerous for some birds to live in a home without their wings clipped, but I'm a staunch advocate of flight — my birds aren't clipped, and they live inside my home. Fortunately, there are options between clipping and flight.

Some people keep their birds clipped for only part of the year. Because the wings grow out only during a molt, which happens once, maybe twice a year, some parrot guardians allow their birds to have a couple of months of flight and then clip the wings a bit when the weather becomes nice enough for the windows to be open.

Another option is to clip only a few of the flight feathers — the first two to four — to allow the bird some flight. Most parrots won't be able to get too high with this modified clip but will still be able to fly.

Situations exist where a parrot can fly in a safe place, such as in an aviary or habitat. This type of housing is becoming very popular these days. I encourage you to consider this option. You can even build an aviary or habitat in an apartment, albeit it will have to be a small one.

If you are unable to house your parrot in an aviary or habitat, you may want to clip his flight feathers. Many people lose their birds to an open window or deadly accident that happens when the bird is able to fly freely in the home. Even the best birdkeepers can't predict an accident, and all it takes is turning your back on the bird for one moment. I hate to encourage this option, but I have to at least present it.

Tips for clipped and unclipped parrots

If you do decide to keep your birds flighted, here are some important tips to follow:

- ✔ Know where your birds are at all times. Supervise, supervise, supervise!
- ✔ Never take your flighted bird outside without a carrier.
- ✔ As you walk around with a flighted bird, keep your thumb over its toes as it perches on your hand. If it tries to fly in a room where it's unsafe, you can gently direct the bird toward the floor.

✔ Teach your bird to come to you when you call — a certain whistle or phrase, along with encouragement to fly to you, will train a bird to come when you request.

If you decide to clip your bird's wing feathers (for all or part of the time), here are some tips to keep him happy and safe:

✔ Make sure that your groomer does a proper clip (or that you do). A rough clip can lead to plucking, because the ends of the feathers can irritate the skin on the body.

✔ Don't clip too many flight feathers. Best to be conservative at first and clip more if necessary.

✔ Remember to allow enough feathers to remain so that the bird does not have a hard landing if he falls or tries to fly.

✔ You only have to clip your bird's feathers when they come in after a molt, generally once or twice a year.

✔ Make sure your clipped bird is getting enough exercise.

✔ Move your clipped bird around from room to room as you move around. This way, he can be with you and have a change of scenery. Clipped birds tend to get bored.

Proper Clipping Technique

If you've opted to clip your bird's wing feathers, your best bet is to find a professional who will clip them initially and then show you how to do it yourself. Many owners are squeamish about clipping their own bird's wings, though, and opt to have someone else do it each time. If you have an avian veterinarian in your area, that's the best person to regularly schedule wing clipping with. That way, you have the added bonus of the veterinarian seeing and handling your bird, and developing a relationship with it. Of course, you can always clip your bird yourself and may want to learn how.

Holding the parrot properly

The first thing you have to do when clipping wings (or toenails) is be able to hold your parrot properly and safely.

You can't simply grab a bird any which way, stretch out a wing, and clip. This can be very dangerous. A parrot has fragile bones that can break if you're too rough or don't hold him properly. Also, a bird breathes differently than we do, and it's possible to prevent a bird from breathing by holding him around the chest area, even lightly.

Grasp the bird around the neck and the back, leaving the chest free. You can use a thin towel if you don't want to do it barehanded — this is called *toweling*. Your thumb should be on one side of the bird's neck, bracing the bottom of his jaw, with your index finger on the other side doing the same (see Figure 9-2). The parrot should look like she's resting with her back in your palm. Of course, she'll be struggling — you can place a washcloth over her feet so she can grasp onto something.

Clipping the flight feathers

Once you feel that you're holding her properly, have someone else gently extend her wing and clip the first six to seven feathers (the long ones at the end of the wing), beginning at the point where the primary feather coverts end — those are the feathers on the upper side of the wing that end at the midpoint of the primary flight feathers (see Figure 9-3). With a sharp scissors, clip each feather, one by one, making a very clean clip so that the clipped end of the feather falls just under the primary covert. Clip both wings. If you don't, your parrot may become distraught, not to mention clumsy. Make sure that the ends of the clipped feathers are blunt. If they are sharp, they can cause irritation under the wing, which can lead to itching and plucking.

Figure 9-2:
Proper toweling technique used for clipping and examination.

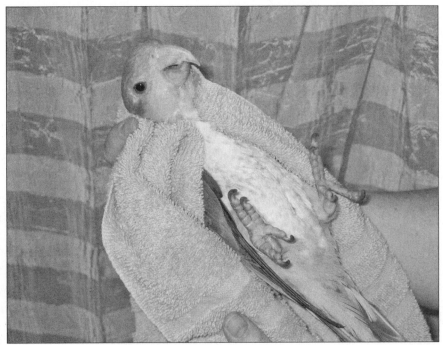

Photo by Vicki Johnson

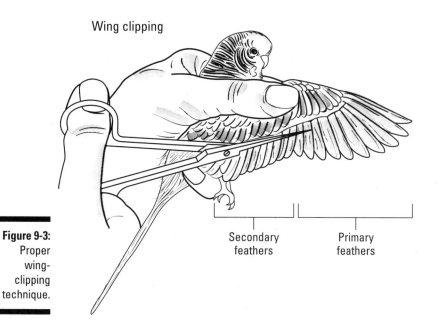

Wing clipping

Secondary feathers

Primary feathers

Figure 9-3:
Proper wing-clipping technique.

Don't ever clip your parrot's wings until you've watched someone do it in person and have had them show you how to hold your bird properly and which feathers to clip. Don't take a pair of sharp scissors to any part of your bird until you know what you're doing. And remember: Never clip *any* feathers other than the wing feathers, because your bird needs those for insulation and balance.

Some people like to leave the first two or three primary flight feathers intact so that when the wing is pulled into the body, it looks like there's no clip. This may be good for aesthetics, but it's not great for those feathers, which are very vulnerable to breaking. The strength of the wing isn't in the individual feathers, but in how those feathers work together to form a larger unit. The feathers themselves are fairly fragile.

Check regularly for new feather growth on the wings. Individual feathers that grow back are prone to breaking, because they're not protected by the strength of the other feathers. Never clip a brand-new feather, however, because it still has a blood supply. Let the feather mature for a few weeks before trimming.

Special considerations

African grey parrots need a far more conservative clip than most other birds. They are quite heavy and tend to get injured from falls more easily than other birds when too many wing feathers are clipped. Four to five primaries will do. Very light birds, such as cockatiels and budgies, will need a more copious clip to keep them from flying high (they can still fly *distance,* even when clipped, but not fly too far *up*).

Toenail Clipping

If you provide your parrot a variety of perches — especially a rough concrete perch wide enough so that your bird's feet have to open significantly for him to stand on it — you won't need to clip your bird's toenails all that often. However, if you have sensitive skin or if a child regularly plays with the parrot, you might want to keep those toenails blunt.

Clipping a bird's toenails is an easy procedure. A bird's toenails are much like ours. Part of our nail is without blood supply and is easily clipped off, while the other part has blood and is very painful when broken. In a parrot with light or pink nails, you can easily see the part that's "dead" and the part that's "living" — the sensitive part, called the *quick,* looks like a pinkish vein following the curve of the nail. It's more difficult to see the quick in a bird with dark or black nails.

Only cut off the "dead" part of the nail. Never, if you can help it, cut into the quick — the part of the nail that has the blood supply. Whenever you trim nails, you should always have a styptic powder on hand in case of bleeding. You can use regular styptic powder from the drugstore or get some from your pet shop. Styptic powder should only be used for bleeding from the nails. It burns if you put it on skin. Baking flour that you probably have in the kitchen also acts as a coagulant and will stop bleeding from small wounds. Nails may bleed a lot, more than you'd imagine, but most birds will stop bleeding well before it becomes a true health hazard. However, for smaller birds that don't have a lot of blood, like parakeets, one drop represents a significant amount. Always take bleeding seriously.

To trim a parrot's nails, hold him the same way you would if you were trimming the wings, and have someone else grasp the foot firmly. Don't let the foot wiggle. Next, with a regular human nail clipper (a clipper for a baby works well, as does one for cat claws), snip the very tip of the nail off, making sure not to cut into the quick (see Figure 9-4). If the nail is dark, and you're unsure where the blood supply is, cut off only the very tip, and repeat the procedure in a week. Better to leave more on the nail than risk bleeding.

If you're squeamish about cutting your bird's nails, you can file them down with either a Dremel tool (an electric filer that you can get at the hardware or craft store) or an emery-board–type filer. Don't file too much or too hard, however, or you can file right into the quick. Of course, your avian veterinarian will be happy to trim your bird's nails if you're not up to it. You can have them trimmed when you take your parrot for grooming or a checkup. Using the Dremel tool takes skill and practice, so you're better off letting an experienced groomer do it.

Because toweling a bird can be traumatic, I like to sneak up on my birds for a quick toenail clip. I hold the bird on one hand while we're interacting, and with the other hand, I sneak up on one toenail with regular fingernail clippers. I quickly snip off the very tip of one nail, and before the parrot knows what happened, I palm the clipper and pretend like I didn't do anything at all. I clip one nail a day like this, so it takes about a week to get them all done, but it's easier and far less traumatic this way.

Figure 9-4:
Proper toenail-clipping technique. Be conservative when you clip so that you never cut into the quick — the living part of the nail.

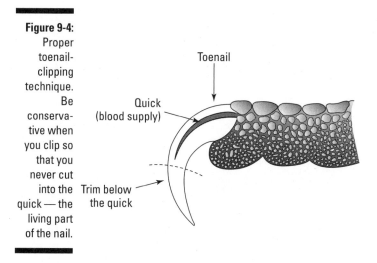

Grooming the Beak

If your parrot has crunchy things to eat, plays heartily with his toys, and is healthy and in good condition, he shouldn't need to have his beak trimmed. The beak, made of the same material as the nails (keratin), should wear down as your parrot engages in eating and playing.

A parrot with an overgrown beak (see Figure 10-4 in Chapter 10) may have a medical condition that is going untreated or may be suffering from malnutrition. If you notice that your bird's beak is growing too long or that it's misaligned, make an appointment with your avian veterinarian. Do not *ever* attempt to trim or correct your bird's beak yourself, because you could seriously injure him. The doctor or someone with this kind of experience should be the only person to ever trim a beak.

The beak naturally flakes as it grows, so your groomer or avian veterinarian will file the beak to remove this growth and then will oil the beak, making it nice and shiny. This is generally done with an electric filing tool and/or metal filers on larger birds. Smaller birds' beaks are done only with the handheld filers. Please don't attempt this yourself!

Beak breaks

Sometimes, a beak breaks due to an injury. Often, the part of the beak that broke just grows back. In other cases, the avian veterinarian has to bond the beak with special material until it grows back. This bonding also helps the beak grow in the proper position.

I once rescued an Amazon parrot whose bottom mandible was completely split in two. When he ate, much of the food would fall through the crack. I took him to the avian veterinarian to fix the beak, but we both decided that the bird didn't need it. Despite the food falling through the crack, the bird was quite porky and definitely didn't look like he'd ever missed a meal.

The misaligned beak

Occasionally, due to trauma, poor handfeeding technique, or illness, a beak will become misaligned. Usually, this comes in the form of *scissors beak,* where the upper and lower parts of the beak are off to the side. In other cases, the bird could have an underbite.

In cases of misalignment, the avian veterinarian can train the beak back into alignment by filing it a little bit each week or two over a few months and allowing it to begin to grow properly. This generally takes about six months in a healthy parrot.

Bathing Your Parrot

Most parrots love to bathe (see Figure 9-5).

Bathing softens dirt on the feathers and skin and encourages preening. If you bathe your parrot regularly, you will notice that his feathers will begin to become waterproof due to his preening duties. Bathing is important for parrots, whose skin can become dry and itchy, leading to plucking. It's also important that any pollutants be removed from the bird's feathers so that it doesn't ingest any toxic stuff while preening.

Here are some bathing tips:

✔ In warm weather, or when you can provide enough warmth after a bath, you can mist your parrot with a handheld spray bottle that you can buy in any drugstore or supermarket. If he's interested in the bath, he'll spread his wings, put his head down, shake around, and delight in every drop.

Figure 9-5: Most parrots, like this caique, don't need much more encouragement to bathe than a container filled with clean water.

Photo by Tanya Johnson

✔ Try misting above the bird so that the water simulates a rain shower. You can do this outside (in a safe place) with a hose for larger, ardent bathers.

✔ In the summer, you can completely soak your parrot to the skin a couple of times a week. This is very good for your bird.

✔ In very cool weather, keep bathing to a minimum unless you can offer heat after the bath. A bird lamp will do.

✔ Bathe only in the daytime hours — a bird that goes to bed wet can catch a chill and will be uncomfortable.

✔ Some companies make a suction-cup shower perch that you can use to shower with your parrot. Many of my birds love this, and it allows us more time to spend together. Make sure, though, that the water isn't too hot and that the bathroom is parrot proofed. If the parrot doesn't like to bathe in the shower, merely being in a steamy room will add moisture to the skin. Always supervise your parrot when the water is running. See Figure 9-6 for an amusing alternative showering method.

✔ Washing dishes is another bathing opportunity. Put your parrot on your shoulder during this time, and he may hop into the sink for a bath under the faucet. Make sure the temperature of the water is mildly warm.

✔ Never spray a bird that's freaked out by the whole affair. This bird will need to come to bathing on her own. Allow her to be near a stream of water (in the shower on a shower perch) and enter the water by herself.

✔ Don't blow-dry your parrot. Some blow-dryers contain nonstick coating on the heating coils, which can be deadly to your bird.

✔ For the reluctant bather, a flat plastic or ceramic dish filled with wet spinach, watercress, curly kale, or other greens may encourage bathing (the greens are also fun to play with and are good to eat).

Don't ever use soap on your bird unless it's for a *very* good reason — for example, if he gets oil on his feathers. Make sure to use very mild glycerin soap, and rinse your bird thoroughly. Wash only his body (not the face), and don't scrub. Your best bet is to fill a plastic tub with warm soapy water about chest-deep to your bird and set him in it, if he'll tolerate that. Remember, when doing anything unnatural, such as a genuine bath (not a mist or shower), be gentle and compassionate, and realize that your bird may become frightened. When in doubt, call your avian veterinarian.

There are bathing products that you can buy in your local pet shop that contain ingredients such as aloe that are good for the skin. Personally, I'm a fan of tepid, clean water for bathing. Many of the store-bought products can irritate the eyes and contain unnecessary fragrances.

Figure 9-6:
There's more than one way to bathe a parrot.

A parrot's chest muscles contract rapidly and repeatedly after a bath. This looks like shivering, but it's not. It's actually the way the parrot creates body heat after getting wet, and it's nothing to be concerned about.

Caring for Molting Parrots

When birds *molt,* they shed their feathers, making way for new ones. A molt can happen once or twice a year, depending on the amount of seasonal light and warmth where you live. In general, a parrot goes through one major molt a year, losing about a third of its feathers. In the lesser molts, which happen once or twice a year, it only loses a few feathers.

Molting is very stressful for a bird. Your parrot may become cranky and not want to be touched. The newly growing feathers can be itchy or painful. You will notice that little "pins" begin to stick out from between your parrot's other feathers (see Figure 9-7). These are called *pin feathers.* The pin is a sheath of material (keratin) that grows over the new feather until it is ready to fully emerge. Your parrot will spend time removing these sheaths but will not be able to remove the ones on his head. If he'll allow some head scratching, you can gently remove them for him. Bathing also helps soften these sheaths and allow the new feathers to emerge.

Molting parrots will not lose all their feathers at once. Most molts are many weeks or months long, with feathers being replaced gradually. If you notice bald patches on your bird's body, or if his feathering is becoming so thin that you can see his skin beneath, take him to your avian veterinarian right away. Some illnesses involve feather loss.

A molting bird needs some special care to make this time easier. Frequent misting with warm water is often helpful in softening the pin feathers. Offer your parrot an extra-nutritious diet at this time, including a protein source, such as hard-boiled eggs, egg food, and even pieces of boiled chicken. This will help fortify him and keep his energy level high. A molting parrot uses 30 percent more energy than when she's not molting, so she'll need some extra resources. In general, you shouldn't notice a difference in the way your parrot behaves, eats, plays, or reacts to things during a molt. Just realize that there is the *potential* for him to be a little "off" while new feathers are coming in. Don't force playtime. Adding the stress of forcing him to play is not going to be good for his overall health.

Figure 9-7: This bird is going through a molt. Note the pin-feather sheaths peeking out from under the feathers.

Photo by Rikki Paulsen

Blood Feathers

The pin feathers and very new feathers that have just emerged from the sheath of protective keratin still have a blood supply and will bleed if injured or broken. This often happens with a wing feather, especially in a clipped bird. If the bird was fully flighted, the other wing feathers would protect a new feather, but a clipped bird does not have that luxury. Some parrots, such as cockatiels, are also prone to cage thrashing, especially at night, and can break wing and tail feathers that way.

In a thick feather like the wing or tail, you can actually see the blood supply clearly, a dark red strip going down the vein of the feather. If this feather breaks or is cut, it will bleed copiously.

If you notice a bleeding feather, don't panic. Simply pull the feather straight out from the root with one slow, methodical tug. This will stop the bleeding immediately. A pair of needle-nosed pliers is good for this use and should be kept in your birdy first-aid kit. If you're squeamish about pulling out feathers, put some regular baking flour on the wound, and get your bird to the avian veterinarian as soon as possible.

Chapter 10

In Sickness and in Health

There's an old myth that a parrot will hide its illness until one day, it's belly up in the cage before you even knew anything was wrong. Why? If a parrot in the wild shows that he's ill, a predator will take notice. Often, very ill birds will eat well until their dying day. So the myth isn't entirely false — parrots are very good at hiding their illnesses. But if you're attuned to your parrot and know what his healthy state is like, you'll more easily be able to tell when he's ailing.

This chapter shows you how to recognize illness, discusses common avian illnesses, and suggests how to prevent and identify them. You'll also find out about the most common accidents for companion parrots, as well as how to help an ailing or injured bird.

Before I go on, I have to offer a disclaimer. This chapter is by no means meant to help you diagnose your parrot. Only a qualified avian veterinarian can do that. The info contained here is only meant to give you an idea of what kinds of ailments are possible. Parrots can have similar symptoms for a variety of diseases, and you can't diagnose illness without thorough testing.

Anatomy of a Parrot

To understand how to keep a parrot healthy and how to recognize if he's ill, you have to know something about your bird's bodily systems. Parrots are very complex and have a lot of intricate organs and systems, too many to detail here. But here are some of the important aspects of a bird's body that you should be aware of:

- ✔ **Eyes:** A parrot has one eye on either side of its head, allowing him to see nearly 360 degrees. This helps him notice predators and avoid other dangers. Parrots don't see better than humans, but they do notice images faster. They have worse depth perception than humans, which is why they're always cocking their heads to get a better angle. A parrot's eyes are very large in proportion to its head — if humans had eyes that large, they'd be like tea saucers. Parrots also have a third eyelid called a *nictitating membrane* that acts as a kind of squeegee for the eye, keeping it moist and uncontaminated.

  Parrots have different eye colors, depending on the species. Some eye colors indicate gender, as in the Goffin's cockatoo, where the female's eyes are brown and the male's black (though this is not always a reliable method). Also, in many species, eye color changes as an immature bird becomes an adult. A healthy eye is clean, moist, and free of discharge. A parrot with an eye problem may squint, scratch the eye with its foot, or rub the eye on the perch or bars of the cage. Look for swollen eyelids, cloudy eyes, excessive blinking, discharge, and excessive tearing. Any eye condition must be treated immediately.

- ✔ **Ears:** Your parrot's ear is located just behind the eye and looks like a small opening in the head. It is covered by a small flap of skin and generally by feathers, unless the feathers have been lost due to illness. You may see the ear after your parrot bathes, when the feathers around the head are wet. In most parrots, the feathers over the ear are a different color — either vastly different or just a slight shade darker or lighter than the other cheek feathers. Parrots cannot hear in the same range of sound that humans do, but they do hear sound in greater detail.

- ✔ **Feathers:** Feathers are a remarkable evolutionary construct, unique to birds (see Figure 10-1). Feathers regulate a bird's body temperature, help it remain waterproof, and allow it to fly (in most cases). The colors and patterns of feathers also facilitate mating rituals and, in some parrots, help birdkeepers know males from females. Parrots have fewer feathers than other orders of birds, but their feathers are stronger. See Chapter 9 for a lot more information about feathers.

- ✔ **Preen gland:** Parrots have a *preen gland* at the base of the tail (on the rump), officially called the *uropygial gland,* which secretes an oil that the parrot spreads on its feathers during preening. This oil helps keep the feathers supple and waterproof, though it's not necessary for water-proofing in parrots — Amazon parrots do not have this gland, and neither do hyacinth macaws, Lear's macaws, or Spix's macaws. The oil from the gland also contains precursors to Vitamin D. When sunlight hits the oil on the feathers, it turns to Vitamin D, and the bird ingests some of the oil during preening. Most problems and infections associated with this gland occur as a result of malnutrition and vitamin deficiency.

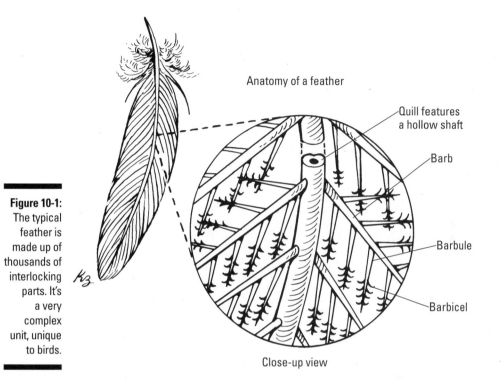

Anatomy of a feather

Quill features
a hollow shaft

Barb

Barbule

Barbicel

Close-up view

Figure 10-1:
The typical
feather is
made up of
thousands of
interlocking
parts. It's
a very
complex
unit, unique
to birds.

✔ **Feet:** Parrot's feet are *zygodactyl,* meaning they have two toes pointing forward and two pointing backward (see Figure 10-2). This is a first-rate design for grasping and climbing. Parrots also use their feet to regulate body temperature. When it's cold in the bird's environment, a parrot can decrease the amount of blood circulating to his legs and will often draw one leg up into his body and stand on the other. When a parrot is warm, he can increase the blood flow to his legs to cool off.

✔ **The beak:** Parrots are called *hookbills* because the beak is curved. This kind of beak is perfect for eating a wide variety of foods. The beak is made of the same material as human fingernails, keratin, which grows over a honeycomblike structure that is basically hollow, a good design for a bird that needs to be light enough to fly (see Figure 10-3). The beak acts as a crushing and cracking device but is also delicate enough to peel the skin off a pea. The beak also functions to help your parrot climb and move around, kind of like an additional foot. The beak may not look sensitive, but it is. Your parrot should be able to keep its beak trim through eating and playing. If the beak is overgrown (see Figure 10-4), your bird may have a nutritional disorder, or other illness or injury.

Never trim your parrot's beak yourself. See Chapter 9 for more about grooming the beak. If the beak is flaky, it could be a sign of underuse or illness.

✔ **The cere:** The *cere* is the fleshy spot just above the beak where the nostrils, or *nares,* are located. In some species, like the parakeet, the cere is prominent; in others, the cere is covered by feathers. Both the cere and the nares should be clean and free of debris. If you notice a discharge, a crust, or bubbling around the cere or the nares, contact your avian veterinarian immediately.

✔ **Tongue:** A parrot's tongue is fleshy and muscular, with a hard plate beneath the tip. It has about 350 taste buds — humans have about 10,000 (interestingly, rabbits have about 17,000, pigeons around 40, chickens roughly 24, and catfish 100,000). This is why parrots love sharp-tasting foods, such as jalapeño peppers. A parrot can manipulate its tongue during speech to make different sounds, something that previously was thought to be something only humans could do. Lories and other parrots that feed on nectar have brushlike organs on the tip of the tongue, making it easier to eat pollen and nectar from flowers.

Figure 10-2:
Parrots' zygodactyl feet make for good grasping and climbing.

Photo by Roberta Kendall

Figure 10-3:
A parrot's beak is made of two parts: the upper and lower mandibles.

Photo by Roberta Kendall

Figure 10-4:
An overgrown beak can indicate malnutrition or mites. This condition deserves a trip to the avian veterinarian.

✔ **Neck:** A parrot's neck is relatively much stronger than a human neck. A parrot's windpipe is fully ringed with bones, allowing for the stress of turning the head so far around. This is why the proper way to hold a parrot is basically around the neck — you will not prevent a bird from breathing this way, but you will prevent it from breathing by holding it around the chest area.

✔ **Skin:** A parrot's skin is much thinner and more delicate than a human's.

✔ **Syrinx:** This organ, located at the back of the throat, is the parrot's "voice box," allowing her to sing, make noises, and talk. It can become infected, especially if the bird has a respiratory-tract issue. Prevent this with proper nutrition and medical care.

✔ **Skeletal system:** Most of a parrot's bones are hollow, making it lighter for flying. A bird's skeleton makes up a very small percentage of its body weight. If the bones were solid and heavy, the bird would have to expend more energy. Some of the bones are *pneumatic* and aid in the breathing process, so they are actually part of the respiratory system. This is why it's so dangerous for birds to break certain bones, including the skull, pelvis (hips), upper wing bone (humerus), keel bone (sternum), clavicle, backbones, and shoulder.

✔ **Muscles:** Parrots are extraordinary athletes and are able to fly for miles a day, resulting in a well-muscled bird. The muscles a parrot uses for flight are "red meat," tough and oxygen-rich. (This is why a chicken's breast muscles are "white meat" — it doesn't need to fly.)

✔ **Respiratory system:** Your parrot has a very sensitive respiratory system, susceptible to airborne irritants such as aerosol sprays, fumes from heated nonstick cookware, and tobacco smoke. Coal miners used to take birds, primarily canaries, into the mines, and when the canary keeled over, it was time for the miners to leave.

Parrots are prone to respiratory illness and distress because their system is more complicated than that of humans. They do not have lungs that expand and contract like ours do. Parrots take two breaths to complete the breathing cycle — the first fills nine air sacs, located in hollow spaces in the body and in some of the bones, and the second pushes the air into the lungs. Same goes for exhalation. If you notice your parrot panting or having respiratory distress, call your avian veterinarian right away. You may be able to identify a respiratory infection by a change in your parrot's breathing and, in severe cases, bubbling from the mouth or nostrils. A parrot laboring to breathe may "bob" its tail as it pants. If you observe these symptoms, take your parrot to the veterinarian right away.

✔ **Digestive system:** After food is crushed and chewed by the beak, it is swallowed and goes to the *crop,* a saclike organ near your parrot's breast. Parrots do have saliva, but their saliva doesn't have enzymes like a human's saliva. For humans, digestion begins in the mouth, but for parrots, it begins in the crop. After being softened in the crop, the food goes to the stomach *(proventriculus)*; then it goes to the gizzard *(ventriculus)*, which grinds the food, and moves on to the *cloaca,* where feces and *urates* (urine) collect before being eliminated through the *vent.* It takes about three hours for food to make it from the beak to the vent, depending on the type of food and the bird's health. Many digestive disorders can occur in parrots. If you notice a change in your bird's eating habits or droppings (color, frequency, or odor), contact your avian veterinarian at once. See Chapter 8 for a good illustration of the digestive tract.

✔ **Circulatory system:** Birds have a four-chambered heart, like humans, but it is much larger proportionately — it has to be very strong to pump oxygen-rich blood at a rate faster than needed by humans.

✔ **Reproductive system:** Female parrots have two ovaries, though only the left one is functional. Birds don't get pregnant the way female humans do. They get "eggnant." All parrots reproduce by means of eggs. Females can lay infertile eggs and don't need a male around to be inspired to start a little egg family. The male has similar organs to a human male, but they are hidden internally. Later in the chapter, I discuss illnesses of the reproductive tract.

Indications of Illness

A major part of making sure your parrot remains healthy is being an observant guardian. Make an effort to get to know your bird's everyday, healthy behavior so that you'll be better able to tell when something's wrong.

Birds can be very sneaky when it comes to their illnesses and injuries. They would rather no one notice, especially a predator. A sick parrot doesn't want to be picked out from the crowd. This is why it's often difficult to tell if a bird is sick until he's *very* sick — sometimes when only a few hours are left of its life. But an observant owner will be able to see early signs of illness, including:

✔ **Excessive sleeping:** An ill parrot may sleep too much, especially during the day. Sleeping on the bottom of the cage is a particularly significant symptom. Look for any odd changes in sleeping patterns.

✔ **Sleeping on two feet:** A well parrot generally sleeps with one foot drawn into its belly.

✔ **Fluffed-up appearance:** A fluffed-up parrot may be trying to maintain his high body temperature and fight off an illness. Or it just may be too cool in the room.

✔ **Loss of appetite:** You should know how much food and what types of food your parrot consumes each day. If you notice that your bird is not eating or is eating far less than usual, there could be an illness present.

✔ **Change in attitude:** If your parrot seems listless and is not behaving normally, or has become very cranky or limp, call your veterinarian.

✔ **Lameness:** If your parrot can't use his feet or hold up his head, there's something very wrong.

✔ **Panting or labored breathing:** May signify respiratory illness or overheating.

✔ **Discharge:** If you notice runniness or discharge on the eyes, nares, or vent, the bird may be ill.

✔ **Change in droppings:** No good parrot book would be complete without an in-depth discussion of poop. Your parrot's droppings should consist of a solid green portion, white urates (over the green part), and a clear liquid. If the droppings are discolored (very dark green, black, yellow, or red), and there has been no change in diet (such as feeding beets or blueberries), there may be a problem. Also, if there's a pungent odor or the droppings seem far more liquid than usual, call your veterinarian immediately.

✔ **Debris around the face or on feathers:** Indicates poor grooming or vomiting, potential signs of illness.

✔ **Bobbing tail:** A bird sitting on the perch and panting will have a bobbing tail. This is often a sign of respiratory illness.

✔ **Messy vent:** If the bird's vent is crusty or damp with fecal material, there's a problem.

Choosing an Avian Veterinarian

Your parrot has the potential to live for many years, and in that time it is likely that he will experience an illness or an injury. These things occur to the birds of even the best bird guardians. The most important relationship you can foster (beside the one between you and your bird) is the relationship between your parrot and your avian veterinarian. When your parrot becomes ill or injured, you may only have a few hours before the situation becomes critical.

A bird isn't *really* supposed to be living in a home, where danger lurks around nearly every corner. Having your parrot become a regular patient at your local avian veterinarian's office is the best bet to keep your parrot healthy and alive in case of an emergency.

A regular veterinarian can treat some ailments in birds, but an avian veterinarian sees all kinds of bird illnesses and injuries, and is better able to diagnose and treat these problems. An avian veterinarian's office is equipped with the latest technology for diagnosing and treating birds of all kinds.

If you live in or near a large city, you should have no problem finding a doctor specializing in birds. You may have to travel a bit if you live in a rural area.

Find an avian veterinarian near you by calling the Association of Avian Veterinarians at (561) 393-8901, or go to the Web site at www.aav.org.

When you first get to the office, make a mental note of the cleanliness of the rooms, and talk to the staff to make sure they're friendly. Ask to see the back rooms, where the animals (specifically the birds) are kept. You'll want to see these in case you have to leave your bird overnight. The staff may not let you see the back rooms because of the potential spread of diseases, but that should be the only reason. If the office is filthy, and the staff is rude or careless, consider changing veterinarians. Here are some other things to look for:

- Is the veterinarian a member of the Association of Avian Veterinarians, or has he or she been practicing medicine solely on birds for many years? Ask if the doctor is board certified in avian medicine. Many veterinarians claim to be able treat birds, but they aren't really experienced enough to do so.

- Does the veterinarian have a good bedside manner? Do you feel comfortable with the doctor?

- Does he or she handle your bird with gentleness and confidence?

- Does he or she explain procedures being performed on the bird?

- Ask the veterinarian whether he or she has pet birds at home, or make a note of any birds in the office and inquire about them. If the doctor has birds at home, that's a pretty good sign. If not, ask why not.

- Is the doctor familiar with treating your species of parrot? Some parrots have specific health issues that should be addressed.

- Are the doctor's fees are reasonable for your budget? Ask about fees when you make your appointment. The vet should consult with you before doing any expensive procedure unless you've given consent for any treatment, no matter how costly (I've done this plenty of times!).

- Is the vet available to treat emergencies, even when he or she is not in the office? It's important that you develop a relationship with your avian veterinarian while your bird is well. The doctor will be more likely to see a known patient in the middle of the night than a new one. Many offices have a rule that new patients will not be seen on an emergency basis.

- Is the doctor willing to send you and your bird to another vet if he or she is unable to deal with a medical problem? Not all avian vets are specialists. Your bird may need someone to deal with an eye injury or specialized surgery and will need to go to another doctor for that.

✔ Does the office schedule regular, timely appointments? If they keep trying to schedule you weeks in advance for a wing trim, consider another office.

Make a note of the hours your avian veterinarian works. and hang the schedule and the office's phone number on your refrigerator for easy reference.

The moment you suspect that your parrot is ill is not the ideal time to find an avian veterinarian and begin building a relationship. You should schedule a "well-bird check-up" within the first three days (or sooner) of bringing your bird home. If you've had your bird for a while and have never taken him to the avian veterinarian, do so immediately.

At the well-bird check-up, the vet will weigh him, thoroughly look over his entire body, and may perform some tests. All this information will be recorded in the bird's chart. Then, if you begin to notice an illness later on, the doctor will have a reference point for your individual bird — the bird's healthy weight, feather condition, and so on. You can also use this opportunity to talk to the doctor about nutrition, grooming, and anything else you're concerned with. Schedule a well-bird check-up every six months. You can combine the visit with a grooming visit, if you like.

When you take your parrot to the veterinarian for the first time, be prepared to answer questions. Here are some you may encounter:

✔ How old is your parrot?

✔ What sex?

✔ Where did you obtain the parrot?

✔ Do you possess other birds at the moment?

✔ How is your parrot housed?

✔ What does his diet consist of?

✔ How much time does your parrot spend out of the cage?

✔ Is he active, and in what manner?

✔ Have there been signs of illness or unusual behavior?

✔ Has your parrot been exposed to any household dangers?

✔ Is your parrot in a breeding situation?

✔ Has this parrot seen another avian veterinarian?

✔ What did that veterinarian say about the bird?

✔ Were there tests taken?

✔ What's the phone number of the other clinic (to get previous medical records)?

Holistic care

Holistic care has become very popular for humans in recent years and is becoming so in the bird community as well. Many veterinarians use holistic care along with Western medicine in their practices. I encourage you to do some more research and reading about holistic care for birds — but not to abandon Western medicine in the treatment of your ill bird. A combo of both is generally pretty effective in treating most medical conditions.

Treating your bird holistically doesn't have to begin when it becomes ill. A lot of good information is available on the Web about feeding and caring for a bird holistically so that you can *prevent* illness. Check out www.holistic bird.org and www.landofvos.com/articles/kitchen.html for some helpful info on this aspect of parrot care.

Here are a few questions *you* should ask about your parrot and her treatment:

- ✔ What do you think is wrong with my parrot, if anything?
- ✔ What kinds of tests are you going to do to/for my parrot?
- ✔ When do the test results come back?
- ✔ How do I treat my bird at home?
- ✔ What can I do to make my bird more comfortable?
- ✔ What are the costs of the procedures you're going to perform?

Common Health Disorders

There are many health issues that can plague parrots, but some are more common than others. Many parrot illnesses stem from a basic lack of nutrition and vitamins, which can break down the immune system and leave the parrot open to all kinds of diseases and ailments. I encourage you to heed the advice in Chapter 8 and do some nutritional research on your own. After nutrition, filthy and damp housing conditions are next on the list of why birds become ill. Keeping your bird's area clean goes a long way toward preventing illness.

Nutritional disorders

Wild parrots are very active and do not have a tendency to put on extra weight, whereas your house parrot has nothing to do but eat all day, which can lead to a porky bird. A parrot that's sitting around all day eating seed may become obese, which can lead to tumors and to liver and kidney disease. This is one of the many reasons why a complete, balanced diet is so important.

Other symptoms of nutritional disorders can include overgrown beak, poor feather quality/color change, feather plucking (see Figure 10-5), weak bones, trouble laying eggs, and yeast infections, among other symptoms.

Parasites

Parasites are not a huge problem with parrots, but they do occur. The minuscule *feather mite* is not common in parrots but can infest birds that live outdoors in filthy conditions.

The *red mite* eats blood and is highly communicable, though not very frequent in parrots. Mites, as wells as feather lice, can cause itching and discomfort; may cause your parrot to pick at his feathers; and may even make the feathers bleed. If you suspect mites, don't try to treat them yourself — see the avian veterinarian. The mite protectors sold in stores are ineffective and can even harm your parrot rather than help him.

Figure 10-5: Sometimes, plucking can be an indication of illness rather than of frustrated behavior. As with this cockatoo, or any bird that is mutilating its feathers, the guardians should begin solving the issue by visiting an avian veterinarian.

Photo by Maryann Jaschick

Roundworms can be found in parrots and should be tested for on your first veterinary visit. If they're discovered, regular testing and treatment is essential; eliminating them is difficult because of their complex life cycle.

Giardia is a one-celled protozoan parasite that can affect your parrot, other animals in the house, and even you. Giardia is contacted through contaminated food or water, and it causes distress in the digestive tract. You may notice diarrhea, itching, failure to digest foods, weight loss, and other symptoms. Your veterinarian can test for giardia and treat it effectively.

Bacterial infections

Mycobacterium avium is accountable for the tuberculosis infection and is transmitted through food, water, or filthy housing. Avian tuberculosis *can* be transmitted to a human infant or someone with a compromised immune system. Transmission is via airborne particles shed from infected birds. Although this type of infection in humans is a respiratory disease, it's chiefly a digestive disorder in parrots. Symptoms include weight loss and digestive distress. Good nutrition, clean surroundings, and minimized stress levels can help manage this disease in birds.

Psittacosis, also called *chlamydiosis* and *parrot fever,* is also transmittable to infant humans and those with suppressed immune systems, and causes respiratory distress symptoms in both human and parrot. It's a strange organism, because it is treatable like a bacteria, but it behaves like a virus. Psittacosis is transmitted through droppings and infected secretions. Some birds can be carriers of psittacosis without displaying symptoms. If it's caught early, this infection is highly treatable. Ask your avian veterinarian to test for this disease, especially if a person with a weakened immune system is going to be in contact with your parrot. Symptoms include limey or yellowy droppings, listlessness, labored breathing, and nasal discharge.

Viral infections

A virus is a treatable, though incurable, disorder. Several viruses regularly affect parrots:

Psitticine Beak and Feather disease is an incurable, communicable (to other birds) disease that involves feather loss and beak lesions. Diagnosis is through a blood test, and euthanasia is normally suggested when there's a positive result. This disease is terminal. Symptoms include feather loss, abnormal feather growth, and a generally ill condition.

Polyomavirus affects young parrots, though adult birds are carriers and transmit the disease to their young, which perish around the time that they should be fledging from the nest. This disease occurs in breeding birds, though households with many birds are susceptible. As of today, there is no treatment for polyomavirus, so prevention is key. A vaccine is available, so ask your veterinarian about it.

Pacheco's disease is a viral hepatitis affecting the liver. This disease is terminal and is primarily diagnosed upon death, which happens quickly. This is a highly communicable disease and can be transmitted easily when bringing a new bird into your home. Enforce strict quarantine at all times. You can find out more about quarantine in Chapter 7. Roughly, it's a period of 40 days (or more) where you keep new birds away from your established birds. Ideally, the new birds should be in a location with its own air supply, and you should wash up and change your clothes after servicing the cages of the new birds.

Fungal infections

Yeast infection or *candidasis* generally affects the mouth and digestive tract, and can even involve the respiratory system. Your parrot has the fungus yeast in its body normally (as you do), but when the bodily systems become unbalanced — for example, when a parrot is undernourished or after a treatment of antibiotics — the yeast can grow to a surplus, causing illness. Symptoms include a sticky substance in the mouth and white mouth lesions. Regurgitation and digestive problems may occur as well. Treatment by a vet is essential, as is a diet rich in Vitamin A. A yeast infection is not immediately fatal, but if left untreated, it can cause the bird to perish.

Aspergillosis is a fungal infection causing respiratory distress and is very often deadly. Changes in your parrot's breathing, changes in vocalization, or gasping or wheezing may indicate this infection. Aspergillosis is difficult to treat and may take months of medication. Prevent it by keeping your parrot's environment sanitary and dry. If you see hairy black mold growing anywhere near your bird's environment, he can get this fungal infection.

Fungal infections are more apt to affect undernourished birds than they are to affect birds with healthy immune systems. Be sure to feed your birds lots of fresh fruits and veggies rich in Vitamins A and C. Fungal infections are not contagious from bird to bird or bird to human.

Foot disorders

Your parrot is on his feet all the time (if he's not, worry!), and there are several disorders of the foot you should watch out for:

Gout is a painful condition of the legs common in birds not receiving proper nutrition. Symptoms include visible swellings on the legs and lameness.

Bumblefoot is an infection of the bottom of the feet connected with poor nutrition and obesity. The skin on the bottom of the foot is inflamed and red, and may become scabby, resulting in lameness.

Lameness and *weakness* in the feet is occasionally linked to hens that become egg bound (when an egg becomes stuck or crumpled inside the hen), but there can be multiple reasons for lameness, including tumors.

Feather disorders

Several illnesses can affect feather quality. If you notice bald patches on your bird (with the exception of under the crest in cockatoos and cockatiels), feather bleeding, and torn and ragged feathers, see your avian veterinarian right away.

Self-mutilation (feather plucking and chewing) is common in some species of parrots, including African greys, cockatoos, eclectus, and others, generally occurring due to illness, confinement, unhappiness, or fear. Often, a parrot will pick his feathers over an area that is irritated due to an illness or para-site. Sometimes, a bird may become very unhappy with her housing or cir-cumstances and will begin a nervous habit of plucking at her own feathers, either removing them from the skin or chewing them off. This is an ugly habit and is difficult to correct.

The first step is to run the gamut of veterinary tests on the bird to determine whether something is awry healthwise. If all is well, take a look at the bird's circumstances. Has something changed recently? Is the housing situation too small or dark? Perhaps another bird is chewing the feathers off of this bird. Is there enough stimulation in the cage, toys, and so on? Has anything new moved into the environment, even for a short time, like party favors, bal-loons, or a Christmas tree? All of these things are potential causes for feather plucking and chewing. See Chapter 14 for more details on the causes and treatment of feather plucking.

Reproductive disorders

Hens (females) of any species may have difficulty laying eggs if they are under-nourished or have laid too many eggs in a row, leading to calcium depletion in the bones. *Egg binding* is when an egg becomes "stuck" inside a hen and she is unable to lay it. She may be weak, the egg could be misshapen, or she may have a tumor or other disorder of the reproductive system. Symptoms of egg binding include panting, squatting, and lameness.

Keeping your laying hens healthy and nourished, and resting them between clutches (bunch o' babies), will help prevent egg binding. Consult your veterinarian immediately if you suspect egg binding. If it's late in the night or you can't get to the veterinarian's office immediately, place your hen in a warm hospital cage (see toward the end of this chapter for how to create this) or incubator at around 90 degrees Fahrenheit, and put a few drops of mineral oil (or olive oil) in her vent and one drop of olive oil in her mouth. Be gentle! You can easily asphyxiate a smaller bird by putting oil in the mouth, so if you can get her to take it willingly, that would be great. The oil in the vent and/or mouth may help her pass the egg. Even if she does, take her to the veterinarian as soon as you can. She may need a shot of calcium or other treatment.

Older male parrots can develop tumors on their testicles. Regular veterinary check-ups should help find and treat any developing problems of the male reproductive system.

Common Dangers to Companion Parrots

The home is a dangerous place for any bird, especially for a curious, agile bird like the parrot. I can't begin to tell you how many horrible, tragic situations I've heard about and even witnessed involving parrots, from flying away to being mauled by the family dogs or wild predators. Knowing how to avoid dangerous situations is the first step toward keeping your parrot safe. The second step is knowing how to deal with certain situations when they occur. Like the Boy Scouts of America, be prepared.

This section outlines the most common parrot injuries and accidents, shows you how to prevent them (or at least how to try to prevent them), and gives valuable emergency tips in case all your forward thinking isn't enough to keep your parrot safe. Accidents happen to the best of guardians, but it's how you react to accidents that makes all the difference in the world.

Predators and animal bites

Parrots are prey animals, meaning they are hunted by other animals for the purpose of eating them. Your parrot instinctively knows this, which is why he's always on the lookout for the family cat or dog. Even if your other animals are very well fed, even porky, they will prey on your bird.

Even a brief encounter with a cat or dog can be deadly. If contact occurs, take your bird to your avian veterinarian *immediately*. DO NOT wait until the next day to see how the bird is doing. She could be dead by morning.

Snakes also pose a danger to your parrot. Snakes are a bird's natural preda-tor. Birds are so fearful of snakes that it's not even a good idea to make a shushing sound when trying to calm your parrot. Snakes are notorious for sneaking into cages, swallowing a bird, and being stuck inside because of the lump of the bird in its body — not fun to wake up to on Sunday morning.

Other pets, such as ferrets and rats, will not think twice about eating or injuring your parrot. If you keep your bird outside, take precautions so out-door predators — such as opossums, raccoons, and hawks — can't get to your parrot. You can do this by keeping the cage only in a wired-off space and double-wiring the cage with two layers instead of one, keeping the outer layer about one inch from the inner layer — a cage within a cage. This keeps preda-tors from pulling your parrot's feet and legs off through the bars. Your imme-diate response to an animal bite should be to call your avian veterinarian or *any* available veterinarian immediately. You can flush a small wound with a weak solution of hydrogen peroxide and water before you leave the house for the veterinarian's office. If the wound is large, leave it alone, and rush the bird to the veterinarian.

While I'm on the topic of other pets, bird-on-bird aggression can cause severe injury, even death. Keep large or aggressive birds clear of other birds that they can harm.

Standing water

Parrots are attracted to water and can drown easily by falling into deep water while trying to take a bath or drink. A clipped parrot isn't quite as balanced or agile as a flighted one, and it can slip easily into water and be unable to remove itself. Here are some dangerous bodies of water:

- **Toilet bowls:** Close all toilet lids, even if you think your bird can't get to the bathroom, and especially if he can. If you shower with your bird, this is especially important.

- **Pools and Jacuzzis:** If your bird has access to these recreational items, keep a close eye on him when he's out of the cage. I once had a parrot fly into the center of my pool, and I had to go in fully clothed to retrieve him! Fountains and ponds hold the same danger.

- **Dog bowls:** If you have a large dog with a large dog dish, your parrot might find its way into the center of it and not be able to get out.

- **Fish tanks and fish bowls:** These can be mesmerizing for a parrot, who might want to bathe in it. Keep all tanks and bowls securely covered.

- **Drinking glasses:** A half-empty drinking glass may entice a parrot to drink, and he may fall in and be unable to remove himself. This is an absolutely tragic circumstance. Imagine turning your back for a moment and finding your bird drowned in your glass! Awful.

> ✔ **Standing water in the kitchen:** Full sinks and pots boiling on the stove pose grave dangers for your birds. Keep an eye on the sink when you're soaking dishes, and keep all cooking pots tightly covered. The same goes for your large appliances, such as the dishwasher and washing machine. Your parrot could fly in unnoticed, and you might turn on the machine.

Nonstick cookware

Nonstick cookware, when heated, emits a colorless, odorless fume that kills birds immediately. There used to be a rule that only nonstick cookware that was burned or overheated emitted the fume, but there have been cases where birds have died from normal cooking temperatures. I don't own a piece of nonstick cookware, and I will never bring it into my home. Why take the chance? A bird dying of this kind of poisoning dies a horrible, agonizing death, and there's no antidote.

Birds have also died from self-cleaning ovens during the cleaning process. Make sure you remove your parrot from the house during your oven's self-cleaning, and ventilate the house well before bringing him back inside.

Nonstick surfaces can be found in the items in the following list

Heat lamps

Portable heaters

Plates on irons

Ironing-board covers

Stove-top burners

Drip pans for burners

Broiler pans

Griddles

Cooking utensils

Woks

Waffle makers

Electric skillets

Deep fryers

Crock pots

Popcorn poppers

Coffeemakers

Bread makers

Nonstick rolling pins

Lollipop and other candy molds

Stock pots

Roasters

Pizza pans

Curling irons

Anything considered nonstick

Common household products

Products that you regularly use in your home can be deadly to your parrot. These products include cleansers and candles — items you wouldn't think of as poisonous. When cleaning your bird's cage, rinse it thoroughly before placing the bird back inside. Or you can opt to use safer cleansers, such as baking soda as an abrasive cleanser and vinegar or grapefruit seed extract as a disinfectant. These things will not harm your bird.

Here's a partial list of common household products that you should keep far away from your parrot:

- ✔ Barbecue items, charcoal, and lighter fluid
- ✔ Cleansers, soaps, and detergents
- ✔ Scented candles, candle "beads," and air fresheners
- ✔ Gasoline, kerosene, and other fuels
- ✔ Liquid drain cleaners
- ✔ Insecticides, rodent poisons, and roach and rodent traps
- ✔ Paint, paint thinners, and turpentine
- ✔ Crayons, markers, pens, and pencils
- ✔ Fertilizers

Symptoms of poisoning include vomiting; paralysis; bleeding from the eyes, nares, mouth, or vent; seizures; and shock. Bird-proofing your home should help eliminate the danger of poisoning; however, accidents can occur even in the best of circumstances.

If you believe your parrot has come into contact with poison, call your veterinarian immediately and then call the National Animal Poison Control Center's 24-hour Poison Hotline at (800) 548-2423, (888) 4-ANIHELP, or (900) 680-0000. Rushing to your avian veterinarian is key to saving your bird's life, though rapid first-aid from you with the help of the NAPCC can be critical to saving your bird.

Poisonous houseplants

Most people have houseplants, and most parrots are curious — not a good combination. Your parrot will not hesitate to nibble (or even feast) on your houseplants, and some of them can be deadly.

Never, ever let your parrot have full run of your houseplants, and be careful about the tree limbs that you use as perches if you are inclined to make your own. Fresh tree branches are a wonderful addition to a parrot's environment, but only if they are from a safe tree and are free of pesticides and fertilizers. Wash all plants and tree parts thoroughly before placing them near your bird.

Some plants and trees that could harm your bird include the amaryllis, caladium, holly, hyacinth, iris, juniper, larkspur, oleander, philodendron, poinsettia, rhododendron, and wisteria. For a much more thorough list of unsafe plants for parrots, see www.liparrotsociety.org/non-toxi.htm and www.cockatielcottage.net/houseplants.html.

Ceiling fans

Birds instinctually fly to the highest point they can reach, and this is often the ceiling fan. A whirling ceiling fan and a bird flying around the room are a deadly combination. In a tangle, the fan will win every time.

Make sure your ceiling fan is off when your bird is out of the cage.

Toxic foods

Most foods are fine to share with your parrot, but some can be deadly or at the very least make him sick. Here's a list of foods never to share:

- **Alcohol:** Alcohol is toxic for birds (for humans too, actually). Some people think it's funny to give their bird a sip of an alcoholic beverage. Not only is it not funny, but it's also deadly.

- **Chocolate:** Chocolate is toxic to birds. I've seen a particular macaw in a pet shop offered chocolate candies with no immediate ill effect, but I don't know what happened to that bird in the long run.

- **Caffeine:** Caffeine is toxic for birds. No coffee or tea for Roxy.

✔ **Avocado:** There's a substance in avocado that's toxic for birds. Don't share your guacamole!

✔ **Pits:** Some seeds and pits are toxic for birds, such as those in peaches, nectarines, and plums. Remove them from fruits before serving.

✔ **Rhubarb:** There's evidence that rhubarb is toxic for parrots. I've never needed to offer it to my birds, so I don't really know for sure about this one, but better safe than sorry. I've heard that it's the skin of rhubarb that's particularly toxic.

✔ **Raw onions:** There's no evidence that raw onions will kill a bird, but they might make him ill. Cooked onions are okay in moderation if they're in something that you're eating and want to offer your bird.

Electrocution

Most parrots are curious and love to chew. They might think that the "rope" is a new toy when it's really an electrical cord. A determined parrot can chew right through an electrical cord and electrocute itself. Keep all cords wound up and tucked neatly away, out of the reach of your bird.

If there are some cords that you can't put away, buy a length of plastic tubing from any hardware store, slice it open lengthwise, and fit it around the length of the cord.

Feet and doors

Allowing your parrot free-roaming privileges on the floor is a good way to get him crunched. Someone might not know he's there, or you may lose sight of him, and the next thing you know, he's under your shoe. Many birds have been killed this way. It's worse when your bird is similar to the color of your floor — if you have an albino cockatiel and white carpeting, for example (though I don't know any bird guardian that would have white carpeting!).

A parrot roaming the floor also has the potential to be crunched in a closing door (or being eaten by another pet). The floor is an unnatural place for a bird, who feels safest in a high spot. You can play with your bird on the floor, but please supervise.

Lead and other heavy metals

Stained glass and chipping paint can both contain lead, and your curious parrot may want to see what those things taste like. The same holds true for jewelry parts, lead weights, and fishing lures. Metal poisoning is difficult to treat and causes an agonizing death. Keep all metals away from your bird.

Many people make bird cages from galvanized wire because it is rust resistant. This wire is dipped in zinc, which is deadly to birds, who are likely to hang on to the bars of their cage and ingest the zinc particles. Scrub any new caging material vigorously with a wire brush and cleanser, and rinse thoroughly before housing birds inside a cage made from galvanized wire.

Mirrors and clean glass

A squeaky-clean windowpane may be invisible to a parrot, who might think that it's his chance to go winging to the great outdoors, only to find himself with a broken neck. A clean mirror also looks like a clear flight path. The good news here is that you may now officially keep your windows and mirrors dirty. Yes, that's right — having a bird gives you a great excuse never to do windows again. You can also purchase stickers and place them on your windows or hang an attractive *plastic* window decoration (not stained glass).

A young bird that's not a skilled flyer yet might even bump painfully into walls and furniture. Don't let your young bird have full flight in the house until he understands his flying abilities.

Night thrashing

Some parrots, cockatiels and ringnecks somewhat more than other species, engage in *night thrashing* or *night frights.* This is when a parrot, for no reason clearly apparent to its human friends, throws itself violently against the cage bars at night, often resulting in broken feathers and injured eyes and feet. The reason for night thrashing is unknown, but it may be caused by a scare in the night. Even something as minor as a car door slamming in the neighbor's driveway can cause a thrashing episode.

To prevent or stop night thrashing, add a nightlight to the room where your parrot sleeps. This will enable him to see in the darkness and feel a little more secure. If you cover your parrot's cage, leave one side of the cage uncovered so that there's some light getting through.

Temperature changes

Parrots can stand a wide temperature range — say, between 55 and 99 degrees Fahrenheit — but are prone to chill, frostbite, or overheating when the temperature goes to an extreme beyond the comfort range. Avoid this by making sure that your parrot lives in a controlled environment where the temperature is constant — 70–85 degrees Fahrenheit is very comfortable for a parrot. Fluctuations in temperature, like the kind that happen in a kitchen or bathroom, should be avoided on a long-term basis.

Frostbite

Frostbite may cause the loss of toes or feet, or even cause death. If you keep your parrots outdoors during the cold time of year, consider bringing them inside on the coldest nights. Your parrot will carry the painful frostbitten foot as though it were broken. The frostbitten area will eventually die, and the flesh will change to a dark color. If you discover this condition, place your bird in a warm hospital cage, and call the veterinarian immediately (see later in this chapter for instructions on making a simple hospital cage).

Overheating

Overheating is a little simpler to deal with, especially if you catch it early enough. If you notice your parrot panting, standing with his wings open, or lying on the floor of the cage or carrier, he may be overcome with heat. If you know it's going to be hot where your parrot is, keep a spray bottle handy, and lightly mist him with cool water, repeating the misting until he's soaked to the skin. Watch him closely until his manner seems normal. In warm weather or when traveling in the summer, make sure that your bird *always* has cool water to drink. Parrots should by no means be kept in full sunlight unless they have a shaded spot where they can get out of the sun.

If your parrot does not respond to the cool misting, remove him from the warm spot immediately, and place him in a cooler location. If you have a fan, place the flow of air on the cage, and mist him again. As he recovers, move the flow of air so that it's not directly on him. Put small drops of cool water into his beak if he's unable to drink, but be careful not to choke him. Call your avian veterinarian right away.

Oil on feathers

Oil on the feathers makes it impossible for a bird to regulate its body temperature and is a serious condition that must be treated by an avian veterinarian. According to Murphy's Law, if there's one place where your parrot will land, it's in a pot of oil, and ideally, that oil won't be hot!

If your bird gets soaked in oil, dust him with flour or cornstarch; blot him with paper towels; and then give him a warm bath in a tub filled with warm water and some very mild, grease-fighting dish soap. Do not scrub the bird or dunk its head. Simply allow him to soak, and repeat the bath several times. Place him in a warm hospital cage, and take him to the avian veterinarian as soon as you can.

Broken blood feathers and bleeding nails

A broken feather and a bleeding nail are small wounds and can often be treated successfully at home. Styptic powder or a styptic pen used to be the way most birdkeepers dealt with the situation, but that stuff can be quite stinging on skin. Instead, use regular baking flour or cornstarch. Apply a small mound of the flour directly to the wound, and that should stop the bleeding immediately. You can use styptic powder for nails only.

Physical injuries and seizures

Fractures, beak, eye, and foot injuries and seizures are all cause for calling your avian veterinarian right away and rushing to the office for treatment. In the meantime, place your parrot in the warm hospital cage, and make him feel comfortable. Transport him in the hospital cage if you can. Leaving him in his regular cage can cause more injury if he thrashes against the bars or toys.

An unconscious bird may be suffering from a toxin in the air — ventilate the room well, and try to revive your bird by taking him to a different area of the home. If he doesn't revive quickly, contact your avian veterinarian right away.

Flying away

I can't tell you how many people I've known who have lost a bird to an open window or door. It has happened to me three times over the years, and I consider myself a very careful guardian (two of the birds actually returned).

If your bird is unclipped, or if you suspect that the clip is growing out, be very careful about open windows and doors. Even a clipped parrot can get pretty far if the wind is right. Keep screens on your windows, and make sure your bird is in her cage when you open the door. Never, ever take your parrot outdoors on your shoulder. You'd be surprised at how far she can get, and there's always the danger of a hawk swooping down and grabbing her. Some people use a "flight suit" or a harness, but many parrots won't tolerate such items. Taking your bird outside, including to the vet, means using a carrier (see Figure 10-6).

This yellow collar macaw is one of the so-called "mini macaws." It is smaller than its larger cousins, though this bird isn't tiny, by any means. *Photo by Andrea Carter*

The hyacinth macaw is one of the giants of the macaw family. These birds are not for the beginner, though they make loving companions for those who can care for them properly. *Photo by Bob and Liz Johnson*

Here are some macaws and Amazons in the wild. *Photo by Bonnie Zimmerman*

The eclectus is one of the most unique of the commonly kept parrot species. The male is bright green, the female bright red. It wasn't until a few decades ago that breeders realized that these weren't two different species.
Photo by Nancy Giacomazzi

The little parrotlet (shown here in the blue mutation) is a popular companion, though it can be feisty and isn't recommended for the beginner or someone who is going to be shy around birds.
Photo by Chantell van Erbe

The Hahn's macaw is the smallest of the macaws and is often mistaken for a conure.
Photo by Gary Rose

The male eclectus. *Photo by Paul J. Robinson*

This yellow-naped Amazon is one of the best talking species, though it can be a tough bird once it hits maturity, and it needs a sensitive guardian with a lot of fortitude.
Photo by Cyndi Baker

The Quaker parrot comes in a variety of mutations and is found feral in the wild all over the United States. It is one of the noisier parrots. *Photo by John Lapinski*

Which is the baby eclectus and which is its stuffed animal pal?
Photo by Essi Laavainen

Parakeets enjoy being kept in a bonded pair.
Photo by Johanna Middleton

The rainbow lory comes in over 21 known subspecies, and is one of the most beautiful parrots, though one of more difficult to care for and one of the messiest. *Photo by Sally Lamar*

The highly intelligent African grey parrot can learn to communicate cognitively with its human guardians. This is the author's African grey, Hope. *Photo by Nikki Moustaki*

The little Meyer's parrot is a member of the poicephalus family. It is affectionate and known as one of the quieter parrots. This is the author's Meyer's parrot, Jesse. *Photo by Nikki Moustaki*

The peachfaced lovebird is the most popular of the nine species of lovebird. It is feisty, but loyal and loving, and breeds readily. *Photo by Nikki Moustaki*

The Senegal parrot is the most popular of the African poicephalus parrots. *Photo by Rikki Paulsen*

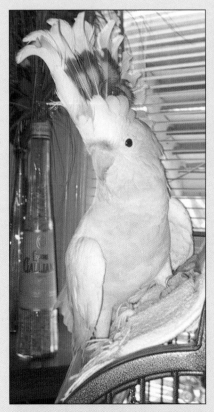

The Major Mitchell's cockatoo (also called the Leadbeater's cockatoo) is arguably one of the loveliest in the cockatoo family. *Photo by Sherlynn Hogan*

Pretty in pink — that's the rose breasted cockatoo (also called the Galah), one of the smaller of the species. *Photo by Sherlynn Hogan*

The sun conure, a South American species, is loving and sweet when handfed, but can be persistently noisy. *Photo by Susan Dzieweczynski*

The Australian cockatiel is just second to the budgie (parakeet) in all-around popularity. It is sweet, easygoing, and relatively quiet (though not silent by any means). *Photo by Susan Dzieweczynski*

The Bourke parakeet comes in several pretty mutations. It is not known as a great hands-on companion, but handfed individuals do make loving pals.
Photo by Vicki Johnson

Caiques are known for their clownish, bouncy personalities. They can be "beaky," though, so shy guardians need not apply. *Photo by Vicki Johnson*

The hawkheaded parrot is an unusual bird, not often kept as a companion, but it is definitely a fancier's bird. It has a colorful head crest that it raises when it's excited or fearful. *Photo by Tom Richardson*

The large cockatoos, like this Moluccan, are very loud and can be a handful for a guardian with any level of bird experience. *Photo by PetProfiles*

The scarlet macaw is one of the beauties of the South American rainforest. *Photo by PetProfiles*

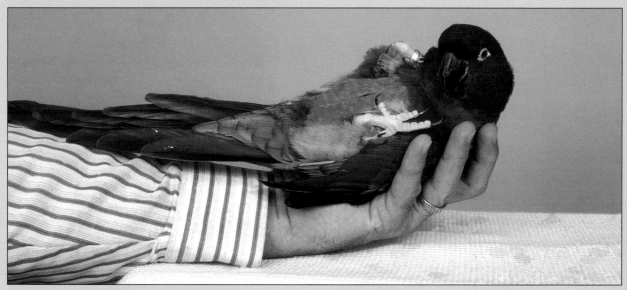

Patagonian conures are lovely and loud. They tend to be "one-person birds," but they are also incredibly affectionate. *Photo by PetProfiles*

The blue and gold macaw is the most commonly kept of the large macaws. *Photo by PetProfiles*

These Alexandrine parakeets look almost like their feathers are painted on. They are good talkers, but they tend to be noisy as well. *Photo by PetProfiles*

Jardine parrots are in the poicephalus family, are known to be quieter than other parrots, and have a solid temperament, making them good companions. *Photo by Robin Miller*

Figure 10-6:
When you visit the avian veterinarian, be sure to take your bird there in a safe, sturdy carrier.

Photo by Angela Cancilla Herschel

Watching your parrot fly away is a tragic experience — one of the worst moments in a birdkeeper's life. If you keep your parrot's wings clipped, there will be less of a chance that you will lose him. But even if your parrot flies away, all hope is not lost — many people ultimately retrieve their birds. Here are some tips on how to do that:

✔ The first thing to do is note which direction your parrot flew, and try to keep him in sight as long as you can. Knowing the general direction will help later in trying to get him back. If you can, go to the spot where you think he went. If you can see him, try to tempt him down with a piece of millet or some nuts.

✔ A cagemate is also a big temptation to return, so if you have other birds, bring them outside in a safe carrier.

✔ Don't yell or throw things at him. Be cheerful and encouraging.

✔ Take his cage outside (or a smaller cage that he knows), and fill it with his favorite foods and lots of water. He may come down and enter the cage when he gets hungry.

✔ A good thing to have on hand *before* this happens is a tape of your parrot's vocalizations so that you can play the tape back to him. This may get him to come down from the treetops.

✔ If your parrot hasn't come down by nightfall, and you have an idea of where he is, you can climb up and catch him. A bird net is really helpful at this time. Birds don't see well at night and are easier to catch then.

✔ If you don't retrieve your bird by the first evening, it's time to create signs. Post the bird's photo on the sign, or clip out a picture of a similar-looking parrot from a book. Parrots can fly long distances, so you'll want to cover a large area.

✔ Call your local bird club and pet shops, and tell them about your lost bird in case someone contacts them about a bird they've found. Post the loss and his picture on the Internet as well. You can also take out an ad in your local paper. Offering a reward is a good way to get your bird back.

In most cases, a tame parrot will fly to someone when he gets hungry or lonely. He may land on someone's shoulder, and ideally, that person will be conscientious enough to check the local paper for a lost bird.

Microchipping a parrot is pretty common these days — my birds are chipped. The veterinarian injects a small microchip about the size of a grain of rice into the bird's chest muscle. The chip is encoded with information that will track back to you. Most shelters and veterinary offices have a scanner that can read the chip. I encourage everyone to microchip their larger parrots. Better safe than sorry.

Unsafe toys

Toys with unsafe parts that can get caught on your parrot's toes, feet, neck, and beak are a big safety issue. Make sure that all toys are the appropriate size for your parrot and that your bird can't fit its head into any of the rings on the toy. Make sure that all metal parts are stainless steel and that all of the clips close securely with a thread (like a screw), not a spring. Also, avoid toys with jingle bells, because the slots can catch a small toenail or beak.

Toys made of fabric material can be deadly for your bird. Not only can the parrot ingest this material, but it may also chew a hole into it and hang itself. Cotton rope toys are fine, but make sure to trim all strings as they come unraveled. See Chapter 6 for more information on safe and unsafe toys.

Humans

Humans are by far the most deadly household danger for a parrot. Whether through neglect or abuse or accident, most parrot injuries and deaths are directly attributed to humans. Children, the inebriated, and guests who know nothing about birds all pose risks. Keep your bird safe by creating strict rules and sticking to them.

Don't leave your parrot unattended with people who may pose a threat to him. If you have a party where alcohol is involved, move your bird to a safe, locked room. Drunk guests may try to do something strange to the bird or try to feed him alcohol or other unsafe foods.

Emergency Tips

What constitutes an emergency? Any time you feel, for one moment, that your bird has been injured or is in danger, it is considered an emergency. Parrots are sensitive birds that can go into shock from an event that you may consider minor, such as a bleeding toenail or flying into a wall and seeming to recover. Would you rather lose your bird because you took a cavalier attitude toward a seemingly minor accident?

Make up several index cards with important birdy phone numbers on them, including your own phone number, your avian veterinarian's number, the number of a 24-hour animal medical service, a taxi company's number, a neighbor's number (if they're familiar with your bird), the number of your bird sitter, a family member, and the number of someone who has keys to your home. Keep one card with you at all times; place one by each phone in the house; hang one on the refrigerator; place one in your parrot first-aid kit; tape one to your parrot's carrying case and one to your bird's cage; and give one to your bird sitter, one to your neighbor, one to the concerned family member, and one to the person with your house keys. You can also print some very basic bird-care tips on to the backs of the cards.

Buy "In Case of Fire" stickers (available in most pet shops), indicate the types and location of your animals on them, and post the stickers on each door in your home.

Often, when you have to medicate or examine your bird, you will have to "towel" her — that is, wrap her safely in a towel so that she can't move or bite you. For proper toweling technique and a photo of a properly toweled bird, see Chapter 9. For tips on how to socialize your bird to the towel, check out Chapter 16.

Medicating Your Parrot

If your avian veterinarian has treated your parrot and sent you home with medication, be diligent about giving the proper amount and continuing the medication for the allotted time. Make sure that your veterinarian shows you the proper way to administer the medication and that you are clear on how to do it before you leave the office.

If you're not comfortable giving the medication in a certain manner — injections, for example — make that concern known. Most likely you will simply be mixing something up into the water or giving a bit of medication orally with a needleless syringe. You will have to learn to hold your parrot properly to administer oral medication properly, so be sure to ask your veterinarian to show you how.

Never, ever give your parrot human medicine at any time. In my practice as an avian care expert, I can't tell you how many times people have called or e-mailed me that they've been offering their bird antihistamines, antacids, and leftover human prescriptions. A great many human medicines are toxic and deadly to parrots, and there's absolutely no reason for anyone to be trying to treat a bird himself. That's what the avian veterinarian is for. Also, an inquisitive parrot may be able to break through pill packaging to get to the "seeds" inside. Keep all medicine out of reach of your parrot!

Creating a Hospital Cage

A *hospital cage* is essential for comforting an ill or injured bird. It offers warmth and a safe space to recuperate. Your parrot's regular cage may have items such as toys that he can injure himself on, it might not be warm enough, or the cagemates may pick on him while he's ill.

To make a hospital cage, line a ten-gallon fish tank with a few layers of white paper towels. These are easy to replace, making cleaning the cage easy. Place a screen on top and a dark towel covering ½ to ¾ of the cage top and sides. Do not cover the entire cage with the towel. Place a heating pad on medium heat under half of the cage. Your parrot should have the option of moving away from the heat. Place a cup of seeds and millet spray in the cage, as well as a very shallow dish of water. A weak bird can drown in even a half-inch of water.

Do not place toys or perches in the cage, but you can place a rolled-up, regular, cotton hand towel in one corner so that your bird can perch or snuggle up to it if he wants to. Place the hospital cage in a quiet, safe place where your bird can recuperate undisturbed.

Creating a Parrot First-Aid Kit

Always have a parrot first-aid kit on hand for any emergency. Buy a small tackle box or other container to keep all the items in so that you won't have to go rushing around the house in search of something you need. Keep it near or inside your parrot's travel cage, which you should have ready to go at a moment's notice. Don't ever try to treat a serious emergency yourself, though in some cases, the veterinarian might talk you through a procedure on the phone. Here's what a parrot first-aid kit should contain:

- Antibiotic ointment (for small wounds; nongreasy)
- Eye wash
- Bandages and gauze
- Bottled water (you may need clean, fresh water to flush out a wound or clean your bird)
- Baby bird formula (can be used for adults that are having a difficult time eating)
- Cornstarch and baking flour (to stop bleeding on skin)
- Cotton balls
- Q-Tips
- Nongreasy first-aid lotion
- Dishwashing detergent (mild)
- Heating pad (always allow a bird the option of moving off of a heating pad)
- Hydrogen peroxide (always use in a weak solution with water)
- Nail clippers
- Nail file
- Needle-nosed pliers (for broken blood feathers)
- Penlight
- Pedialyte (great for reviving a weak bird)
- Saline solution
- Sanitary wipes
- Sharp scissors
- Syringe (without needle)
- Styptic powder for nails (to stop bleeding)
- Small, clean towels (for holding or swabbing)
- Spray bottle (for misting)
- Alcohol (for tools)
- Tweezers
- Veterinarian's phone number
- A sealed bag or can of your bird's base diet (in case of evacuation due to extreme weather or other circumstances)

What to do if a parrot breaks your skin

There's no known transmittable disease that a human can get from a bird bite, even if it breaks the skin. Most diseases passed from bird to human are airborne. A parrot's mouth is basically dry, so the chance of infection from bacteria the bird is harboring in its mouth is slim. If I had a dime for every time I've been nipped by a bird, I'd have at least five bucks. Simply wash your wound, apply some ointment and a Band-Aid, and learn from the experience.

Part IV
Parrot Behavior Made Simple

The 5th Wave   By Rich Tennant

"He loves his ball and string, but once in a while
he'll pick up the trombone and play 'Under Paris
Skies' over and over again."

In this part . . .

Parrot behavior simple? Hardly. These creatures can seem as complex as a billion-piece puzzle. This part gives you the picture on the box so that you can figure out how to put it all together. Chapter 11 is all about instincts and wild parrots. Chapter 12 details your parrot's normal behaviors, things you can expect from every bird. Chapter 13, for those with more than one parrot, helps you keep the peace. Finally, Chapter 14 details the terrible behaviors that can plague ill or unhappy parrots. You find out how to recognize the beginnings of unwanted behaviors and how to temper them.

Chapter 11

Understanding Your Wild Child's Instincts

*P*arrots in the wild and parrots in a human home have a lot in common in terms of natural instincts, though they lead very different lives. Understanding something about how parrots exist in the wild and how their instincts work will help you better care for your bird. If you can get inside that bird brain, you have a better shot at having a mutually fulfilling relationship.

Most scholars agree that birds are modern-day dinosaurs. They are certainly descended from dinosaurs and share some remarkable similarities, such as hollow bones. Species in the *Psittacosaurus* genus had a beaklike mouth 100 million years ago. Remember, parrots are in the *Psittacidae* family. The first bird, archaeopteryx, was really a dinosaur with featherlike constructions on winglike limbs. Your parrot pal has roots going back a long time.

Daily Life of Parrots in the Wild

Wild parrots living in different places in the world lead very different lives. Even though a parrot lives in your home, she is still programmed with the behavior she needs to survive in her native habitat. These distinctions may not be completely clear if you're keeping parrots as companions, but people who breed parrots know quite well that not all parrots nest in the same manner. Here are a few interesting examples:

- ✔ Patagonian conures burrow deep into limestone or earth cliffs to nest.
- ✔ Quaker parrots build elaborate, giant, communal stick-nests.
- ✔ Some lovebird species (and Quaker parrots) are the only parrots to actually build nests. All others find or dig holes in trees and other places.
- ✔ Brown-throated, Aztec, and half-moon conures excavate termite mounds and make nests in them.

The climate and terrain that parrots live in also contribute to their behavior, nutritional needs, and housing requirements. Here are a few distinct examples:

- ✔ New Zealand's mountain parrot, the Kea, lives in high altitudes in the cold and snow.
- ✔ Lories have brushlike tongues that help them eat pollen and nectar from flowers.
- ✔ Blue-crowned hanging parrots sleep hanging upside down.
- ✔ The night parrot of Australia is nocturnal, and feeds and drinks after dark. It is also one of three ground parrots that are entirely terrestrial.
- ✔ Bourke's parakeets become active at twilight and are known to fly around on moonlit nights.
- ✔ Hyacinth macaws eat a fatty diet primarily consisting of nuts. They even eat nuts that have been digested by cattle (yes, they eat them right out of cow patties).
- ✔ Some macaws, Amazons, and conures eat clay at "clay lick" cliffs in South America (see Figure 11-1). It is supposed that these clay cliffs contain minerals that the parrots need or that the clay purifies the parrots' systems due to the toxic vegetation that they eat. The act of eating dirt is called *geophagia*.

As you can see, some parrots lead very different lives in the wild. Knowing something about the habits of your parrot's species can help you better care for her.

The daily life of a wild parrot is different for every species. Species that live in similar environments generally share similar habits. For example, the budgie, cockatiel, and other Australian grass keets forage, drink, and nest in the same areas.

Figure 11-1:
In South America, wild macaws like this blue and gold regularly visit a mineral "clay lick."

Photo by Bonnie Zimmerman

In general, there's a breeding season and an off season. Some parrots have to deal with periods of drought, the end of which usually triggers the breeding season. Some parrots nest, rear, and wean young in a matter of months — for example, the budgie. Others, such as the hyacinth macaw, have their young around for years.

The last Spix's macaw

The last Spix's macaw *(Cyanopsitta spixii)* disappeared from the wild in 2000. The 19-year-old male, living in Brazil, had paired with an Illliger's macaw *(Ara maracana)* and was being closely monitored by conservationists. He disappeared and was eventually assumed dead. He was the last wild Spix's. Captive-bred Spix's have been released into the wild, but the results have yet to be productive, with some individuals dying or disappearing. There are fewer than 60 Spix's macaws left in the world. In 2002, a fortunate and serendipitous event occurred — a 25-year-old Spix's male, Presley, was discovered living as a pet in a Colorado home. After losing its Amazon "mate," the bird's human family decided to give him up and add him to the sorely lacking Spix's gene pool. He is now living in Brazil. The Spix's is the most endangered parrot in the world.

The Carolina parakeet

The only true native parrot to the United States was the Carolina parakeet *(Conuropsis carolinensis)*, now extinct. These 12-inch parrots vaguely resembled the jenday conure and could be seen in large flocks from Nebraska to New York to Florida. Because they frequently raided crops, farmers killed them in large numbers because they were pests, and milliners (hat makers) killed them in flocks for their feathers (to put on the hats). By the mid-1800s, their numbers declined drastically, and they weren't seen outside of Florida. When it was clear they were becoming extinct, the remaining specimens were killed ruthlessly for their skins. The last flock of them was seen in Florida in 1920. In 1918, the last Carolina parakeet in captivity died in the Cincinnati Zoo. The species was declared extinct in 1939. You can see stuffed specimens of Carolina parakeets at the Smithsonian Museum in Washington, D.C.

Much of the day for a wild parrot is spent foraging for food. Some species fly for miles to find a fruiting tree. Some parrots eat more than 75 types of plant material in the wild — far more than any guardian can ever hope to offer in captivity. Many fruits are eaten just before they ripen, some are eaten just after, and some fruits are opened only for their seeds. Most parrots feed in the morning, take an afternoon siesta, and then feed again close to dusk. Some forage all day, especially those that live where a wet season brings abundant food. Some parrots feed high in the rainforest canopy; others feed on the ground.

The Plight of Wild-Caught Parrots

In 1992 the United States passed the Wild Bird Conservation Act, which banned the importation of wild-caught parrots into the country. Quarantine stations that served as holding places for these birds were closed. I happened to attend one of the last bird auctions at one of the last quarantine stations in South Florida. Thousands of wild-caught birds were there, all crammed into small cages, numbered, and being sold to the highest bidder. Many of the larger birds were plucked, injured, and in bad shape. These birds had known freedom not long before, but now they were a long way from home, up for bid to anyone who had the money to take them home. It was a very sad scene, but it represented an end to the plight of wild-caught parrots in the United States. That was a huge victory for conservationists. The only parrots that can be caught and brought into the United States now are those that aviculturists petition for because they are endangered or threatened with extinction. The petition can take years.

The closing of the quarantine stations was a bittersweet victory. Capture and exportation of wild-caught parrots continue as Europe and other parts of the world still accept them into the pet trade. Also, poachers and smugglers continue to raid nests, steal babies, and capture adult birds. Many of these birds do not survive the first few days in captivity. Many don't know how to eat the food provided and starve to death. The babies are improperly fed and die either from infection or from choking on the food. The parrots that do survive are often improperly packed for the long trip to Europe or other ports, and many die in transit. Of the individuals that make it to their destination, many more die from improper care and handling, or from the stress of their ordeal. There are no humane means of capturing a parrot, and it is critical that this trade not be supported. If you suspect a smuggled bird, please contact your local Fish and Game or Fish and Wildlife authorities.

It's not only the plight of the captured parrots that's a concern. The remaining parrots in the wild are also compromised. Poachers chop down hollow trees that are irreplaceable nesting sites. With fewer nesting sites, the parrots don't go back to nest. When adult birds are captured, one of a pair may remain, and this lone bird has to find a new mate and begin nesting all over again. These factors add to the declining parrot populations all over the world.

The reason for the success of this industry isn't because its commodity — parrots — is beautiful and intelligent. Business is business, and the bottom line is money. The end user — the consumer — may love parrots, but to the trappers, the parrots represent a job. Unfortunately, their job is deadly.

In some cases, wild-caught birds can make good companions. I've had many myself, but only one really enjoyed my company: a mealy Amazon, tamed long before I got him. The others, always skittish or vicious, were rescues I took on after their previous guardians couldn't handle them anymore.

The Shyne Foundation

Bob and Liz Johnson, owners of the Shyne Foundation, a free-flight sanctuary in West Palm Beach, Florida, have a lot of experience with wild-caught birds as companions. They have 130 birds flying in an enclosed multiacre free-flight habitat. The large enclosure mimics the environment the birds would have in the wild, complete with trees and dense foliage.

"Out of our 130 free-flighted birds, about 35 of them are wild caught. Some of them make nice companions, but it's still hard on them," says Liz Johnson. "They go though torture when they're removed from their natural habitat. Trapping has a lot of emotional impact on the birds, and to be removed from everything they've ever known — their environment, friends, and food — is horrible."

One of the Johnsons' first avian friends was Lotus, a large hyacinth macaw. "Lotus came in from Brazil with five young hyacinths in 1977," says Liz Johnson. "The people bringing them in didn't realize that they were too young to eat on their own. They had barely any feathers when they came in and were very ragged looking. Lotus had one ragged tail feather — that's it. He wouldn't eat anything, and we had to force-feed him with a syringe. I had to back him into a corner, and he was scared to death. I'd just hope I got the syringe in his mouth. I finally got him to eat Brazil nuts. Two of the hyacinths he came in with died."

Today, Lotus is a fully feathered, handsome fellow who rules the roost at the Johnsons' habitat. He was lucky to have fallen into their hands — most are not as fortunate. The Johnsons also have a Moluccan cockatoo that was smuggled into the United States by a pilot. "When we first got him and would walk by him on the porch, he would get so scared that he would literally fall on the floor, passed out as if he was dead," says Liz Johnson. "Twenty-six years later he still hasn't overcome his fear of people. He wouldn't bite if his life depended on it, because the person that smuggled him used to hit him when he bit. Now he just makes a hissing sound if I go to pet him. He will step onto my hand, but he's still scared of his shadow."

Differences between wild caught and captive bred

Aviculture has made giant strides in the past decade, and handfed baby birds have flooded the pet trade, especially in the United States. Handfed babies make superior companions to wild-caught birds simply because they are socialized to humans and to human sounds and objects from the time they open their eyes. They are exposed to the germs on our hands and in our environment, and build immunity to them, giving them an advantage over their wild cousins. Though handfed babies have instincts that are a sort of shadow memory of the jungle, a handfed baby knows only humans and their ways if it has been properly socialized, though many babies aren't.

This is not to say that captive-bred babies or adult birds are perfect. They're still birds, just a couple of generations away from their parents, who may have been wild caught. All parrots are still wild animals, and taking one into your home is a huge commitment. However, if you're bringing a bird home, you definitely want to begin with the best animal you can find, and if you're looking for a companion, a captive-bred, handfed bird is going to be much easier to handle than a bird that has been ripped from the rainforest.

How can you tell a wild-caught bird from a captive-bred bird? It's not always easy. For starters, you can look for a closed band on the bird's leg. A *closed band* is one that was slipped over the bird's foot and onto its leg when the bird was a tiny baby. This kind of band isn't possible to slip onto an adult's leg. The band will have numbers and letters on it, indicating where the bird was hatched, the year, and the breeder's initials. An *open band* is one that was clamped onto an adult bird's leg and is often associated with wild-caught birds, though this does not offer conclusive proof. Bands are easily cut off, so a bird without a band isn't identifiable as wild caught or captive bred.

Finding a knowledgeable bird breeder with a good reputation is a great way to find a captive-bred, handfed baby. It is unlikely that a small breeder is involved in the wild-bird–smuggling trade, though not impossible. There are unscrupulous people in any business. Beware very inexpensive birds that should fetch a much higher price.

Conservation organizations

If you want to become involved in parrot conservation, check out what some organizations are doing to help the plight of wild parrots:

- **The World Parrot Trust:** www.worldparrottrust.org. Restores and protects populations of wild parrots and their native habitats; promotes awareness of the threats to all parrots, captive and wild; opposes the trade in wild-caught parrots, educates the public on high standards for the care and breeding of parrots; and encourages links between conservation and aviculture.

- **Project Bird Watch:** www.indonesian-parrot-project.org/index.php. An all-volunteer group committed to the conservation of Indonesia's parrots and cockatoos. The nonprofit corporation's mission is to help conserve endangered Indonesian cockatoos and parrots.

- **Rare Species Conservatory Foundation:** www.rarespecies.org. A nonprofit organization dedicated to developing conservation strategies for saving endangered plants and animals, with the ultimate objective of restoring critical species in the wild.

- **The Macaw Landing Foundation:** http://unix.ipns.com/~mlf/. Promotes and applies scientifically based information from the field to the propagation of endangered macaws, to wildlife management, and to environmental education, while building public awareness and supporting other organizations that work to preserve macaws in the wild.

- **World Wildlife Federation:** www.wwf.org. Leads international efforts to protect endangered species and their habitats.

Feral parrots in the United States

You don't have to travel to South America or Australia to see parrots in the wild. Populations of wild feral parrots live and thrive all over the United States. No one really knows where these parrots came from, but the suspicion is that they aren't handfed companion parrots, but wild-caught parrots that escaped once they reached the United States. In most places, the parrots do not displace other species and don't destroy native flora, so they aren't a nuisance (though some feral Quaker parrots build extensive nests on power lines and cause power outages — Maui, Hawaii, is monitoring its flock of feral mitred conures in case the parrots begin to displace native species). The most famous feral parrot population is the "Wild Parrots of Telegraph Hill" in San Francisco, a flock of cherry-headed conures (see Mark Bittner's book on the topic, as well as the film about it released in 2005). San Francisco also has a flock of Brotogeris parrots. In South Florida, you'll find huge flocks of Quaker parrots, as well as in Connecticut, Alabama, Texas, Delaware, Illinois, Virginia, Louisiana, New York, New Jersey, Oregon, and Rhode Island. South Florida also has flocks of nandy conures, Amazon parrots, and macaws. Some suburbs of Phoenix, Arizona, have flocks of hundreds of peachfaced lovebirds.

Understanding Your Parrot's Instincts

Instincts are an inborn patterns of behavior or responses to specific stimuli. *Reflexes* are part of instinct as well. For example, when an object flies at your face, your reflexes force you to close your eyes — it's impossible keep them open. Reflexes are immediate reactions to stimuli. Instincts include more complex automatic behaviors. Humans have an instinct to make a crying child stop — crying is designed to get adult human attention. Parrots have all kinds of reflexes and instincts that rule their behavior, too.

Your parrots' instincts are pretty much going to remain intact; you won't be able to modify them much. Parrots do have an incredible capacity to learn and modify their behavior based on their environment, but reflex and instinct nearly always take the front seat. For example, a parrot can become used to the family dog, a predator, but that doesn't extend to every dog. If a strange dog comes over, the parrot may fear it as it would any predator.

Prey versus predator

All parrots are *prey* animals — meaning predators, like hawks and snakes, will eat them. This is one reason parrots can see nearly 360 degrees around them. Most parrots are fearful or suspicious of quick movements, which is why children really need to be taught to move slowly and talk quietly around parrots.

Predators are quick, and parrots instinctively know that they have to be quicker to get out of the way or risk being lunch.

Most animals have a *fight or flight* instinct. When cornered by something dangerous, they choose to either flee or physically defend themselves. Your parrot would certainly rather use the *flight* option. However, a parrot with clipped wings can't. Sure, it may be able to flutter away or run as fast as its little birdy feet will carry it, but that's not quite good enough. This is why many parrots choose *fight* — or *bite*. Fully flighted parrots that are allowed to have some self-direction are less likely to bite.

Finding a high spot

Parrots like to be in the highest spot they can find. They know instinctually that they can see predators better from there. This is why the curtain rods are such tempting perches. Some parrots do forage and dig on the ground, but these species are particularly attuned to movement and sound, and fly up and away at even the slightest hunch that danger is nearby.

Flocking

For the most part, parrots travel in *flocks,* social groups ranging in number from a handful to many hundreds of individuals. There's no real flock leader, but there are family groups of parents and siblings that live in the vicinity of other family groups. These groups forage together and help one another remain safe from predators. When one bird senses a threat, it sounds an alarm cry. Those parrots that forage on the ground, like grass keets and African greys, are particularly sensitive to movement and can become alarmed easily.

Parrots in a large flock are also safer because the movement of many birds tends to confuse predators, making the birds harder to catch. Parrots that roost in flocks are also safer from nocturnal predators because one bird can warn hundreds with a warning call. Because parrots are so dependent on other members of the flock for survival, they tend to languish in homes where they don't get enough attention. A lone parrot tends to be a lonely parrot unless its human guardians give it an extraordinary amount of hands-on attention.

Most parrots are incredibly tuned in to their flockmates. Some people even report that their parrots seem to be psychic. Now, I tend to doubt that, but I do know from experience that my parrots have an uncanny ability to "read" me. The oddest thing I've ever experienced with any parrot continues to happen every day with my African grey. Every morning, the nanosecond that I wake up, my grey begins to vocalize. Now, if he was vocalizing before I woke up, I'd hear him and wake (I'm a light sleeper). I sleep with two walls and an air shaft between me and this bird, as well as with the door closed and a white-noise machine going. How does he do it? I can only assume that his senses are incredibly attuned to his flockmate.

Sleeping

Parrots retire to their favorite tree or nesting site just after dusk, settle in for the night, sleep quietly, and arise with the sun. Most parrots nap in the daytime, particularly those in warm climates where it doesn't pay to be flying around in the afternoon heat (see Figure 11-2). Some parrots, such as lovebirds, actually chatter in their sleep in the daytime. Scientific studies on finches have shown that birds actually dream of their vocalizations while asleep. No one is really sure if parrots do this, but it's an interesting theory.

Figure 11-2:
This cockatoo is sleeping with one foot drawn up into its belly and its head tucked onto its back. This is normal napping position. However, if your bird is doing this all day, with two feet on the perch instead of one, it could be an indication of illness.

Photo by Sherlynn Hogan

Vocalizing

Parrots vocalize most at dawn and dusk. In the morning, they tell other flock-mates that they're okay and have made it through the night. In the evening, they're telling flockmates that they've found a safe perch or are in the nest and that everything's okay. Okay, I admit that this is a *very* simplistic explanation of why these two times of day are so chatty for parrots, but because no one really knows what they're saying, it's as good an explanation as any. Maybe they're vocalizing for sheer joy.

Harvard biologist Michael Schindlinger has spent years studying the vocalizations of yellow-headed Amazons and has come to the conclusion that they have a complex and varied vocabulary. Each species has its own "language," as does the same species of parrots living in different places. The language is passed from generation to generation. Parrots of the same species have the same basic vocalizations, but there are variations from area to area, kind of like a dialect. Schindlinger believes that studying the sounds of these parrots can help determine from where smuggled parrots were illegally poached. See www.freeparrots.net/parrots/ for more information on Schindlinger's Oratrix Project and his video *Stalking the Wild Amazons.*

Mess

Well, mess isn't an instinct, but it's worth mentioning here because it's something that wild parrots do. Wild parrots are just as messy as captive ones, but it's okay to be messy in the rainforest or on the plains. In these settings, food and chewed items that fall to the ground below become natural mulch or food for other animals. But the real benefit for wild parrots is that they never really have to come in contact with their feces — a much cleaner situation than the average home. This is part of why it's important to use a cage with a grate.

Camouflage

Most parrots are colored so that they blend into their environment. Green parrots blend incredibly well into the canopy of the rainforest. Brightly colored birds in reds and blues, like the female eclectus, blend well into the shadows of dense foliage and in their nesting holes. Parrots that live in grasslands, such as budgies, often have stripes or blocky patterns similar to their environs. Those big white cockatoos may seem like they'd stand out on the Australian plains, and indeed they do, but when they're all together in a flock they tend to blend together, confusing a predator that needs to be able to distinguish one individual in order to pursue it. It's hard to believe that these large birds blend anywhere, especially with their antics — see Figure 11-3.

Figure 11-3:
Parrots are
natural
acrobats.
Their feet
are built for
climbing
and
hanging.

Eye contact

Intense eye contact can be intimidating for a parrot, especially one that's skittish. Avoid staring directly at your parrot, or glaring. You can certainly look at your parrot, but don't make a point of staring him down unless he's doing something you don't want him to do. Then a hard squinty glare should stop him in his tracks. Don't over do it, though, because your aim is just to let the bird know that you're not pleased with him, not to frighten him.

Chapter 12

Normal Companion Parrot Behaviors

*B*ecause the parrot is still essentially a wild animal, he comes into your home with all kinds of strange behaviors. A parrot is not like a dog or a cat in the sense that it can be trained out of certain behaviors. A dog can be trained not to bark at the mailman or to go potty in the yard, but you're going to be hard pressed to teach your parrot not to vocalize loudly while you're on the phone. Instead of becoming angry at your bird for a natural and instinctual (or inadvertently taught) behavior, it's a good idea to simply accept that he may whistle incessantly while you're making a long-distance call — so leave the room if you want a quieter conversation.

Wild parrots behave in a certain way to maximize their potential for staying alive and nesting successfully. Those are their primary goals. *Your* parrot has similar goals, even though he's in quite a different environment. Your parrot will do some adapting to become a companion bird, but it's more likely that you'll have to adapt to his instinctual behaviors. Don't get mad, frustrated, or emotionally injured at your parrot's behavior — he's just being a bird, after all. It's not personal.

Many an avian veterinarian has seen a healthy parrot come through the office attached to a frantic guardian. This is not to say that you shouldn't take your bird for medical care if you suspect there's a problem, but it is helpful to know what your parrot's normal behaviors are so that you can save yourself a trip. I discuss more about unwanted or "bad" behaviors in Chapter 14. For now, this chapter gives you the rundown of basic, normal behaviors that can sometimes be puzzling.

Flying

Flying is the most natural behavior for a parrot. However, it's one that many guardians typically take away from their parrots. There's a widely perpetuated myth that a bird whose wing feathers are intact (not clipped) will not remain tame or will be difficult to handle. From a strictly behavioral standpoint, this is absolutely false. Yes, a bird may require clipping during the taming process to keep it from flying out of your hands. But a tame bird that is fully flighted may actually be much friendlier and more at ease than one that's clipped.

Flying has tremendous health and psychological benefits too, as outlined elsewhere in this book. It also has its safety pros and cons. But in terms of behavior, there's no reason why a parrot needs to be clipped. When a parrot can realize his full potential as an individual, he is happier, more self-directed, and healthier, as long as he has a safe place to fly.

Even though I do advocate clipping a bird's wings during taming, even that's not necessary if you've got the right situation. For example, untamed birds in a free-flight habitat or large aviary (where you can enter and mingle among them) may take cues from the tame birds living with them. If the tame parrots land on you and choose to have physical contact with you, many of the untamed parrots will most likely check you out as well if you seem like a trustworthy creature. This won't happen with every individual parrot, of course, but it does happen.

Climbing

Parrots naturally want to be in the highest spot they can find, and if they can't fly there, they'll climb. Their instinct tells them that the higher they are, the safer they are, because they can see potential dangers from a lofty perch. Your parrot is no exception. She's most likely going to choose the highest perch in his cage as her sleeping spot.

Climbing around a cage does offer some exercise for your parrot, but it's not enough. Still, it's more than a lot of companion parrots get. If you can, offer a few ladders and safe rope for some climbing fun. You can also buy a hanging gym — some come with great climbing potential. For your parrot's safety, get a *ceiling protector,* a slippery plastic rod that you attach between the gym and the ceiling to prevent your bird from climbing to the ceiling and chewing on the paint or plaster.

Ground Foraging

Some parrots — particularly African grey parrots, cockatiels, cockatoos, and grass keets (which comprise a large group), — forage on the ground for some of their foods. This is why some of these parrots like to dig in their cage tray; it's a natural instinct. Parrots are in more danger on the ground, certainly, but there are generally sentinel parrots in the group that keep an eye out for danger and give an alarm call if necessary.

People who keep parrots outside in a habitat know that they do spend a lot of time on the ground, foraging, playing, digging, or eating soil. Wild parrots have been observed many times eating soil and sand, though no one really knows why they do this. Presumably there are nutrients in the soil, or perhaps it's used as grit. Some parrot guardians use grit for this reason, but the fact is that the grit sold in stores is generally made of oyster shells or a type of gravel that they wouldn't naturally find in the wild. Many veterinarians have seen parrots die from too much grit, but it's doubtful that anyone has ever seen a parrot die from lack of grit.

Most veterinarians will tell you not to allow your bird to touch the ground for any reason. There's a fear of parasites and illness from filthy conditions. However, parrots that are allowed on the natural ground get the benefit of the earth's biomagnetism (which is healthful for everyone). It's unfortunate that most places where a parrot could potentially roam, like a backyard, are often sprayed with chemicals that have leached into the soil. The grass, plants, and dirt in the average yard aren't safe. If you had a safe place to allow your parrot to wander around on the natural earth, he would probably really appreciate it. Supervise carefully!

Chewing

Parrots love to chew and enjoy whittling away at a wooden toy or branch. This chewing behavior is completely normal and should be encouraged. In the wild, parrots chew bark and other vegetation seemingly to take nutrients out of the sap (it's not certain why they do this). In your home, your parrot will also chew things to bits, even if there's no nutritious sap to be had, like in a paperback book (well, if it's a romance novel, perhaps it's sappy).

Some owners become frustrated that their parrots destroy household items. This destruction is part of the parrot's *job*. If you want to keep your wicker and wooden furniture intact, please keep your parrot away from it. Don't expect that your parrot will know the difference between his playstand and the legs on your antique piano.

Provide your parrot with plenty of toys and perches to chew. I've heard inexperienced parrot guardians say, "I'm not going to keep buying my parrot these expensive toys/perches, because all he does is destroy them." Well, yeah, that's what he's supposed to do!

If you have a real chewer on your hands, you can find some creative ways to help him get all of that energy out:

- Buy a coconut with all of the coco fiber still on it. Chop the whole thing in half, and put it in the cage. (This follows the advice of parents in tropical regions everywhere — if you want to keep a kid quiet and occupied for a few hours, give him a coconut to crack.)

- Buy natural woven baskets, and let your bird chew them up. Make sure no chemicals were used in making the straw or the baskets and that there's no shellac on them.

- Make a parrot piñata. Take a small, new cardboard box, and fill it with nuts, dried pasta, sisal knots, tiny rawhide bones, and other fun things. Punch a hole in the top of the box, and push a thick piece of sisal rope through it; then knot. Close the box by putting each flap over the other (so that you don't need tape). Cover the box with white tissue paper, tucking it into the flaps (no tape). Hang the box in the cage, and let the bird go at it! You can do the same thing using a clean brown paper bag, too.

- A pad of blank newsprint makes a great chewing toy, as do a roll of calculator paper and a roll of white, unscented toilet paper or paper towels (once the parrot is done with the paper, take away the roll, because some cardboard glues contain lead).

Freezing

No, I'm not talking about a parrot-popsicle. Predators are attracted to movement, so freezing in place is one of the many defense mechanisms that the parrot uses to protect himself. Many predators can't see an animal if it's completely still. The parrot hopes that freezing in place will help him become invisible to predators, but it's a funny behavior to humans, because we can still see the bird — doesn't work very well on us, does it?

Vocalization

Parrots in the wild vocalize to tell the other parrots that everything's okay, to warn the others of danger, to establish territory, to interest a mate, and to signal that food or water has been located. Your companion parrot vocalizes for many of the same reasons.

At dawn (or when you uncover the cage and let the light in), a companion parrot will begin to call its flock to say that he has made it through the night and that everything's all right with the world. Because your family is your parrot's flock, it's a nice gesture to call back to tell your bird that you're okay, too. You can do this by whistling or by calling out to your bird, using his name and telling him that you're also awake.

At dusk, the wild parrot will vocalize again to indicate that a sleeping location has been found and that all is safe and well with the world. This is a noisy time for a parrot, so be patient with him if he's screaming all throughout dinner. Bring him to the dinner table with you! I discuss more about abnormal vocalization in Chapter 14.

Contact calling

During the day, wild parrots *contact-call* to one another. This helps locate a mate or offspring among a crowd or in a vast space. Your parrot will contact-call you throughout the day to make sure you're in hearing range and that all is well with you. You should call back to him, letting him know you're fine. This will make him feel safe and may help quiet him down if he's being noisy. If you don't call back to him, he may continue calling until you do. This can lead to frustration on his part, and he may begin a habit of screaming and carrying on all day. Parrots don't like to feel that they're alone.

Screaming

A screaming parrot is cause for concern. There's a difference between insistent vocalization and screaming. Loud, insistent vocalization may be a call for attention or a response to external stimulation (such as a song on the radio or the vacuum cleaner). Genuine screaming is cause for alarm and is usually caused by pain, fright, or loneliness.

If you hear your parrot screaming, rush to his location to see what's wrong. Occasionally, a bird will learn that screaming draws his owner's attention. He may pretend that something's wrong to get a reaction out of his owner — for example, that his foot is caught in a toy or that he's frightened. In general, though, a screaming parrot is legitimately calling for help or is so lonely that it has taken to screaming to get one iota of attention, even if that attention is a guardian screaming back. I discuss screaming and how to quell it in Chapter 14.

Hissing

Hissing and spitting is the parrot's way of saying, "Back off." Cockatiels and Amazons often do this. A frightened parrot, or one that perceives a threat, will back away from the offender in a crouched posture, hissing and making little spitting noises. A very tame bird is unlikely to do this, but a semitame or untamed bird will use these techniques to ward off intruders to his space.

In general, hissing and spitting are bluffing behaviors, used to threaten the intruder and make her go away. The next response, if the intruder continues the advance, is generally flight. If the parrot is caged and can't get away, it will have no other choice but to thrash and bite. Be kind and gentle with a parrot displaying these aggressive vocalizations. This is a bird that's scared and will do anything to protect himself.

Growling

African greys are known for growling, particularly those who were wild caught or parent raised. Rarely does a handfed baby grey growl. Growling is a warning, just as it is in dogs. Quakers growl as well, as do some Amazons. Unless you want a sharp bite, don't get too near a growling bird. He's afraid and will likely defend himself.

Begging

Handfed baby parrots and young parrots beg using a kind of sheeplike baying that stops once the parrot is fed or cuddled. Parrots that weren't weaned properly or were handfed for too long also beg like this, and the begging can go on for quite some time. Head bobbing can also accompany the sheep noise.

I had a client once whose eight-month-old African grey parrot consistently and loudly made the sheep noise and bobbed every time she passed the cage. As it turned out, the client was still handfeeding the bird with warm formula every day, even though the bird was eating on its own. I told her to offer the bird the formula mixed with warm oatmeal in a bowl and leave it in the cage, rather than feed it to the bird. Within two days the begging noise stopped, and the bird was eating all on its own.

In particular, baby Quaker parakeets (also called monk parrots) are known for their begging behavior. A baby Quaker will toss its head back, bob up and down, "quake" (hence the name), and make a sheeplike baa-baa noise. Some Quakers will do this for quite a while after weaning and may also revert to it when ill (other parrots may revert back begging when ill as well).

Beak Clicking versus Clucking

Beak clicking is when a parrot makes a sharp click with its beak, similar to the sound of someone clipping their fingernails, but a lot louder. This noise doesn't come from the syrinx, as do most parrot noises, but is instead produced mechanically by the beak to indicate fear or aggression.

Clucking, on the other hand, is a noise that says, "Come here; I like you; pet me!" It is similar to the sound humans can make by sticking the tongue to the roof of the mouth and pulling down sharply — like what you'd do to make a horse giddy-up.

Preening

Preening is the activity of cleaning and ordering the feathers. Your parrot isn't picking lice off of his body or pulling feathers during normal preening activity. He's making sure that everything's in order so that he can regulate his temperature, fly, and look pretty for the opposite sex. You can encourage preening with regular misting with warm water, but make sure your bird will be dry before bedtime.

Your bird preens more when she's molting. Molting isn't a behavior, but a physiological event that happens once or twice a year. When a bird molts, it loses feathers all over its body a few at a time and replaces them with new feathers. During normal molting you won't see bald patches on your bird, but lots of feathers all over the floor and in the cage tray. Your parrot may behave crankily at this time and may sleep more often. Molting takes a lot out of a bird, and he needs more rest and more protein at this time.

Yawning

Birds yawn for much the same reasons that humans do. First, yawning clears the ears. Second, they may yawn to get extra oxygen, though scientists haven't proved yet that this is the real reason why humans yawn. Finally, they may yawn to scratch an itchy throat or ear passage. If you think that your bird is yawning too much, it may be worth a trip to the avian veterinarian.

You can make a tame bird yawn by gently rubbing in a circular motion over his "ear-ways" as you pet his head. This is a funny reaction, and it gets them every time!

Beak Grinding

A healthy, sleepy parrot will grind the two parts of his beak together as he's drifting off for a nap. The "gritch-gritch" sound this makes is strange and can seem like an abnormal behavior to us humans, because teeth-grinding can be a sign of something awry. This behavior isn't like teeth-grinding at all but is a sign of a content parrot. Experts aren't really sure why birds do this — it may have something to do with conditioning the beak.

Regurgitation

Parrots show their affection for another bird and for a human guardian by regurgitating (see Figure 12-1). This may seem odd, but it is an indication of a truly exceptional relationship between human and bird.

Males are more likely to regurgitate to show affection. It is unlikely that anything actually comes up into the mouth during the behavior, which is indicated by a series of up-and-down head bobs and then the bird leaning over to the guardian's mouth or part of a hand, or even to a beloved toy. Sometimes, a small amount of food does come up. Simply thank your bird, but don't encourage this behavior too often.

If you notice that your parrot is vomiting when he's alone and that there's debris sticking to his beak and face, it's time to call your avian veterinarian. Rather than bobbing up and down to regurgitate, a vomiting bird shakes its head from side to side to clear the debris out of the beak. This is an indication of illness.

Figure 12-1:
Birds "in love," nesting, or parents feeding chicks regurgitate for one another as a sign of affection or a mating ritual, or to offer partially digested food.

Photo by Priscilla Schmidt

Beak Wiping

Your parrot doesn't have a napkin to wipe his face after a messy meal, so he'll use a perch, the bars of his cage, or a toy. Parrots are fastidious about their cleanliness, and wiping the beak to remove debris is just another way to keep themselves clean. Clean perches weekly to remove debris.

Beak wiping can also be an aggressive or warning behavior meaning, "You're in my space, pal." It's just one in a series of territorial behaviors that a parrot will do to show another parrot or a human that they'd better back off.

Tail Behaviors

A parrot that has just done a bit of exercise may sit on his perch and bob his tail because he's breathing hard. If you notice that he's bobbing his tail and has not exercised and/or you see a discharge coming from his nostrils or mouth, he may have a respiratory problem.

Fanning of the tail feathers can indicate excitement, the beginning of a preening session, or aggressive posturing. Amazons in particular fan the tail in an effort to seem larger during *display* (see later in the chapter for details on display).

A wag of the tail indicates a contented bird and is also a behavior that releases tension. Parrots also wag after a preening session, just before or after ruffling and shaking out the feathers.

Breeding Behavior

Parrots in male/female pairs (and sometimes in same-sex pairs) have their own body language and behavior exclusive to a bonded birdy couple. They spend a good deal of time preening each other — called *allopreening* — and sitting close to each other on the perch (see Figure 12-2). Parrots mate for life (though they aren't always faithful!).

Male parrots often do a sweet little mating dance to impress their mates, including perch hopping, banging on the cage bars with the beak, and lots of vocalizing. It's heartening to watch a closely bonded pair. See Chapter 17 for a lot more info on mating rituals and pair behavior.

Figure 12-2:
These "three amigos" are preening each other gently, called *allopreening*. They are a sun conure, a nanday conure, and a caique.

Photo by Rikki Paulsen

Often, guardians don't even know that they're encouraging breeding behavior in their parrots, which can lead to behavior problems. Here are some tips for the single bird:

- ✓ Don't offer a nest box, cardboard box (for play), hut, or any other enclosed object that can be considered a nest.

- ✓ If your parrot is exhibiting strange behaviors in the springtime, reduce the amount of light he or she receives to about 12 hours a day. Often, 11 hours is best to settle a hormonal bird. Parrots are prompted into breeding condition by light, so when there are more hours of light than darkness, the hormones start pumping.

- ✓ Egg laying for the single hen isn't a problem unless the laying is excessive. A few eggs a year is okay, but if she's laying an egg every other day for weeks, she's going to deplete her calcium supply — cockatiels in particular are known to do this. Let the hen sit on her eggs for a week or two, and deal with her protective behavior, but then remove the eggs eventually, or she'll sit on them for weeks with no result. Don't remove them too soon, or she'll just keep laying. Allowing her to finish out the clutch and then start sitting on them should cease egg laying (though not always). If she's laying the eggs in a food dish, remove it, and get something smaller. Reducing her daytime to 11 hours should help control her hormones.

- ✓ If you see your bird rubbing its vent repeatedly on a perch or special toy, and the behavior bothers you, remove the toy or perch. Some birds will also want to do this on your hand, which you should not allow. This is mating behavior and can lead to worse behaviors, like territoriality and biting.

Eating Habits

Birds are hungriest in the morning, after a long night of fasting. The parrot's fast metabolism compels him to find food soon after he wakes. This is a great time to offer your parrot healthy foods. Birds also feast again just before dusk so that they can last the night hours without eating. Again, this is a good time to fill your bird's dish with the healthy stuff.

Shiny things

Parrots are drawn naturally to shiny, colorful objects. They may persist in removing your earrings or in pulling at a metal chain around your neck. A larger parrot can easily break a watch or other jewelry. Be careful of leaving your jewelry unattended, especially when you're cleaning it with a toxic cleaning solution.

Bathing

Most parrots love to bathe and do so with gusto. A parrot will stand on the edge of a bowl of water, dunk its chest and head, and then shake and spray the water everywhere. This is a normal behavior and should be encouraged. A dirty bird may become annoyed at the dirt on its feathers and begin plucking or chewing them.

Your parrot may appreciate a mist of water that comes from above, like a light rainfall, or he may jump into the kitchen sink while the water is running and bathe in the "waterfall."

Breast quivering after bathing is normal and is a result of the breast muscles contracting over and over to create heat. This is nothing to worry about.

Sleeping

Healthy birds sleep on one foot with the head either tucked into the feathers on the back or simply hunched down into the body. This is normal for nighttime sleep and for daytime naps. However, if you see your parrot sleeping all day like this, especially if he's sleeping on two feet instead of one and is puffed up, the bird might be ill.

Scratching

Parrots scratch to remove dirt from their feathers and to get rid of itches, of course. If you notice excessive scratching resulting in poor feather condition or feather loss, call your avian veterinarian.

Just like when you gently scratch over your parrot's ear holes, when he scratches them, he'll yawn or open his mouth wide and stick out his tongue. This is normal.

Sneezing

Birds sneeze for the same reason we do, to clear the nasal passages. Sneezing is normal unless you notice that your bird is sneezing very frequently or you notice a discharge from the nostrils.

One note about your parrot's nose: Most birds have a very shallow nostril, and it might look to you like the nostril is plugged. Do not *ever* attempt to remove anything from your parrot's nose. If you sense something is wrong, do not hesitate to seek medical help.

Nipping

There's a difference between *nipping* and *biting*. Nipping, or *beaking,* is a normal behavior that some baby parrots do to test the things in their world, even your fingers. It hurts, but it's not done out of aggression. Adult parrots also give warning nips to let you know when to back off. A warning nip is not as hard or long as a real bite.

Biting is actually *not* a normal behavior. In the wild, birds do bite at each other, but they're generally warning bites that are aimed at getting the other bird to go away. In captivity, clipped birds can't just go away when frightened, so they bite — hard. Biting can be prevented by learning to recognize the signs of aggression in your bird and by socializing your parrot properly. I discuss biting in depth in Chapter 14.

Body Language

Learning to recognize your parrot's healthy body language will help you know when he is feeling fine or when he's ill, as well as when he wants attention or food. It will also help you avoid receiving a nasty bite.

Most parrots are an open book in terms of body language. Once you know the signs, it's not difficult to tell when your bird is happy, sleepy, terrified, or simply excited just by noticing his stance.

- **Flapping wings:** Clipped parrots will often hang on to a perch, the side of the cage, or a dowel on a playgym and flap, flap, flap away (see Figure 12-3). Flapping is exercise for your companion parrot and can indicate that he needs a little more activity or wants your attention.

- **Crest position:** Cockatoos, cockatiels, and hawkheaded parrots have a wonderful way of showing you how they feel: a head crest (see Figure 12-4). When the crest is mostly back, with just the tip of it sticking up, the bird is generally going about her business, content and relaxed. When you're playing with her, she may lift her crest, excited by playtime or something new and interesting. If the crest is standing high at attention, it's an indication of excitement or fear. An absolutely terrified cockatoo or cockatiel will slick her crest down flat and may also crouch and hiss.

Figure 12-3:
Birds flap
their wings
to get some
exercise. It
probably
also feels
really good!

Photo by Pet Profiles

✔ **Fluffing and ruffling:** Parrots will perform a quick feather ruffle to release tension, much like when humans take a quick moment to lean back and stretch before we go on to the next task. Parrots also fluff their feathers after a preening session so that all of the particles of dirt they have just removed will fall away. You may notice a fine dust of powder emanating from your bird after he does this, especially if you have a grey, a cockatoo, or a cockatiel. A parrot that stays fluffed for a longer period of time may be chilled or not feeling well.

✔ **The "please" dance:** A parrot that wants attention will clamber around the cage near the door and may sit right in front of the door, moving his head back and forth. This means he wants out. If he does the please dance while he's out, he wants your attention or something you have.

✔ **Head down:** If your bird is used to being scratched on the head or neck, she may put her head down and ruffle her feathers, giving you the perfect spot to scratch.

✔ **The attack stance:** Displays of aggression can be normal at times for a companion parrot, though they can be unpleasant. Many aggressive displays are merely posturing. A bird would much rather fly from a fight than actually engage in one, unless it's defending its nest. Unfortunately for the companion parrot, there is often no place to escape, and the aggression must be acted upon. Aggressive postures include fanning of the tail; crouching or standing tall and swaying from side to side with the crest held tightly back; hissing and spitting; fluffing the back feathers; and crouching with the beak open, ready to pounce and bite (see Figure 12-5).

✔ **Stretching:** Parrots stretch for the same reasons we do, to lubricate our joints, to release tension, and primarily because stretching feels good. You may notice your parrot stretching one wing and one leg on the same side of his body at the same time. This classic birdy stretch that resembles something from yoga called *mantling*.

✔ **Bowing and bobbing:** Bowing and bobbing is an attention-getting technique used by tame parrots. It can become a neurotic behavior for a constantly caged parrot. Also, ill parrots bow and bob, so you'll have to watch your bird carefully to distinguish an attention-getting strategy from illness.

Figure 12-4:
For cockatoos, cockatiels, and hawk-headed parrots, raising the head crest can mean excitement, fear, and joy, among other things.

Photo by Pet Profiles

Photo by Essi Laavainen

Figure 12-5:
This African grey is in "attack stance." I wouldn't put my fingers in this bird's face at this time.

✔ **Head shaking:** Some parrots, particularly African greys, shake their heads as if there's water in the ears. No one really knows why they do this, and it seems to be normal. If your bird is doing this a lot, it may be a sign of an ear or nasal infection.

✔ **Leaning forward, wings shaking:** If the wings are quivering, and the bird is staring at you, it's about to launch itself at you. This is typical "I'm going to fly!" posture.

✔ **Quivering wings:** A parrot that's shivering or has quivering wings may be frightened, overly excited, or in breeding mode.

✔ **Beak language:** An open beak, crouched posture, and hissing or yelling is prime biting posture. This is a frightened or displaying parrot.

✔ **Potty language:** Backing up a step or two or crouching on the perch, lifting tail, and even making a little noise. You can catch "poop posture" before the poop happens and move the parrot to another place if you want him to poop elsewhere.

✔ **Chicken scratching:** African greys and sometimes other parrots will "chicken scratch" at the bottom of their cage or on the carpet. Greys in particular do this because digging is part of their natural wild behavior. If you don't mind the mess, you can give your grey a sandbox (or litter box) to play in, using clean sand from the toy store.

✔ **Eye pinning (dilate/contract pupils):** A parrot whose pupils are pinning in and out is excited and may be in bite mode. Some parrots do this when they're excited about something they like, such as a new toy or good food.

✔ **Wing drooping:** Wing drooping can be part of a mating dance, but in a listless bird, it can indicate illness.

✔ **Wing flipping:** A parrot will flip its wings up and down to indicate frustration, get attention, or indicate aggression. It may also happen during molting, when it's trying to align new feathers or get rid of old ones that may be hanging or ready to fall out.

✔ **Blushing:** Some parrots blush — the blue and gold and the Buffon's macaws, for example. It's not for the same reason that humans blush, however. It's more about excitement and mating ritual.

✔ **Back down, feet up:** Some parrots play on their backs. If the bird isn't breathing and is stiff . . . well, get the shoebox ready.

Flocking behavior

Bob and Liz Johnson of South Florida, owners of the Shyne Foundation, a free-flight avian sanctuary, have had the unique experience of living for many years with over 100 large, free-flying macaws, as well as a handful of Amazons, lories, Quakers, greys, and conures. The Johnsons have built a free-flight "rainforest" so that their birds, primarily rescues, can fly and live in as close an approximation of the wild as possible. Here are some of their observations about the behavior of their "flock":

"We have never observed any sign of a flock leader nor organized structure within the large group. There is the occasional aggressive or assertive bird, but none behaves this way in all situations nor to all individuals. These particular birds are avoided by the others. When a bird defers to one of these individuals, it is not out of acknowledgement of his position, but rather avoidance of bodily harm.

"Within what appears to be a flock are duos and small groups, which are dynamic and periodically changing. For example, one group of four hyacinths, whom we affectionately refer to as 'The Fearsome Foursome,' daily reconfirm their alliance by clasping beaks while nodding their heads in turn, much as we humans shake hands. They defend what they perceive as their territory, and seldom do they accept another member into their group.

"Within such a small group there often can be found a most popular member. These birds are often the most gentle and do not appear to dominate in any way. The others defer to this individual voluntarily out of what appears to be admiration and respect. They did not acquire their status through dominance over the others, nor do they assume the highest physical post. In fact, the birds at the highest areas vary from moment to moment. The shyest birds are more often seen up high, probably because this is where they feel more secure. Birds perched high in the trees or on a human head or shoulder have never in any way shown any inclination to dominate us or any other bird. Since the tendency is to fly up when anything frightens them, such as a hawk flying overhead, height seems to signify security rather than dominance.

(continued)

(continued)

"Our observations of these macaws show an astonishing similarity to the 'flock behavior' of humans at a restaurant or rock concert. An alien observer would conclude that humans are flock animals, and therefore, there surely must be a flock leader. But is there? On closer scrutiny, one would see that within this mass of humans there are small groups, probably most containing an assertive, shy, popular, or even nerdy individual, but each group is basically uninvolved with adjacent groups. Should someone yell 'Fire!' they would all run out as a 'flock,' and our observer would now feel certain that his assumptions were correct, that these are definitely flock animals. What he wouldn't see is that each unit would proceed to its own territory, in this case a house or apartment. We see this same behavior in our macaws.

"This entire controversy is merely a matter of rationale. In actuality, birds living in captivity do need to have limits and boundaries set, and must be taught certain behavior modifications, much as would a child, in order to function harmoniously in our environment. The rationale for training a child, however, is not that he would otherwise think he was the group leader and thus attempt to dominate us. Instead, we attempt to enhance a child's self-image and encourage self-direction while still setting limits on his behavior. Companion birds need direction as well, but perhaps the reasons why they behave as they do needs to be reexamined in order to more fully understand them and better direct their behavior."

When Your Parrot Is Training You

How much of parrot behavior is normal and instinctual, and how much is learned and adapted? In the case of the larger, very intelligent parrots, much of their behavior is learned as they have modified themselves to life in a particular home. They are so smart and so interested in getting their needs met, most are very successful in "training" their guardians. Sometimes, that training is self-destructive, exasperating, and lands them in another home or a shelter.

Depending on the parrot, this training can be distressing to the people she lives with, because no one brings a parrot home wishing for an animal that's going to scream, bite, and pull out her feathers. But those are the extremes. A demanding bird can be more subtle in her training methods and will use several approaches to get her humans to come to the cage or move away, bring food, offer hands-on attention, and perform any number of other tasks.

When a human is feeling trained by a parrot, there is generally something that the human is doing to allow the training to occur. Parrots learn by positive reinforcement, and the only way to have a fulfilling relationship with a parrot, one that is mutually rewarding, is to learn what parrots want and don't want and to modify your behavior accordingly. It's no fun to have to run to your parrot every time he opens his mouth. Every relationship has give and take, and that holds true for human/avian relationships, too.

A parrot's typical condition is noisy, messy, fussy, demanding, and moody, depending on the bird. Some parrots are faithful companions, a joy to be around, and would never dream of biting or screaming. Their humans boast that they have the perfect feathered friend. That's great. But for most parrot people, this isn't the case. Many parrots are given up because they are excessively noisy, bite viciously, or pluck and chew their feathers. These behaviors aren't natural to a parrot but are instead learned from the environment and human interactions.

Most parrot behaviors that produce an action on the part of a human reinforce a bird's behavior. Most annoying parrot behaviors are done simply to get attention. Sometimes a parrot screams as a warning, because its food or water dish is empty, or because it's ill, but a persistent behavior that makes humans respond to the bird in a certain way is the parrot's best "training" technique.

When a parrot learns what makes you tick, it uses that knowledge to its advantage. You and your bird should ideally have a relationship based on mutual understanding, and when one half of the relationship is manipulating the other half, the relationship can go sour pretty quickly. This is not to say that you should manipulate your parrot instead. A parrot, above all, should be allowed to be a parrot. It should have license to vocalize loudly at times, mess its surroundings, and flee if it feels threatened. These behaviors are a problem only when a parrot becomes unreasonably demanding. Ask yourself whether your parrot is just being itself, a normal bird, or whether it is truly managing your actions.

Training method 1: Noise

A parrot's primary training method is noise. Excessive vocalization is an easy way to get attention. Parrots don't distinguish between positive attention and negative attention. Telling your parrot that you love him is the same as telling him he's a noisy rat that will go into the soup if he doesn't shut up. Either way, there's attention being directed at him, and he loves being the center of attention. When he screams, and you scream back, go over to his cage, or pick him up and put him in the cage as punishment, he has gotten what he wanted: your sole focus. Parrots are social creatures that do not thrive on being left alone. If screaming works to get your attention one time, the parrot assumes it will work the next time. After you've responded to a screaming parrot a few times, the parrot knows how to get you to jump. You're trained.

The best way to avoid this kind of human training is to ignore any unwanted noise. Remain calm, and don't display irritated behavior. Leaving the room is a good idea. When the parrot is quiet again, come back into the room, and praise the bird. Remember, praise the behaviors that you want, and ignore the ones you don't. Only praise a quiet bird or one that's making noises you like.

Some birds are known to be persistently loud, and there's not a lot you can do about it. Cockatoos, Amazons, cockatiels, ringnecks, conures, and other birds may seem like their vocalizations are excessive, when in reality they are just doing what comes naturally, especially at sunrise and sunset.

When a parrot is lonely, it might scream, his response to avoiding the pain of being alone. If you come running because you're trying to avoid the pain of hearing the parrot scream, and you know he'll shut up if you're in the room, you've just shown him, in very clear terms, that when he screams, you'll come. If the bird is truly lonely, it's reasonable for him to scream, but you should only enter the room or give him attention when he has stopped screaming, if only for a moment. I discuss screaming more in Chapter 14.

Training method 2: Display

Parrots *display* when they're excited, territorial, frightened, or in full mating mode (see Figure 12-6). A bird in full display puffs itself up; spreads its tail feathers; pins its eyes; and, in the case of cockatoos or cockatiels, raises its crest. It may also make threatening noises and flit its wings up and down. In the case of a parrot training its human, display can deter the human from approaching the cage or from picking up the bird. When a parrot displays and the human walks away, frightened of being bitten, the bird knows that when it behaves in a threatening manner, it gets what it wants. It will display again, even if it's just bluffing, because the behavior has been positively reinforced.

Your bird should allow itself to be picked up when you ask. There may be a time when it's in danger and has to be picked up, but if it has you trained to walk away, you won't be able to help. You should also be able to have access to the bird's cage any time you like. If you are always respectful of your parrot and its space, there's no reason why it should refuse you.

If you've asked your bird to step onto your hand, and it refuses and begins to threaten you, use a dowel or a perch to pick up the bird, even if you're just going to pick up the bird for a moment. A sharp "Hey!" or "Ep-ep!" followed by saying "Step up" will often work to get the bird's attention, and he may step up for you then. But if you walk away, you show the bird that you're not really serious about anything and that it doesn't have to mind you. A parrot should be allowed a great deal of freedom and self-direction, but every relationship has its boundaries. What if you had to pick up your bird because there was something dangerous around, but you have taught it that it can ignore you whenever it wants? Remember, however, that some parrots, such as certain Amazons, go into full display mode a lot during breeding season. Give these birds a wider berth, and try to understand the hormonal surge that they're going through.

Figure 12-6:
This Amazon parrot is in full display. Note the flared tail, open beak, and raised neck feathers. If you were there, you'd see this bird's irises pinning in and out, a sign of extreme excitement. Don't put your fingers near this bird!

Photo by Cyndi Baker

Training method 3: Biting

Biting is a great training method for a bird, because not only does it get a person to move away quickly, but it also creates a huge reaction, usually screaming and jumping around, which the bird loves. Biting doesn't happen often in a natural setting when wild birds can just fly away from one another, but a bird in a home might get many opportunities to bite and will learn quickly that it's quite effective.

The best way to avoid reinforcing biting behavior is to avoid the bite in the first place. Learn your bird's body language and biting patterns so that you can tell when a bite is coming. Teach your parrot to step onto a stick or hand-held perch to move the bird away from an area where he feels comfortable (like the cage), because he's less likely to bite you there. If you do get bitten, walk away calmly, and curse up a storm in another room, where the parrot can't see or hear you. If biting doesn't work for the bird, he will be less likely to habitually do it. I discuss biting more in Chapter 14.

Training method 4: Plucking

Plucking can be an attention-getting device, but that's not always the case. Birds that pluck or chew their feathers may be ill, not getting enough attention, have a poor wing clip, be improperly housed, or have other problems. If you've ruled out those options, the bird might be plucking because the behavior gets your attention. When someone sees a bird pluck a feather out, it's natural to say, "Don't do that!" Eventually, the parrot realizes that every time it plucks a feather, it gets a reaction. That may be what it wants, so it becomes a habit that's difficult to break.

Do not ever reinforce a plucking bird. Ignore the behavior, and praise when the bird isn't plucking. Offer the bird a better diet, more attention, larger housing, and something to do other than pluck. Get the bird to a qualified avian veterinarian right away as well, because plucking is often a sign of serious illness.

Once a behavior is entrenched in a bird's routine, it's hard to break, but not impossible. Simply "retrain" yourself not to give in to your parrot's every whim — but do take its real needs seriously, whatever you do. Learn to be calm when the bird is driving you crazy. A bird that's praised for being good will be good more often than a bird that gets more attention when it's behaving badly. I discuss plucking more in Chapter 14.

Chapter 13

Multiple Parrot Households

● ●

In This Chapter

▶ Catching the "parrot bug"

▶ The pros and cons of having more than one parrot

▶ Dealing with a jealous parrot

▶ Parrots in love

● ●

*D*espite the education I have gained from many years working with the bird community, despite the hard-earned, hands-on knowledge and careful tutoring from mentors in the top of their fields in aviculture, rescue, and behavior, people still don't take my best advice: *Only get one or two parrots* — for starters, at least. People sometimes spend hundreds of dollars to remedy their avian issues — they'll break out the credit card for new housing, toys, supplements, lighting, and anything else that may solve the problem, but they won't listen to the fewer-is-better recommendation.

Okay, I admit, that's a little strict. A lot of homes can support several parrots happily. Some can support dozens. And the exception to the parrot-limit suggestion, of course, is pairs that get along (true pairs) and smaller birds that live in an aviary or flight cage. But that's not what I'm talking about here. I'm talking about "part of the family" parrots, birds that want to have a human companion and require a lot of attention, a complex diet, and lots of out-of-cage time. These parrots are so much fun, so affectionate, so part of the family, it's natural to want another one. So another one arrives. Then another, and another. Pretty soon the first one isn't getting much attention, the second one injures the fourth one, and the third one starts biting and plucking. What went wrong?

Parrots are social animals that crave attention from a mate/family. Parrots are programmed to spend most of every single day with a mate. With each new parrot you bring into your home, you cut the attention the first parrot gets by half. If you were able to spend three hours a day interacting with your first parrot, a second parrot will cut that down to one-and-a-half hours. A third parrot cuts the first and second parrots' time down to one hour each. No wonder behavior problems result.

More Than One

Once you're a parrot person, it's tough to keep your parrot quota to one, or even two or three. There's always that pretty feathered face in the bird shop, and of course, the more research you do on parrots, the more parrots you'll want. There are so many beautiful, spunky parrots out there, all with unique qualities. This one talks up a storm; that one is superaffectionate; this other one is bouncy and cute. Parrots can live 15 to 80 years with proper care. That's a lot of responsibility.

It may seem like I'm putting the kibosh on having multiple parrots. I'm not. I'm trying to show that it's better to have one or two parrots that get truly exceptional care than ten parrots that are each a tad neglected, not because you're a bad parrot parent, but because it's tough to give these sensitive creatures everything they need.

The pros

The big pro to having more than one parrot (or a bunch of them) is that each parrot doubles the birdy love in your life. True bird people understand what that means. There's something magical about parrots. When one chooses you as a friend, it's incredibly flattering.

Multiple parrots do keep one another company. There's always someone to squawk with, especially if they're of the same species (though even if they aren't, they still respond to each other). There's no guarantee that they're going to get along, but when they do, it's wonderful for them.

Even if the birds don't get along enough to have physical contact, some parrots thrive in a flocklike setting, enjoying the sounds and movements of other parrots. Sometimes, a problem bird will calm down when there are other parrots around.

The cons

Unfortunately, there are more cons to having multiple parrots (or parrots in general, really). Here's a list to consider:

> ✔ **Longevity:** Parrots live a long time. Even the smaller ones can live upwards of 15 years. What happens when your lifestyle changes? Johnny goes off to college; an aging parent moves in and needs care; finances get a little wobbly, and you have to take a second job — these are all reasons why parrots are typically neglected or given up. This is actually a good reason to have a true pair (male and female bonded parrots of the

same species), or two parrots that get along very well and can keep each other company, instead of one (but I'm supposed to be discouraging you from getting more parrots here, aren't I?). Pairs can share the same housing and require only each other for company, so having two isn't that much more work.

✔ **Vet expenses:** Having more parrots increases veterinary bills. Not only does each bird need a well-bird check-up each year, but there also are increased accidents and injuries, illnesses, and fighting when you have a flock. Prepare to have your checkbook handy.

✔ **Other expenses:** More parrots means shelling out more money for supplies, housing, food, supplements, and everything else they need.

✔ **Mess:** More parrots equals more cleaning. You'll have double the work with two parrots, triple with three, and so on. If one pair lives in one housing area, great. But if they're spread all over the house, the cleaning duties become quite time consuming.

✔ **Time, time, time:** This resource is at a premium in a multiple-parrot household. There never seems to be enough time to give as much attention to each parrot as it would like (this is true of a one-parrot home as well!). Again, this is a good reason to have a pair that get along and that don't need you as their only company.

Parrots Interacting

One of the reasons why people get another parrot (or multiple parrots) is to have a "friend" for their current parrot. Most of the time, the first parrot has entered sexual maturity and has copped an attitude. Perhaps this first parrot is biting, screaming, plucking, and being downright hostile. Because of this change in attitude, the parrot isn't getting a whole lot of attention, which makes the problem worse. The guardian feels sorry for the bird and makes the only logical decision to remedy the parrot's loneliness: Get another parrot.

Imagine: parrot utopia. You get another parrot, and they love each other. It could happen, and it often does. But it's not as easy as bringing in another parrot and sticking it with the established one. That's a perfect recipe for a trip to the veterinarian.

Parrot pals

Sometimes the "getting a friend" scenario works, especially if you know the gender of your bird and can find the opposite gender of the same species. This doesn't always guarantee a match, but it's your best way of getting close (see Figure 13-1).

Figure 13-1:
This eclectus and caique are buddies, but their guardian is sure to supervise all interaction. This might look like a battle, but it's really all in fun.

Photo by Carol Frank

Some parrots start out as close pals, but then for some reason, the relationship devolves. Sometimes they don't like each other from the start and develop a close relationship over time. Sometimes it's love at first sight. Sometime parrots will become acquaintances but not bosom buddies. Some parrots will not acknowledge that you have brought another parrot into the home, even if you place the cages right next to each other. You never know what you're going to get.

There's no way to ensure that your established parrot and a new parrot will like one another. There are, however, really bad combinations. Some parrots tend to be very aggressive toward other parrots, even toward birds of their species, including lovebirds, cockatoos, Amazons, and lories. Though this isn't always the case, birds of the same basic size and from the same basic area have a better shot at getting along than do birds that originate from very disparate places. However, if birds are raised together as babies, they will nearly always get along, no matter the species, at least until sexual maturity. Then all bets are off (see Figure 13-2).

A break in routine can cause tenuous relationships to break. For example, moving residences, boarding the birds elsewhere, or removing one bird from the residence for a while, for whatever reason, can create tension between the duo. This break in routine is enough to make one (or both) of the parrots "rethink" the relationship. Always have an extra cage on hand in case you need to separate them.

Figure 13-2:
These two species originate from extremely disparate places, Australia and South America, but because they met when they were young, they get along well.

Photo by Sherry Killen

Parrot enemies

Some individuals will never get along (see Figure 13-3). They don't like each other, for whatever reason (competition, jealousy, and so on), and will fight if they're placed in the vicinity of each other. Some parrots are bullies and will take every opportunity to attack the individual that they don't like. It's crucial to keep these birds in separate housing and to supervise their interaction carefully. Parrots are known to kill each other, and it doesn't take much of a chomp of that strong beak to cause a lot of damage. Sometimes it's possible for warring parrots to come to a stalemate. They may coexist peacefully, but not closely.

Romeo and . . . Romeo

Often, parrot guardians want to get the opposite gender as a friend for their established parrot. This isn't absolutely necessary. Females will bond with females, and males will bond with males. In some cases, though, these same-sex combos are deadly, so you have to supervise carefully and always give each bird its own housing.

Figure 13-3:
Even though these ringnecks are the same species, their interaction can be charged and territorial.

Photo by Gail Olsen

One-sided love

Sometimes one parrot will absolutely adore another one who can't stand the sight of the adoring one or who will attack the "stalker." Sometimes the object of the affection will tolerate the lovesick bird but not return its advances. The Romeo will often become bored with the unresponsive bird and turn its affections elsewhere — to another bird, you, a toy, or another object.

Keeping the peace

The best way to keep the peace is to give each bird its own housing unless the birds are a *true pair*. With some species, such as cockatoos and macaws, even pairs that have been together for years have been known to break up, usually by violence and with the death of or serious injury to one of the birds. This extreme usually happens during breeding season, so keeping your parrots out of breeding condition will help avoid this (you'll find more information on this in Chapter 14).

Always supervise "friend" birds when they're out of the cage and interacting, especially if they are of vastly different species or sizes. Never force birds to be friends, and never, ever force them to live together. Allow them to come to the idea by themselves.

Falling in love

Most parrot love happens at first sight. The birds see each other, and in a moment — boom! — fireworks. The eyes start pinning with excitement; the tails flare or wag; vocalization begins. These parrots want to be together.

There's a common myth that parrots mate for life. Most do, but there are dalliances and even divorces. Even a parrot in the tightest of pairs may have a roving eye when a newcomer arrives on the scene. This may cause a rift in the initial relationship, which may or may not survive the dalliance.

If two parrots are bonded and deeply in "love," don't break them up! It's cruel to split up two parrots. These birds can bond for life. Some breeders split up parrot pairs to get different results in the babies. Most parrots will pair up with the next pretty face. They are social animals and would rather choose a new mate than be alone.

Introducing a New Parrot

The first thing you *must* do when you bring any new bird into your home is *quarantine* it. You'll find more information on quarantine in Chapter 7. In short, quarantine is a period of at least 40 days during which you keep the new bird isolated from your established birds to ensure that there are no diseases being passed from new to old.

After quarantine and a clean bill of health from your avian veterinarian, you can begin introductions. Some birds will love each other from the start, taking just a few moments to begin preening and sitting close on the perch. Others take a more cautious tack, watching the newcomer for a while, sizing everything up. Others go in for the attack right away. Here's an introduction protocol to follow. Remember to always err on the side of caution:

- Allow the birds to see each other for the first time while both are in their separate cages. Try to read their body language. Do they seem excited? Are they "talking" to each other? Is one ignoring the other?

- When you sense that they're ready, allow them to come out of their cages, and see what they do. Watch the interaction carefully.

- Allow them to play on a playgym together in *neutral territory*. Never, ever put the new bird inside or on top of the established bird's cage. You can put the established bird on the new bird's cage, but it's best to find a neutral place that isn't "owned" by either bird.

- If there's any indication of aggression, separate them immediately. Have a stick and a towel on hand in case you have to break up a fight. Use the stick to try to pry them apart (gently!) and the towel to scare them enough to let go of each other.

✔ Some parrots, like caiques and some macaws, play roughly with each other, beak-wrestling and rolling each other around. This is normal and should not be confused with real aggression. You'll know when one of the birds is being hurt — there'll be plenty of screaming.

✔ The best time of year to introduce parrots is the fall or winter. Breeding season is over, and the introduction won't be as charged as it would be in the spring or summer.

✔ The best time of day to introduce parrots is just after the morning vocalizations are over. The birds will be calmer.

Introduce *only* on a weekday after your avian veterinarian has opened for the day.

Factors in Getting Along

There are some basic factors to whether certain birds will get along. Again, it's really up to the individual birds, but there are some very basic guidelines:

✔ **Age:** Most young parrots who haven't reached sexual maturity will accept a newcomer, if not as a close preening friend, at least as a play-gym pal. Parrots that are hand-raised together do very well as pals. Remember that any birdy relationship can go south at any time, but the majority of pairs remain together peaceably for life, especially if they're not breeding. Introducing mature individuals can be a little trickier. In most cases, it's love at first sight, or else there will be little or no relationship at all. This can, of course, change as breeding season approaches or exits.

✔ **Same species:** Introducing the same species removes a lot of the factors that cause parrots to not get along. Still, there's no guarantee, and some species (and particular individuals) are pretty picky about whom they're going to like and whom they'd like to remove the eyes from. Gender has a lot to do with it, but not everything. A bird may choose not to accept a bird of the opposite sex of the same species for reasons locked inside its feathered head.

✔ **Different species:** Vastly different species can become and remain close friends. However, never, ever allow different species to breed. Some dissimilar species can't produce young together anyway, but some can produce a *hybrid,* a "mutt" bird that is often infertile, often called a *mule.* Hybridizing parrots isn't a great idea, because there's a limited gene pool for most parrots, and this practice dilutes it further. Some hybrids, particularly in the macaws and conures, are standard in the parrot trade, and though they make good companions, they should not be bred.

Breeding pairs

Potential breeding pairs should be introduced in separate cages, side by side. Let the pair get to know each other from afar and long for each other's company. Let them interact through the cage bars. If they try to preen and feed each other, you know you've made a match. If they gnash at each other through the bars, don't put them together. When you finally make the physical introduction, put the established bird into the new bird's cage, not the other way around. This way, you avoid cage territory issues. You can always move them back later after you've refurnished the old cage with new toys, perches, and a nest, making it look different than before. Make sure that the pair are of the opposite sex and healthy, and that both birds are of breeding age. If they are younger, you can introduce them, but you'll have to wait to set them up for breeding.

✔ **Different sizes:** It's cute to see a budgie and a macaw preening, or a conure and a cockatoo — these odd couples do exist. But it's not a great idea to pair up (as friends) birds of such dissimilar sizes. The little bird is always at risk for injury. All it takes is a car backfiring outside during a preening session for the little bird to lose its head. Even close supervision can't prevent a serious injury or death.

Changing Your Relationship

Introducing a new parrot (or parrots) into your home may irrevocably change the relationship you have with your established parrot. You may not get as much affection as before, or your bird may try to bite you, preferring the avian friend. For example, cockatiels may remain friendly no matter how many you have, whereas lovebirds can get snappish and cranky with a human guardian when they're part of an avian pair.

However, many thousands of avian/human relationships survive a multiple-bird household. Once a parrot is bonded to you, it may never give up the bond, allowing the other parrots in the house to be pals but giving its heart to you. It very much depends on the species, the time you've put into the bird, the trust you've built, and the bond you have.

Chapter 14

When Good Birds Go Bad

*P*arrots aren't always easy companions. They can develop neurotic or annoying behaviors that baffle guardians. The top three offending behaviors are screaming (excessive vocalization), biting, and plucking. Beyond those are the one-person possessive parrots, the potty mouths, and the scaredy cats. This chapter will help you recognize problem behaviors and try to fix them, and shows you how to prevent them in the first place.

One word of caution, however: This chapter cannot diagnose your bird's problems, nor can it prevent all issues that may arise. Each situation is different and can have hundreds of different causes and a variety of solutions. The examples that I give here can't possibly apply to every bird. This chapter is designed to give you a basic understanding of what can — and does — go wrong with parrot/human relationships and helps set you on your way toward solving it.

The First Steps

When a parrot is exhibiting unwanted behaviors, the very first thing to look at is the bird's overall health. Has the bird been to the veterinarian for a complete battery of tests? If not, your next phone call should be to the bird doc. Ill parrots are bound to be cranky and potentially noisy, and may pluck their feathers. These are "normal" behaviors for ill birds (actually, most ill birds are quieter than usual, but don't rule out illness as a cause of screaming). Most people want to treat biting, plucking, and screaming as behavior issues, when much of the time, these behaviors are due to illness.

Second, you have to look at the bird's nutrition and exercise levels. Is the bird suffering from a vitamin or mineral deficiency? Inadequate nutrition is definitely a reason for crankiness or plucking. Parrots that don't get adequate exercise are also at risk for behavioral issues. It's important to take care of your parrot's basic needs before you begin looking at your relationship.

Finally, understand that some annoying behaviors are normal and that you're not going to change them. Conures and cockatoos are noisy. Caiques are beaky (nonaggressively nippy). Lovebirds are feisty. African greys learn to mimic annoying household noises. There's not much you're going to be able to do about it. These aren't behavioral problems — they're facts of life when living with a parrot.

Dominance

Before I get too far in this chapter, it's important to mention *dominance*. Dominance is a trait seen often in pack behavior, like that of wolves. There are a dominant male and a dominant female (the *alphas*), and they assert their dominance over the other members of the pack using body language, aggression, and occasionally physical force. When the dominant male and/or female become aged or weak, either may be challenged by another member of the pack for the dominant role. This has nothing whatsoever to do with how parrots behave and interact in the wild or in your home. Your dogs may behave this way (I know mine do), but your parrots won't.

When your parrot isn't doing what you ask, he's not trying to rule the roost. He's not trying to usurp your position as flock leader, because he doesn't know there's even such a thing. When a parrot seems to be pulling rank on a human, it's generally because the human is misreading the scenario. For example, if every time you pick your parrot up off of his playstand, you go straight to the cage and lock him up, eventually he's going to get wise to the routine, and if he's a feisty individual, he may start either refusing to get onto your hand or biting to drive you away. Some guardians think the parrot is trying to be the boss. No way. The parrot is just smart — he doesn't want to go back to the cage. Now, if you mix up your routine a bit, the parrot won't be so sure that you're going to lock him up the minute you approach the playstand — perhaps you're on your way to the kitchen for a treat.

You can indeed be the alpha pack leader in a house full of dogs (or even with one dog). Once you learn dog body language and positive-reinforcement training techniques, you can be the master and elicit certain behaviors on cue. The dog should absolutely do what you ask, each time you ask it (as long as the request is reasonable for the age and training level of the dog, and it doesn't cause the dog pain or discomfort). This will never be the case with a parrot. You may get what you want part of the time, but the parrot will also get its way some of the time, too. As an avian behavior consultant *and* a dog trainer, I live with this scenario every day. My birds get away with far more in this sense than my dogs ever will.

The key is to make what you want and what the parrot wants *the exact same thing.* You do this by using *positive reinforcement,* which you can find out more about in Chapter 16.

In the wild, parrots don't show dominant behavior. They show *territorial* behavior, *resource guarding* (protecting food and nesting areas), and some-times aggression, but there's not a flock leader among a parrot group, nor are there power struggles to be top bird. In captivity, however, a *pecking order* may ensue among parrots in close confines. This has less to do with domi-nance than it does with resource-guarding: The toughest parrot inevitably wins the best perch, first rights to the food dish, and the superior nesting area. This is one of the reasons why it's so important to give captive parrots as much space as possible if they're going to interact. Fights to the death rarely (if ever) occur in the wild, but they certainly do in captivity.

Height dominance

There has been a lot of discussion about so-called *height dominance* in parrot behavior circles. People have thought for a long time that parrots should never be kept in any type of housing that allows them to physically perch above the guardians. It's true that parrots do like to be in a high spot, because that's where it's safest — where they can get the best bird's-eye view. But this has nothing to do with any kind of dominance.

The fact is, though, that it's more difficult to get a stubborn parrot off a tall cage or perch, especially if the parrot knows (or thinks) that he's going back into the cage or if he's afraid of you. He may stand on a high perch and lunge downward at your hand, or he may climb to the back of the cage, where he's impossible to reach. But this isn't about the parrot wanting to be superior. This is about not wanting to be locked up. Parrots kept in free-flight housing don't display any of this behavior. They are actually far less apt to bite as well.

Don't worry about how high your cage and perches are. Instead, work on the relationship between yourself and your parrot by using positive reinforce-ment. For example, when I want my African grey to get back into his cage so that I can leave the house, I simply add a handful of seeds to his dish. I may even lure him with an almond and then give it to him when he climbs inside. Because he doesn't get seeds that often, he makes a beeline for them. Now the cage is an okay place to be for a while, not a place where I've stuck him after picking him up. I always want him to associate my picking him up with something positive. This way, he very rarely refuses to get onto my hand. When he does refuse sometimes, I either insist in a firmer and clearer voice, "Up!", and he complies (I think because I've gotten his full attention, not because I was firm), or I ask something else that I know he'll do, like put his head down for a scritch. When I've got him doing that, I ask him to step up, and he always does. If he and I were working at cross purposes, neither of us would get what we need. When we're working toward similar goals (I want him in the cage; he wants the seeds that are in the cage) both of us win, and the relationship is safe.

Note that I don't shut the bird in the cage every time he gets seeds — he *does not* associate seeds with being shut in the cage. I just know that he'll climb inside for seeds at any time, so it's an easy and painless way to get him there. Know thy parrot! If I closed the door every time he got seeds, he'd eventually learn that the presence of seeds meant being locked up, and that would defeat the purpose of this kind of training. Fortunately, I don't need the seed trick in the evening. When it's bedtime, he naturally goes inside to the swing where he sleeps. This is common for parrots that are kept out of their cages most of the time and allowed to roam in and out at will. Parrots that are confined a lot may find another place to roost, like the cage's top back corner.

There's a common suggestion that you not keep any parrot on your shoulder because of perceived height dominance. This is more a safety issue than it is about dominance. I don't recommend that you keep a potentially aggressive bird anywhere near your face. I wouldn't keep *any* bird with a very powerful beak near my face, based on a couple of nasty experiences with a particular Amazon parrot! But some smaller parrots are okay to ride along on your shoulder, especially if they're known to be gentle. If you get bitten once, you'll just know not to let that little parrot hang out on your shoulder again. But remember that one bite from a Moluccan cockatoo is far different and more damaging than a bite from a parrotlet. Large cockatoos have been known to send guardians to the emergency room with torn-off lips, ears, and fingers. Use your best judgment, and always err on the side of caution.

Aggression

An aggressive parrot is having issues that are far simpler than dominance. Frankly, the bird isn't thinking that hard about its status in your household. It's just trying to get its needs met. An aggressive parrot is most likely having hormonal issues, has been frightened by something, is ill or injured, is being territorial or guarding resources, or doesn't want to go where you want to go (like back to the cage) or to the room you groom him in. Before you solve aggression, you have to figure out what the aggression is about. See the "What's Bugging Your Bird?" section later in this chapter.

One-Person Parrots

The word isn't out yet on whether or not certain species become "one-person birds" or whether their socialization (or lack of it) makes them that way.

However, it certainly seems like some species are more prone to it than others. Some Amazons, cockatoos, lovebirds, and African grey parrots in particular are most blamed for having this trait.

Imagine that your bird loves you to death but becomes enraged, even hostile, when another person is in the room. Perhaps your bird was once sweet to you but has now bonded with another member of the family and threatens to remove your eyes when you approach. Even a stranger to the home can become the object of infatuation, making the favored person the one on the outs. For example, someone with another hair color may tickle the parrot's fancy, as can someone who is the opposite gender of the favored human. Often, these little infatuations are short-lived and will fade once the new crush has left the scene.

In the wild, most parrots mate for life. When danger comes near, perhaps a another handsome male parrot or a predator, the male parrot may snap at the female parrot to make her fly away to avoid the potential threat to her life or their relationship. This isn't *always* the reaction to a threat, but it is one of many possibilities. So if you are the adored person, and the parrot perceives that another person is a threat to you or your relationship with the parrot, you may get a nasty bite when the other person is in the room. "Fly away!" your parrot is saying.

Often, the person who has fallen out of favor with the parrot, or people who were never on its friend-list to begin with, are insulted, baffled, and hurt by the parrot's behavior. It's not personal. The parrot is an animal with animal instincts, and no one really knows why a parrot chooses one person over another. There are best guesses, like the bird's preferring its opposite gender or preferring the gender of the person who handfed it, but those explanations don't always work. Obviously, if someone from one gender harmed the bird at one point, it may not trust that gender — but it may not trust people with brown hair and glasses, either, if that's what the former abuser looked like.

Preventing possessiveness

Before your bird has the chance to exhibit one-person behavior, have someone else in the family (the least-liked person) take over feeding duties, and ask everyone in the house to talk to the bird, make soothing sounds, and give him treats. This may not make the bird love everyone, but it will get the bird very used to everyone. No parrot should be out-and-out hostile to anyone in the house. Everyone in the family should be on at least speaking terms with the parrot. If you've already got a hostile, one-person bird on your hands, see the next section, "Reversing one person-ness."

Here's the kink in the plan for those people who insist that their parrot love everyone: It may not happen, and don't push the issue if it doesn't. Why should the parrot have to have a close relationship with everyone in the house? Do you have a close relationship with everyone at work? Do you trust everyone there enough to pick you up and carry you around to unknown places? Try to see the world from your parrot's point of view. If he doesn't like someone, even if he doesn't like you and prefers someone else in the family, that doesn't mean you can't have any kind of relationship with the bird. It just means you might not have the relationship *you* wanted and expected. Expectations work against the principles of a real relationship, the rules of which should be mutually decided upon. Just because you have the opposable thumbs in the relationship doesn't make you boss.

How you introduce people to your parrot is crucial. Supervise all guests, and make sure they take off hats or any scary jewelry. Show them how to approach the cage, and instruct them not to pick the parrot up, but just to talk to it and offer a nut. Then you can pick the parrot up and place it on the visitor's hand if it seems like the bird will tolerate that. Don't push it! If the bird seems scared or doesn't want to go, don't force it.

If family members are afraid of the parrot and unsure when they handle him, of course he's going to turn into a one-person bird — you're the only one he can trust. Imagine that you have the option of sitting in two chairs, one that's always sturdy and comfortable to sit in, and another that's rickety and always seems to be ready to fall apart. Where would you sit? Your bird can tell which person is going to fall apart. The person's hand is unsteady when holding the bird, or the person moves too quickly. Either way, the parrot is going to have little faith in this person and may even bite when he or she comes near. Often, the biting behavior comes out of the parrot's simply wanting to hold on and steadying itself with its beak. The person feels the beak for a second (not even pain) and then makes a fuss or even drops the parrot on the floor. Confidence is key.

Another scenario for one-person-ness becoming a problem is the behavior's being inadvertently positively reinforced. I'll use an example from my own avian consulting practice: A husband and wife have a little Amazon that they love. The bird is loving and sweet for the first two years they have him. He is fully flighted and has free run of the house pretty much all the time. The problem begins when the bird starts favoring the husband and biting the wife. Every time happens, the wife gets upset, and the husband comes running to "rescue" her from the bird. He picks up the bird and pets it, cuddling it to his chest. After a while, the bird starts dive-bombing the wife, giving her terrible bites on the face and hands. Again, the husband rescues the wife and then pets the bird.

Well, isn't this case clear? The bird learned that biting the wife was a great way to get the husband's attention. I recommended to this couple that they clip the bird's wings for the time being (and let them grow out when the problem was under control) and that the wife take over caring for the bird. I instructed them to *stick-train* the parrot (have it step onto a stick — see Chapter 16 for directions on stick training). Also, the husband was not to come running if there was an altercation. Instead, the wife would unceremoniously put the bird into the cage and shut the door for a few minutes. Then she would go back and open the cage, being the one now to "rescue" it from its prison and give it a treat for coming nicely out of the cage. I'm not sure that they did all of these things, but this prescription was bound to work far better than what they were doing before.

Reversing one person-ness

Reversing one-person-ness isn't impossible, but it takes planning and the cooperation of all family members. Here are some tips:

- Don't reward the parrot for bad behavior — no rescuing, no laughing, no rushing away when bitten.
- Avoid bites — stick-train the bird.
- Have the least-favored people take over feeding and treating the bird.
- Take the bird and the least-favored person into a room the bird is unfamiliar with, and see if the bird will tolerate the person there. Try it with the most favored person both in and out of the room.
- Offer lots of verbal praise for any friendly contact between the less-favored person and the bird.

Mango the fierce

One of my funniest birdy stories happened years ago with Mango, one of my yellow Fischer's lovebirds. My friend Mark was visiting one day and wanted to hold Mango, who is feisty but also very sweet. Mark was sitting on the couch, holding Mango at face level and talking to her. It was such a sweet scene, and somehow, I wanted it to be even more adorable. I told Mark to kiss Mango on the top of the beak. I kissed Mango all the time, and she loved it, of course. He asked me if it was okay to do that. I encouraged him again to do it. Again he asked me if I was sure that a little kiss was okay. *Yes*, I told him, *just do it, it's fine! Do it! Do it!* So he brought Mango to his puckered lips, and CHOMP! She bit his bottom lip so hard, it bled both inside and out. Well, I should have been horrified, but I just about died laughing instead! Mark wasn't amused, but we always laugh about the incident today. It wasn't Mango's fault — it was mine, and the laughing didn't help. I certainly don't encourage anyone to kiss my birds today.

Here's something to think about: If you're the favored person, are you sub-consciously encouraging your bird to be unfriendly with other people? Humans send subtle (and not so subtle) clues to the animals in their lives, and there may be something that you're doing when the bird lunges that's encouraging him to do so. A one-person bird can be flattering — there's nothing like that kind of loyalty. But it's awful for the bird who lives a very small life and who will have a very difficult time being boarded or re-homed. Make sure that you're not inadvertently encouraging this behavior.

Screaming

Screaming is one of the big parrot "offenses" and one of the most normal. Parrots vocalize, sometimes loudly, in the morning and in the evening, and there's nothing you can do about it. Sorry. Get a fish if you can't stand that. If you love your parrot, you'll allow him to be a parrot and do what parrots do.

Okay, I'll step down from my soap box now. I know how annoying parrot screaming can be, as do my former neighbors, who got together and signed a letter saying that they were going to report me to the police for bird abuse because of the sounds emanating from my house. At that time, I was actively rescuing birds and had two mealy Amazons, three red-lored Amazons, one double yellow-headed Amazon, three large macaws, four mini macaws, a bunch of conures, a couple lories, a few Meyer's (who didn't really contribute to the din), some parrotlets, and *dozens* of lovebirds and cockatiels. Well, an animal-control police officer showed up one day and, after taking a tour of my birds, told me he'd arrest the letter-writing neighbors if they bothered me again. Vindication! But it's not fun to be at odds with your neighbors.

In any case, even though some screaming is normal, screaming all day isn't normal. If a too-noisy bird is otherwise healthy, well nourished, and getting enough exercise, it's probably screaming for attention. Just like other unwanted behaviors, avoid inadvertently positively reinforcing the behavior. Offering an attention-seeking bird any form of attention for screaming only makes the screaming worse, because it *worked.* Don't look at the bird; don't yell; don't say *no;* don't talk to it — just ignore the noise.

But the total solution isn't about just ignoring the bird. *Why* is the bird screaming for attention? Is it not getting enough attention or enough of the right kind of attention? If a bird that's lavished with attention screams the second you walk away after playing with him for an hour, you've got an unwanted learned behavior on your hands. If the bird is locked in a cage 23 hours a day and is screaming for someone, anyone, to acknowledge it, you've got to address that. Give the bird some more attention, and the constant screaming may stop.

Making peace with the neighbors

If you're going to get a parrot, or you're moving into a new place, let your neighbors know about your companion, and offer to make introductions. You can even have a new-neighbor potluck party so they can come over and get to know your bird. Explain that they might hear the bird from time to time, but are not to be concerned. Tell them to let you know if the noise ever bothers them. If you're really creative, you can write a letter "from" your bird, staple it to photocopied information about the species, and give it to the people living around you. Because I reside in an apartment in New York City, I'm consistently checking in with my neighbors about any noise (it doesn't help that I have two barky dogs and I play the drums). The only complaint I've had so far was to put new batteries in my smoke detector, which was beeping so loudly that the neighbors could hear it — unfortunately, the beeping was coming from my African grey, and I still haven't figured out where the batteries go.

Another thing you can try is *noise replacement*. I've done this with great results. When the bird makes a particularly awful noise or a very loud call, wait a moment; then respond with a pleasant sound, like a whistle or a nonsense phrase in a high-pitched tone, like *whoot whoot*. You can even try a whisper. If your bird already knows some words or sounds, you can use one of those. A bird that's screaming because you're out of the room or one that's really trying to communicate with you (not screaming out of fear or habit) will pick up the new sound and substitute it for the loud screaming — well, that's the idea. However, you have to stop rewarding the screaming with the new sound as quickly as possible by responding only to the new sound as soon as the parrot nails it. Then ignore the screaming, and respond to the new sound or any other sound you consider acceptable. If not, you'll have a parrot that thinks its screaming is the way to get you to respond with that lovely new sound.

Here are some common antiscreaming remedies that *don't* work:

- **Yelling back:** This only encourages the bird to yell more. *Wheeeee, a yelling fest! Let's all yell as loud as we can! SQUAWKKKKKKKKKK!*

- **Squirting water:** The water-torture punishment is a terrible idea. Water is supposed to be fun, not shocking.

- **Darkness:** Yes, a parrot will shut up in the darkness or with the cage covered, but that doesn't teach it anything, and it's also cruel.

- **Tapping beak:** Some people use this "punishment" for various offenses, and it *doesn't* work! In fact, the beak is very sensitive, and tapping it can hurt. Also, in some species, this can be interpreted as part of a mating ritual and may just cause the bird to become louder.

✔ **Picking up the bird:** Sure, it does stop the screaming, but it also reinforces the screaming, which will begin the minute you put the bird down again. Only pick up a quiet bird.

✔ **Earplugs:** Okay, I'll give you this one. Earplugs work. Buy them for your neighbors, too. When I'm writing, I wear earmuffs that people use on the gun range to protect their ears from gunfire. Can't hear a thing!

Bad Words and Sounds

If you don't want your bird to learn to curse, don't curse around it. But sometimes curses happen, and a quick-witted bird may pick one up and repeat it over and over in front of your in-laws. But that's not the only reason why you shouldn't teach your bird to curse. What if the bird has to be re-homed someday? Not many families can deal with a cursing parrot, especially if they have kids. The same goes for unacceptable sounds.

Both cursing and funny noises often get a big laugh, or at least a gasp, and the parrot loves that kind of attention. The first step toward eliminating unwanted sounds is to absolutely ignore them and to *praise or respond to sounds you like*. Often, bad noises go away on their own once they stop getting attention and the bird doesn't hear them anymore.

You can also use the sound-replacement method detailed in the preceding section, but you can fine-tune it to work with words. For example, find a sound or word that resembles the offending word; then repeat it clearly and with lots of excitement in your voice whenever the parrot says the offending word. For example, replace *hit* with *quit.* You get the idea, right? I changed *bastard* to *mustard* this way. Don't ask how the parrot learned *bastard,* please. It only took a couple of weeks to change the word, and the bird doesn't even say *mustard* anymore.

Biting

Biting is not a natural behavior for wild parrots when they're together. It's more likely that they'll take flight for self-defense rather than engage in real biting matches with other birds of the same species. They will snap at each other to wrangle for a better spot in the tree, but there's no real chomping down or bloodshed. There is sometimes physical violence over nesting sites, but even that's rare. Of course, if a predator tries to enter the nest or corners the parrot, the bird is going to bite. But that's an extreme case of real danger.

Now, think about the times when a parrot has bitten you. Did the parrot perceive danger? Were you doing something the parrot didn't like or want to do? Did the parrot have any other choice? Could it have flown away? This is the primary biting impulse — the bird perceives immediate danger (fear of harm, fear of pain, and so on).

The secondary biting impulse comes from a learned response. Because parrots are intelligent, and because biting works to get the parrot what it wants, a biting parrot will continue to bite unless a guardian works to try to correct that behavior. There are two ways this happens. First, the guardian does something the parrot doesn't want, like pick it up to put it in the cage, so the parrot bites. The guardian pitches a fit, screaming and carrying on. *Wow,* the parrot thinks, *how fun! A song and a dance — I think I'll do that again!* By carrying on, you have just reinforced the biting behavior by giving the parrot a big reward: drama.

Second, when a parrot bites, the bite-ee generally moves away from the parrot. That's what the parrot wanted. Again, the biting works. Now, put those two reactions together, and you have the perfect recipe for parrot training: The parrot does something to elicit a reaction and gets what it wants. So if biting works for one thing (not getting put back into the cage), it may work for another (not getting taken off the shower perch). So the parrot experiments with biting in different situations. Now you have a biting parrot.

The natural reaction to being bitten — or to any pain — is to pull back and move away from it. The natural basic reaction to wanting something away from you is to push, hit, or force it to move away. You know it; your parrot knows it. It's instinctual. So if you have the opposite reaction, you'll throw your parrot off guard, and you'll cause the biting not to work anymore. If the biting doesn't work, the parrot won't do it (unless it's terrified; then all bets are off). Instead of pulling away when the bird bites, *push back.* Push the bird right off the perch if you have to (gently, please). I guarantee you that this will put a look of surprise and shock on your bird's feathered face. He will be genuinely bewildered. Of course, don't go asking for the bites — don't corner a scared bird, and don't force a bird to do anything it doesn't want to do unless you absolutely have to (medical exam, being put into a carrier, and so on).

If the parrot bites while on your hand, you can wiggle your hand or turn your wrist a few degrees to unbalance the bird. He will let go of your hand. If you can anticipate the bite, you can wiggle just before he lunges. Be consistent with this, and the biting should cease. Don't drop the bird to the floor unless you absolutely have to in the case of a huge bird and extreme pain. You can really hurt a bird this way, and it only teaches him that if he bites you, he can immediately get away from you, which is the opposite of what you're trying to teach.

Biting also happens as a result of hormonal surges, territoriality, and possessiveness. Lovebirds, for example, are known for their biting skills. They get very protective over their housing and can become quite wild if not played with for even a few days. In this case, it's not real fear that's motivating the bird; it's instinct. You have to gauge why your parrot is biting to be able to prevent it and correct it. In any case, don't reinforce the behavior.

Then there are cases of snapping *buffalo* birds. A *buffaloing* parrot is one that snaps and lunges, with little intention of really giving you a bite. He's a faker. But this faking works because it's scary. The parrot knows it works, too, because every time it snaps and lunges, the humans move away. This bird is a good candidate for stick training. It often happens that a buffalo bird doesn't bite at all — he's just a very good actor.

In the case of a snappish or *beaky* bird, one that's testing the biting waters or is perhaps in the "teething" stage of babyhood, a sharp "No!" or "Ep-ep" should stop a bite. Not too much drama — just a firm word to get the bird's attention and let him know that you don't appreciate its actions. A moment of silent glaring at the bird with squinted eyes and a mean face works, too.

Of course, the best way to not reinforce biting is to avoid getting bitten in the first place. Learn to read your bird's biting body language:

- ✔ **Eyes pinning:** When the pupils are contracting and expanding, the bird is in an agitated or excited state and can bite.

- ✔ **Glaring:** There's a difference between a bird's merely looking at you with anticipation or curiosity and *glaring*. It's hard to put this difference into words, but you'll know it when you see it.

- ✔ **Erect posture, leaning back, glaring:** This bird feels pressured or fearful and has nowhere else to go. Biting time!

- ✔ **Tightened feathers, neck stretched upward, nervous looking around:** Here's a bird that's looking for an escape route. If he can't get one, he'll bite.

- ✔ **Stooped posture:** Along with other biting indicators, stooped posture and glaring can indicate aggression.

- ✔ **Feather puffing:** Along with stooping, glaring, and eye pinning may come feather puffing — kind of like when a dog's hackles stand on end.

- ✔ **Beak clicking, wonking, growling, or hissing:** Little clicks, odd explosive repetitive noises, growling, and hissing (along with other body language) all mean that you shouldn't get your hand in this bird's face.

- ✔ **Tail flaring:** In some species, a fanned tail, along with strutting, eye pinning, wonking, stooping, and feather puffing, means *stay back!*

Fears and Phobias

Parrots are naturally fearful animals. They have to be, or else they wouldn't survive in the wild. They are instinctually programmed to be fearful of things flying overhead (predatory birds), wires and coils (snakes), and anything bigger than they are that with eyes on the front of the face (predatory animals). In captivity, there's even more reason to be fearful. There are things in a captive environment that a parrot isn't hard-wired to even comprehend.

When you first bring a bird home, you have to introduce it to everything in its immediate environment. Then, after time, introduce it to things in other rooms where the bird may spend some time. Large, unwieldy appliances; musical instruments; artwork; and other odd items may frighten your parrot. Don't push the introductions to these items. You can take the bird into a room for a moment, talk soothingly and reassuringly, offer it a treat, and then leave again. Do this every day until you can come closer and closer to the object. Baby steps.

A phobic bird is a different story. This is a bird that has been conditioned to be terrified of something, usually inadvertently, by its human guardians. In many cases, that something is a person (or people) or hands. This can happen from abuse, improper handling, fearful guardians, and being shuffled from home to home. A phobic bird may have been weaned too early and/or didn't receive enough early socialization. It may also be suffering from an untreated injury, perhaps a broken bone that was never set, foot disorders, chronic pain, and illness. A terrified bird always warrants a trip to the vet, first and foremost.

I once took in an older blue-crowned Amazon that was terrified of hands but would step onto a stick or onto my arm if it was covered in a towel. If I came at this bird with a hand, he would shriek and fly off the playstand. Once on the floor, he'd scramble around until I got a stick and picked him up. Then he was fine. His previous guardians were older people and always used a towel to hold him. He *never* bit me — he was just very scared.

I slowly fed this bird treats from my open hand every day until I got him to touch my hand with his beak. I also used the "whittle down" stick-training method described in Chapter 16. After a few months, this bird started stepping onto my hand with no hesitation. Had I forced him to step on my hand or tried to "break" him, I have no doubt that I would have ended up with a miserable, biting bird.

If you have a phobic bird that's terrified of people or of one particular person, start getting him used to people (or the person) by placing a chair across the room opposite the cage and sitting in it facing adjacent to the bird (not facing it), singing or humming, but not looking at the bird. Do something with your hands if you can, something you can focus on, such as reading a magazine or sewing. As the bird tolerates it, bring the chair a few inches closer. Your focus should not be on the bird. At this point, you're just getting the bird used to your presence without getting in its space (as you must do with feeding and cleaning).

When the bird seems very comfortable with your presence or has at least improved, move the chair back across the room again, this time facing the cage. Don't look directly at the bird, because this can be perceived as a sign of aggression. Again, read or sew or whatever, and move the chair gradually closer. The idea is to get the bird very comfortable with your presence and then get him comfortable with some indirect attention.

If he's responding well to the indirect attention — preening, eating, vocalizing normally, and stretching in your presence — then you can start giving him some direct attention. Talk to him and glance at him, but don't stare. If it seems that he will tolerate it, feed him treats (nuts and sunflower seeds work well), say his name, and tell him he's a good bird. Then go away quickly. You always want the interaction to be short and end on a good note.

Increase the duration you're spending at the cage, offering treats and talking to the bird. Eventually, using this same, slow, incremental method, you'll open the cage, stick-train, hand-train, and so on. The key is to get the bird used to you on his own time. This can take *months,* perhaps even well over a year, and that's fine. Don't expect a fearful bird to come around instantly.

If you're having trouble taming a phobic bird, you can clip its wings, but realize that a clipped bird is bound to be even more fearful. When you clip the wings, you remove a primary source of safety, which can make the bird feel even more insecure. If there's a safe way to keep the phobic bird fully flighted, do it.

Consider the phobic bird's housing, and make it as comfortable and unscary as possible. Place the cage against a wall, and cover another side or two, but make sure the bird can still see what's going on in the home, or he'll be even more frightened. Offer simple toys and perches — nothing too elaborate. Keep the environment uncluttered and as static as possible; this is not the time to get new carpet or a giant fish tank.

Hormonal Issues

All parrots mature eventually, some at less than a year of age, some at a few years. But whatever the case, sexual maturity can cause a change in attitude, preferences, and behavior. This can be startling for guardians, who are often insulted by these changes. As I've said before in this book, it's not personal.

You will generally notice the onset of maturity one spring around the time that the clocks change and the natural light gets longer than the darkness (or if you leave artificial lights on near the parrot for more than 12 hours a day as the parrot matures). Parrots are photosensitive and react instinctively to this change. The daylight of the springtime tells a parrot to get into breeding mode, and its hormones start surging.

Behavior problems during breeding season include:

- ✔ Increased duration of vocalization (screaming)
- ✔ Biting
- ✔ Possessiveness
- ✔ Territoriality
- ✔ Plucking
- ✔ One-person-ness

Breeding season can cause a male parrot to begin courting someone in the house and biting others. He may change his alliances entirely. It can cause a female parrot to become highly territorial of her cage, and she may even lay eggs. If a single hen does lay eggs, allow her to keep the eggs for a couple of weeks and then take them away. If you take them away immediately, she'll just keep having more eggs. You can discourage a hen from laying eggs by taking away anything that resembles a nest or nesting material, even newspaper (make sure there's a grating at the bottom of the cage). Remove all round feed dishes, and replace them with smaller covered dishes. Even this doesn't stop some birds, but it's a start. See Chapter 12 for more information on discouraging breeding behavior.

You have two choices: First, deal with it and realize that this, too, shall pass. Just try not to encourage or positively reinforce any negative behaviors that may flow over into the rest of the year. Second, try decreasing the amount of light that the parrot receives. Generally, if the light hours are slightly fewer than the darkness hours, the hormones should decrease. So giving the bird 11 hours of light and 13 of darkness may work (often, 12 and 12 works, too).

Feather Plucking

Perhaps the most heartbreaking and mystifying unwanted behavior of all is feather plucking. The parrot begins to chew its feathers, pull them out, and even self-mutilate, causing wounds that the bird won't allow to heal. For a long time, people really didn't understand why parrots did this, but as the years have passed and people have started viewing parrots as more than just pretty faces, the answers have become clear. Also, avian medicine and nutrition have advanced exponentially in the last couple of decades, uncovering more reasons for this terrible behavior.

Parrots pluck for a variety of reasons, some medical, some emotional. Here are the primary culprits:

- **Boredom:** A bored parrot can become a plucking parrot. Every parrot needs things to do, toys to shred, television or radio to listen to, and a guardian to interact with. Parrots aren't content with 30 minutes out of a cage a day. They need lots of stimulation.

- **Improper housing:** A cramped parrot may become so frustrated that it begins to chew or pull its feathers.

- **Fear:** A phobic parrot may take out its extreme fear and frustration on itself.

- **Poor diet:** A diet lacking in essential oils, vitamins, and minerals in the proper amounts can lead to dry skin, which can lead to plucking.

- **Illness:** Illnesses that cause pain, itching, or discomfort can cause plucking, especially in the area of discomfort. For example, a parrot with a respiratory infection may pluck over the chest area.

- **Lice or mites:** Any pest plaguing the feathers and skin can cause plucking.

- **Metal poisoning:** Have your vet check for metal toxicity, which can cause plucking.

- **Improper lighting:** All parrots need natural sunlight or artificial full-spectrum lighting.

- **Bathing:** Grease or dirt on the feathers can cause plucking, as can dry skin from lack of bathing.

- **Sexual frustration:** Breeding season's hormone surges can cause a non-breeding parrot to become frustrated and take out the pent-up energy on its feathers.

- **Environmental stimuli:** Something new and scary in the environment can cause immediate plucking, like shiny balloons after a birthday party or a blinky Christmas tree.

- **Environmental changes:** Moving the furniture around or moving the cage can also cause a problem. Parrots like consistency.

- **Nicotine:** Parrots living with and handled by smokers have a tendency to pluck because of the nicotine residue on the bird's feathers.

- **Guardian changes:** Sudden changes in appearance — shaving a full beard, changing hair color, starting to wear glasses, and so on — can cause plucking in a sensitive bird. Also, the primary guardian's going away for a while can cause plucking.

- ✔ **Boarding/bird sitter:** A trip to the bird sitter or a boarding kennel can cause stress-related plucking.

- ✔ **Improper wing clip:** If the ends of the wing feathers are left too sharp or ragged, they can grate against the skin, causing itching, which causes plucking.

- ✔ **Change in household:** Someone leaving the household or someone "scary" moving in. A new baby or pet can prompt plucking too.

- ✔ **The brood patch:** Nesting parrots will pluck a bald patch into the breast feathers to keep the eggs warm. This is normal.

- ✔ **Baby plucking:** Sometimes parents will pluck baby birds. This is normal to an extent — if the parents are doing some real damage to the babies and making them bleed, you'll have to remove them and handfeed.

So plucking can start for various reasons, but like screaming and biting, it can also be positively reinforced. For example, let's say a parrot starts plucking because of a medical issue. Every time it plucks, the guardian yells at it or goes running over to the cage. At the very least, tensions are high when the plucking happens — it makes human guardians cringe. The bird goes to the vet, and the physical problem is cleared up with medicine. But the plucking continues. Why? Because every time the parrot plucked, it got attention. Some parrots *do* need more attention, but they shouldn't get it the second after they've chewed or pulled a feather.

Cockatoos, African grey parrots, Amazons, and eclectus are most prone to plucking their feathers and self-mutilation, though no species is immune to this behavior. Because a bird has the capacity to suffer, it has the capacity to pluck.

The very first thing to do for a plucker is to take it to a good avian veterinarian for a battery of tests and to clear up any health issues. Infections, viruses, fungi, and parasites can all cause plucking. Here are some other possible solutions:

- ✔ **Nutrition:** You have *got* to bolster a plucking bird's nutrition. Supplements are essential for a plucker. I like a site called www.birds2grow.com. It has a lot of great avian supplements and a special kit for birds with feather problems. But supplements aren't enough. See Chapter 8 for a lot more detail on nutrition. There is some evidence showing that plucking birds need more protein.

- ✔ **More direct attention:** Play with the plucker. As long as you're playing with him, he's not plucking.

- ✔ **A job to do:** Give a plucking bird a lot of stuff to chew and shred. Paper, preening floss toys, coco fiber — anything that will keep the bird occupied and off its feathers.

- ✔ **Branches:** Place an abundance of clean, pesticide-free, nontoxic tree branches in the cage. The bird has little choice but to work at those branches until they're whittled away.

- ✔ **Get the bird a mate — not:** I tossed this one in here because it's a common myth, and it *won't* stop plucking. Some parrots will appreciate a birdy friend, though others will see it as a rival or won't pay attention to it at all. If the plucking is due to a medical issue, and you get the bird a mate, how can that help?

- ✔ **E-collar (Elizabethan collar):** As a last resort, you will have to e-collar your bird. You can buy the collar at a pet shop or online, but your best bet is to have the veterinarian put it on. This prevents the bird from plucking. The best e-collar for a bird is clear, so that the bird can see through it. This should be done only if the bird is causing real damage to its skin, such as bleeding and wounds. Please don't try to e-collar your bird yourself — I've heard horror stories of birds dying this way. Only use an e-collar in extreme circumstances. It's a bandage for the problem, not a cure.

What's Bugging Your Bird?

The first place to look when something's bugging your bird is at its health and nutrition. I can't say this enough: Take your parrot to the avian veterinarian for a well-bird check-up twice a year, and take him there immediately if there's any kind of problem.

Maturity

Simple hormones might be what's bugging your bird and causing behavior issues. But beyond that, there may be an issue in how you're treating your mature bird. Puppies and kittens grow bigger and change as they grow, but most parrots are going to have the same basic appearance from 2 to 20. You may be able to turn a baby bird on its back and give it tummy kisses, but an adult parrot may not be interested in that kind of attention. Give your parrot the dignity of growing up, and don't try to treat him like a baby forever.

Other birds

Sometimes, the addition of another "rival" bird into the household can cause behavior problems with the established bird (see Figure 14-1). Now he's got a reason to be louder and nippier, and perhaps even to pluck his feathers. He's competing for your affection. In this case, always tend to the established bird first, and give him the same amount of attention that you did before the new bird arrived.

Photo by Mary Jo Yarberry

Figure 14-1:
These parrots are displaying aggression and/or territoriality toward each other.

Environmental changes

If there's something in your bird's environment that it likes or is used to, and you move it, the bird is going to have an unpleasant reaction. Unfortunately, you're not going to be able to immediately tell which object in your bird's environment is important to him. I've had this kind of thing happen to me only once. I keep a television on for my birds, and one day, I decided to move the TV to another room where they could still hear it, but they couldn't see it. Well, my grey started making a sound I can only describe as plaintive and mournful. It was terrible. It took me about a week to figure out the connection, and when I moved the TV back into the room, the sound stopped.

Additions to the room can also cause problems. I've heard of a bird that started plucking when a computer and monitor were moved into its room. Art and party decorations are often culprits as well, causing fear, screaming, and plucking.

Cage placement

A cage in the middle of a room or up against a window puts the bird in a vulnerable spot, with no protection or safe corner to hide in. This is quite unnatural for a parrot (as is being in a cage in the first place, but that's for another chapter). If something's suddenly bugging your bird, and you've just moved the cage, put it back into the original spot, or try to mirror the original spot by placing towels or sheets over the sides of the cage where the walls were in the other location.

Temperature

A bird that's too cold or too hot, or one that lives with extreme temperature fluctuations, isn't comfortable and can become stressed or ill. Make sure that the room remains a comfortable temperature. If it's chilly for you, it's probably chilly for your parrot. If you're sweating, chances are your parrot is enjoying the weather — but it shouldn't get overheated, and there should always be fresh, clean water available.

Noise

A very quiet house can be stressful for a parrot. The wild is never quiet, not even at night. When it suddenly falls quiet in the daytime, it means that there's a predator nearby — the birds stop chattering so they can listen and remain invisible. You will notice that a bird can catnap in the middle of the day with the television blaring. Of course, loud, sudden noises will startle and stress a parrot, but background noise is actually quite welcome. Some parrots — lovebirds, for example — even sing and chatter in their sleep as a defense mechanism; a chattering, twittering bird doesn't look asleep. Keep the television or radio on low throughout the day.

Sleep

A tired bird is a cranky bird that can develop all kinds of behavioral issues. Keeping a white-noise machine on, or even a fan or air filter, drowns out street noises. It also gives the bird a sense of security, because the environment won't be totally quiet, making the bird aware of even the slightest noise in the house. If you get the sense that the white-noise sound is annoying your parrot, eliminate it.

Total pitch-blackness can be frightening for a parrot. Keep a nightlight on in your bird's room to keep him from becoming startled in the darkness.

How Your Actions Can Help or Hurt

Often, human body language or actions can make parrot behavioral problems worse. Here are some of the top offenders:

- **Come running:** If you come running every time your parrot screams, even if you're looking at her and telling her not to scream, you've just positively reinforced her screaming. Don't be at your parrot's beck and call. Praise a quiet parrot, not a noisy one.

- **Sneaking up:** Don't sneak up on your bird. Always whistle, sing, hum, or talk when you come into the room. Your sudden appearance can be startling to a bird, especially one that's phobic or new.

- **Tone of voice:** Speaking gruffly to a misbehaving parrot doesn't work, and neither does yelling. A simple firm "No!" to get the bird's attention will suffice. Otherwise, talk nicely and calmly to your bird.

- **Roughhousing:** Never roughhouse with your parrot — this will make the bird aggressive or fearful.

- **Noise in the house:** If you have a noisy bird, try to tone down the general noise in the home. Your bird might be competing with the television, the kids screaming, and the vacuum cleaner. A quieter home begets a quieter parrot.

- **Staring:** Staring or intensely looking at a parrot can be unsettling, even for the tamest of birds. It means something ominous to them, even if we're just admiring them.

- **Glaring:** A wicked glare and a mean face can do wonders for telling a bird you're unhappy with it. You only need to do this for a moment for the bird to get the picture. Then stop! Or as your mother told you, your face might stick that way.

- **Punishment:** Punishment doesn't work on parrots. Please see Chapter 16 for a detailed explanation. In the meantime, praise the good behaviors and ignore the bad behaviors.

- **Ignoring:** I mention ignoring bad behaviors a lot in this book. This does not mean ignoring your bird. You ignore a behavior for a period of time long enough for the bird to learn that it doesn't work. For example, when my grey wants my attention, he makes a variety of noises, some of which I like and some of which I don't. When he makes a noise I don't like, I don't respond. I don't look at him or say anything. When he tries another noise, one I do like, I immediately turn to him and say his name or give him other kinds of attention. I have effectively extinguished dozens of noises this way and encouraged dozens of others. I only have to ignore him for a moment for him to realize that one noise doesn't work and that he should try another. You can use this method on any unwanted behavior. Of course, you have to begin with a healthy, well-nourished, and well-adjusted bird for it to work.

Hiring a Behavior Consultant

If you feel you can't tackle your parrot's behavioral issues on your own, it's time to call in an expert. An avian care and behavior consultant, like me, is someone who has extensive knowledge about parrots and their behavior gleaned from years of breeding, rescuing, training, and dealing with companion birds, both their own and those belonging to others, in private and professional settings. A good behavior consultant is up on the latest information about parrot health and behavior, consults other bird experts, listens well, and is intuitive about people and their parrots. Most will talk to you on the phone for a small fee and give you a plan to follow to help solve your parrot's problem. Some will come to your home if you're in the area.

A good parrot behavior consultant:

✔ Will nearly always recommend that you take your bird to an avian veterinarian as the first step toward discovering the problem (though sometimes a problem is so obvious, it doesn't require a trip to the vet).

✔ Will discuss nutrition and housing with you.

✔ Will ask you a lot of questions about your bird's background, life, and environment.

✔ Will never make you feel stupid, blame you for your parrot's issues, or knock you for the type of parrot you have.

✔ Does not bash other consultants or avian experts. We're all in this together.

✔ Does include follow-up calls with the fee.

✔ Does not make a ton of money — generally, the fee is just enough to keep a Web site or Internet list going. It would be nice if we made a lot of money, but alas, that's not the name of this game.

✔ Helps solve your problem (anyone can give advice — it's the quality of the advice that counts).

The Last Resort: Rescue and Adoption

I hope that you will work hard and exhaust every possible avenue to help your bird overcome a behavioral issue. I understand that some people simply can't keep a bird under certain circumstances. Perhaps there's a new baby in the family, and the bird screams all day. Perhaps there's an illness in the family, and no one can care for the bird anymore. There are a lot of reasons why people give up birds, some quite valid.

Parrot rescue and foster organizations are cropping up all over the country, some good, some not so good. Whatever the case, most are overflowing with parrots of all sizes. These places are always short on help and cash, but the parrots continue to arrive daily. If you do place a parrot with one of these organizations, please give a donation. Most of them are thrilled to have volunteers as well. They also need foster homes for parrots.

Here are a few of the larger organizations that can help you find one in your area:

- Foster Parrots: www.fosterparrots.com
- Parrot Education and Adoption Center: www.akpeac.org
- The Oasis Sanctuary: www.the-oasis.org
- The Gabriel Foundation: www.thegabrielfoundation.org
- Midwest Avian Adoption & Rescue Services Inc.: http://www.maars.org/index.php
- Rescue Me: www.rescueme.org

Part V
Taming, Training, and Beyond

The 5th Wave
By Rich Tennant

@RICHTENNANT

"It's 'Feathers', I think she's taking steroids."

In this part . . .

This part is a hodgepodge of the rest of the stuff you need to know about parrot care and behavior. First, you get Chapter 15, all about parrot intelligence. You're going to be surprised at how smart these creatures really are. Chapter 16 is about taming and training — you might want to read this one twice. If you're thinking of breeding your birds, Chapter 17 gives you a realistic picture of what that's all about. Chapter 18 is for those who want to take parrot guardianship to the next level and show their small birds.

Chapter 15

Bird Brains: Parrot Intelligence

• •

In This Chapter

▶ Analyzing parrot intelligence

▶ Chatting with Alex the amazing African grey

▶ Figuring out why parrots talk

▶ Conversing with your parrot

• •

Most people doing any kind of research on acquiring a parrot and those who already live with one or more of them know that parrots are far more intelligent than most people give them credit for. Birds in general are no bird brains.

Smarty Pants . . . er, Feathers

What is intelligence? Well, because there's not enough room in this book to get into a long scientific explanation of intelligence, I'll stick to the basics. Very simply, intelligence has to do with:

✔ Consciousness

✔ Learning ability

✔ Memory

✔ Aptitude

For the most part, *consciousness* has been attributed largely to humans. Animals were somehow left out of this notion — until recently. Research done on chimpanzees shows high intelligence and consciousness. Also, the revolutionary research done by Dr. Irene Pepperberg (see later in this chapter for a lot more on her research) has shown that parrots also possess far deeper intelligence and consciousness than anyone previously thought.

Consciousness also includes an aspect of *self-consciousness.* Adult humans know that they are alive and that they are individuals. But do some animals? Do parrots? There is evidence to show that they may, but it's not certain. Parrots show some forms of self-consciousness, but they don't really show an ego, which is a very sophisticated form of self-consciousness. So the question is: Do parrots know that they have a *self* and know that they are alive?

The basic test for showing self-consciousness is the *mirror test,* whereby the subject is shown a mirror to look at itself. Then something on the subject is changed, and the mirror is shown again. For example, if a colored mark is applied to an adult human's face in a spot that he can see only in a mirror (without his knowing that it was placed there), upon seeing his reflection in the mirror, he will know to touch the part of his body where the colored mark is — he is self-conscious and is aware that the reflection in the mirror is himself. Chimpanzees behave in the same way. Rhesus and other monkeys do not touch the colored spot when shown the mirror, but instead behave as though there's another monkey present. The problem with doing this test on parrots is that there are very few parts of their own bodies that they can't see because of the placement of their eyes. Mirror tests done by Dr. Pepperberg are inconclusive.

So the bottom line is that no one is sure that parrots are indeed aware of their individual *selves,* but there's no question that their ability to learn is vast and that their thinking patterns are quite complex and include concepts that not even two- to four-year-old humans have mastered. But young humans have *Sesame Street* and kindergarten — parrots don't. So their learning curve is stunted unless someone comes along to act as teacher.

What Parrots Really Understand

Research shows that some parrots can come to understand what you're saying and what they're saying in a way that resembles language, but only if you teach them words and phrases in context. For example, a parrot knows inherently that it must drink water to survive, but it doesn't know that the English word for this liquid is *water* and will learn that only if you teach it to associate the substance water with the word *water.* Every time you serve water, give the bird a bath, or it rains outside, tell the bird that these things are water. Once the bird comes to understand that what's in the cup is called water, a talking species may begin to use it in context.

But it still could be argued that this is just an associative response and not really language acquisition. When I take my African grey into the shower, he makes a perfect sound of water going down the drain. My shower doesn't regularly make that noise, but perhaps it made it once, and the parrot began associating the drain noise with the shower. That doesn't mean that he knows what a shower is. I do know that he associates the shower with that noise.

Parrots that are highly attuned to their households will begin to naturally associate certain sounds with other sounds, objects, or interactions. For example, when the phone rings, my grey says, "Hello." This is a common behavior for these parrots. He also tells my dogs "Be quiet!" when they start barking. He does these things because I do them, and he has associated one sound with another. Does he really know why he's saying these things? I doubt that he really understands the true nature of the telephone and why it's ringing. He just knows that I say "Hello" after the ring and that the telephone gets attention when it rings, and attention is exactly what he's after.

When something startling happens, he always asks, "Are you okay?" That's because I always say that when something startles him. So he's just trying to learn the "language of the flock" so that he can communicate with me the way he would use birdy language to communicate with other parrots in the wild. I can't attribute real language to him — yet. The closest we've come is *come here*. He definitely knows that *come here* means that he should come to me when I say it and that I should come to him when he says it. But I spend very little time teaching him language. Read on. . . .

Alex the Amazing Grey

Alex is perhaps the most famous parrot ever. He's an African grey parrot that Dr. Pepperberg purchased from a Chicago pet store in June 1977. Dr. Pepperberg has a PhD in chemical physics from Harvard University and currently studies how individuals learn concepts and communicative behavior, using African grey parrots as subjects. To date, Alex can label seven colors and five shapes, is learning the alphabet, and can count up to six objects. He is also working on identifying objects from photographs. He knows the names of over 100 objects and can ask clearly for what he wants and where he wants to go. If a researcher gives him something other than what he has asked for, he says, "Nuh" (his version of "No"), which is a sophisticated concept for any animal. He also knows the difference between "big" and "small," and "same" and "different," and is learning "over" and "under"; he also has a concept of absence. The other grey parrots in the lab have also shown some evidence of *set making,* a complex skill once attributed only to primates. These are only a few of the vast skills of the parrots in Pepperberg's research lab.

Dr. Pepperberg is also working on developing computer stations for her subject parrots, and they seem to be working well with surfing their own preprogrammed Web sites. If this research seems a bit frivolous, think again. The research has applications for handicapped and autistic children and for others with learning disabilities.

Bird brains in action

Some birds, such as crows, actually use tools to get food and solve problems. If you really want to be floored, check out the short movies of tool-wielding crows at `http://users.ox.ac.uk/~kgroup/tools/media.html`. You won't believe your eyes.

Dr. Pepperberg has had a lot of success with a teaching method called the *model/rival technique.* This technique requires two people and a parrot (or child or learning disabled person). Here's how it works: Two people sit in front of the parrot and handle objects that the parrot is interested in. One human, the trainer, presents the object and asks the other human (the model/rival), "What color?" or "What shape?" and so on. When the human model/rival answers correctly, the trainer gives the person praise and attention. If the model/rival doesn't answer correctly or doesn't say the word clearly (on purpose), the object is removed from sight, and the model/rival is scolded. Then the object and the question are presented again. The person answering the questions is called the model/rival because he/she is modeling the correct behavior for the parrot but also acts as a rival for the trainer's attention.

In Dr. Pepperberg's work, sometimes the roles of the model/rival and the trainer are reversed, and the parrot becomes the model/rival. This change in the environment shows the parrot that interaction goes both ways. Alex often comes up with words and phrases on his own, and researchers always respond to his vocalizations with appropriate actions. If you want to find out more about Dr. Irene Pepperberg's work, check out `www.alexfoundation.org`.

Making Your Bird Understand

As you can see, making your bird really understand takes a lot more than just training him to give you associative responses. For example, when I turn out the lights, my grey says "Night-night" or "Good night," because that's what I've said to him. But he will also say it sometimes when I close the cage door in the daytime. I assume he's associating both the act of closing the cage door and the lights going out with "Good night." These are associative responses. An adult human wouldn't say "Good night" when you shut the front door in the middle of the day, nor would an adult human say "Good night" when you shut off the lights before everyone jumped out from behind the couch at a surprise party. Those are not appropriate responses to either situation.

First, you have to begin with a bird that's capable of real learning and language acquisition. Clearly, African grey parrots are one such species. The larger Amazons and macaws may also have this ability. Perhaps all parrots have it to some degree, but because not much research has been done on other parrots, and there's only anecdotal evidence to back up any claims that other parrots can "understand" the way greys do, I can't assert that you can do this with any parrot. I'm not sure that anyone knows the answer to that yet.

The cool thing about all parrots is their ability to remember and put two and two together. They might not always come up with four, but it's interesting to observe, in any case. If you're not using Dr. Pepperberg's teaching methods, or other methods proved by behavioral researchers to work, it's likely that the only things you're going to teach your parrot are associative responses. You might, however, be able get your parrot to label objects and actions and to ask for them appropriately. When you offer your bird anything — food, petting, showers — say the appropriate corresponding word or action. Be consistent, be patient, and be observant.

Teaching Your Parrot to Converse

Conversing isn't mimicking, nor is it simply talking and repeating words. You can actually have a conversation with your bird. It might be rudimentary, but it will definitely be a conversation. Here's a typical conversation between me and my grey parrot, Hope:

> Me: Hi, Hope!
>
> Hope: (Some beeping and mechanical noises) Are you okay?
>
> Me: Yes, I'm okay, thank you. Are you okay?
>
> Hope: Are you okay?
>
> Me: Yes, I just told you I was okay. Thank you for asking. Are you okay?
>
> Hope: Are you okay?
>
> Me: Yes, I'm okay.
>
> Hope: Hi, Hope!
>
> Me: Hi, Hope!
>
> Hope: Hi, Hope!
>
> Me: Hi, Hope!

Hope: Come here! Come come!

Me: Okay, I'm coming. (I walk over and give Hope a scratch on the head.)

Hope: I love you.

Me: Awww, I love you too, Hopey. (Absolutely melting — bird can do no wrong.)

Hope: (Makes sound of garbage truck backing up, cell phone, loud mechanical noise I can't stand.)

All right, so it's not the Algonquin Round Table. But it's what I do pretty much all day with this particular parrot. He likes talking to me and likes when I talk back, and sometimes it really does seem like we're communicating. But that's wishful thinking, I know. However, if you really put time into teaching your bird, and you have someone who can help you with the model/rival technique, I believe that you can get some form of real conversation out of your parrot.

Why Parrots Talk

Before you can get your bird to converse with you, you have to get him to talk. The way parrots talk is much different from the way humans talk, so it's amazing that they're able to create the same sounds that humans make. Birds don't use the same physiological organs that humans do to produce sounds. Humans use vocal cords to begin the sound and then use the lips, teeth, and tongue to form it into words. Parrots don't have vocal cords in the same sense, but they do have a *syrinx* at the base of the trachea through which air flows, and when the parrot manipulates the syrinx, along with its trachea, glottis, tongue, and beak, certain sounds are formed. Not all parrots use the same organs to produce sound, and some use a combination of different organs. Nevertheless, the result is the same: talking.

Why parrots talk might be of more interest than how they do it. Wild parrots have an intricate communication system that comes close to what humans think of as *language*. Most parrots don't really flock in the way it has often been portrayed, with one leader, a sentinel, and so on. Instead, a group of parrots hanging out together is more like a group of people living in the same neighborhood. They know each other and may be friendly, but they don't necessarily help each other acquire food and housing (there are exceptions, however, like Quaker parakeets, which build and share common nesting sites). The birds of the same species in a certain area, probably the birds within hearing distance of one another, have the same "language," meaning that they share common vocalizations so that they can understand one another. If a parrot from one area was captured and released in another area, the parrot wouldn't necessarily be able to communicate with the birds of the same species in the new location (but it's not clear that this is in fact the case, and the new bird may learn quickly how to communicate, depending on the situation).

Because parrots are social creatures, they need a form of communication to be able to interact. But what if there's no parrot around to talk with? Should the house parrot languish away, waiting for another parrot to share its language? Parrots are fussy creatures, but they aren't stupid. A parrot comes to understand pretty quickly that the humans around it are its social group — its flock, so to speak. Because the humans in the home aren't equipped to learn the parrot's language (nor do most of them want to), the parrot begins to learn the language of its area, of its clan. This is a powerful way for the parrot to become part of the group. In the bird's mind, learning the language of the home is the primary way of getting noticed and getting its needs met. A parrot that talks or mimics other sounds in the home is a parrot that's interested in the humans around it, just as a wild bird is interested in the other birds in the area for nesting, finding food, or watching out for danger.

The first and foremost thing you need in teaching a bird to talk is a good relationship with the bird. A frightened or abused bird is more likely to stay very quiet so that it isn't noticed, or perhaps to scream all day because it's lonely. A happy, content bird is one that makes noise to say, "Hey, I'm here; look at me; play with me!" This is where the first attempts at talking begin. A young bird will make vocalizations that sound similar to sounds in the world around it in an attempt to communicate with its humans, get attention, or at least to fit in. If the bird's human praises the bird for these attempts, the bird will continue to learn.

If you're starting out with a species known as a great talker, like a budgie, an African grey, or an Amazon parrot, simply talk to the bird during your daily interactions with it. When you approach it in the morning, say, "Good morning," and when you put it to bed at night, say, "Good night." The same goes for feeding. Name all the things you give the bird — seed, water, apple, grape, carrot, and so on. When you move your bird from place to place, tell it where you both are going: "We're going to the kitchen." Talk to your bird the way you would talk to an intelligent child, but don't use baby talk, or that's what the bird will learn.

A bird's first attempts at talking may sound like babble. Eventually, the babble will become clearer and will form into words and sounds. In a budgie, talking may come as early as six months of age; in an African grey, real talking may take nine months to over a year, depending on the individual. Amazon parrots should be talked to a lot for the first couple of years — an older Amazon may never learn to talk well if it didn't learn when it was a youngster. Remember, some individuals will not learn to talk at all.

The second most important thing for getting your bird talking, after having a good relationship with it, is praise. Praise can be as simple as turning to the bird, making eye contact, and saying, "Good bird!" Birds love attention from their humans, and you can use that to your advantage. However, you don't want to praise unclear words too highly. Save your highest praise for clearly stated words that you would like to remain in your parrot's vocabulary.

Once a bird is talking freely, you can begin teaching select words and phrases simply by repeating them over and over, but the trick is to use *emphasis*. Make the words sound exciting. Many parrots learn to curse in this way — when you stub your toe, you may spit out a string of curses that will sound exciting to the parrot, because there is so much energy behind them.

There are talking tapes and CDs available online or at your local bird shop, or you can make one of your own. The problem with this is that the bird may become bored or frustrated with listening to the tape over and over. If you do choose this method, make sure that training sessions are no more than 20 minutes twice a day.

Finally, the television and the radio can teach your parrot to talk, though the bird may not always pick up what you'd like to hear over and over. For example, my African grey parrot knows many of the commercials on the television and persistently tells me to "Call right now!" and to "Have your credit card ready to order!" A few times, he even said, "Poland Springs water is the best water on earth. Now we never run out. Call now!" I swear. I should have taped it. It floored me.

Hey, shut up!

Most people that acquire a talking species are delighted when their bird begins mimicking the sounds of the world around it, but some owners aren't prepared for the bird to talk *as much* as it does. Some even wonder how to get the bird to stop talking.

If you have a species of bird that is known to mimic well — such as a grey, an Amazon, a budgie, or a ringneck — be careful what you teach it, or you might be sorry later. Some bird will learn a sound that might not annoy you but then amplify it to the degree that you have to buy earplugs. My grey learned to mimic my cell phone but does the ring about 20 times louder than the real ring — annoying indeed.

But don't worry if your parrot has taken a not-so-nice word or noise and turned it into a booming roar that the whole neighborhood can hear or if it has begun to curse like a sailor. Some noises can be extinguished simply by ignoring them and praising other noises instead. It's important to begin ignoring the unwanted noises and words from the first utterance. When a parrot repeats a curse, the owner is likely to give it some attention for the curse, such as saying, "Bad bird!" or laughing. These behaviors positively reinforce the noise. The cell phone that my grey learned to mimic was easily extinguished from his daily repertoire by changing the ring tone on the phone and by ignoring him when he did it. I used to hear the ring from him *many* times a day. After a while, he only did it a few times a week. Now I haven't heard that ring in months. But I didn't just ignore the noise — I praised noises and words I liked. I've done this with numerous noises with successful results.

If your bird won't talk

A bird that doesn't learn to talk doesn't have to be a disappointment. Many birds won't learn to talk but will be cuddly, affectionate companions that are a joy to be around. If your bird gets to be two or three years old without having uttered a word, it may never learn to speak, but that doesn't mean that you should stop trying. Keep talking to your bird.

Some birds are closet talkers, talking only when no one is in the room. Buy a noise-activated tape recorder, and put it on when you're not home. You may find that your bird is more of a chatterbox than you think. This is because a bird that's lonely will speak in its family's language either to entertain itself or to try to get the family to come back into the room. Many birds do contact-calling, which is when they whistle, scream, or talk to try to make contact with a "mate" who is out of sight. So don't be surprised when you hear a lot of talking from your bird when you're out of the room but very little when you're holding or interacting with your bird.

If your bird is contact-calling, you can get him to stop by simply calling back with a whistle or a catchphrase. I use "I'm here!" when I can tell that he's contact-calling, which is a different sound from his just babbling at the television. That generally puts Hope at ease until I come back into the room.

Chapter 16

Taming and Training Your Parrot

*N*early everyone entering parrot guardianship for the first time (or any time) wants a sweet, tame bird as a companion. Many parrot breeders and those with smaller parrots (like keets or lovebirds) don't mind if their birds aren't *hand tame,* but the average parrot guardian wants a more hands-on relationship with his or her bird.

Fortunately for people buying parrots today, a lot of breeders handfeed their babies, making them tame and sweet. This doesn't mean that the birds *stay* tame and sweet if neglected, which can happen once the birds land in the pet shop and aren't sold for a while. But even a mushy baby bird needs a little guidance. This chapter will show you how to socialize a young parrot and how to tame a bronco bird. You will also discover how to teach simple commands and tricks and to teach your bird to talk.

Beginning Early

The ideal time to begin training a parrot is when it's a youngster. Handfed parrots do not bite when they're young and take readily to handling by a new owner. It may only take a couple of days for the youngster to become accustomed to its new home and new family. Some parrots, like caiques, can be beaky when they're young, but there's a difference between *beaking* and *biting.* It's like the difference between a puppy teething on your fingers and a dog biting aggressively. The puppy (or parrot) isn't being aggressive; it's just testing out the world with its mouth, much like human babies.

When you first bring the young parrot home, give it some time to settle into its new environment. After all, the youngster has just been through a significant change in its life. Everything is new and has the potential to be frightening.

Move slowly around your new companion, and allow the bird to explore the new cage and toys. Tell children to speak in hushed voices and to be very kind to the new bird (see Chapter 7 for advice on parrots and kids).

Some parrots are ready to play just a few hours after being introduced to a new home, though others may need a day or two to adjust. Don't push the new bird into playing until it's entirely ready. Remember that young birds are like toddlers — they may tire easily, and some can be a bit clumsy and may fall, which can create a fearful situation right off the bat.

If you have acquired an older, semitame, untamed, or "recycled" parrot, give him even more time to adjust to his new home. Don't try to tame or train him immediately. Instead, use the first few weeks to establish a trusting relationship without much hands-on training. He will be more likely to accept training if he knows and likes you, and if he begins to realize that you're not out to get him. Keep reading to find out how to start forming a bond with an uneasy parrot.

Socialization

Socialization is different from training. Training elicits automatic behaviors done largely due to repetition, predictability, and consistency on the part of the trainer. With training, the stimulus and reaction are always the same. For example, when you ask a parrot to step up, it does so because you always offer your hand in the same way, praise in the same way, and make the experience of stepping up pleasant. Eventually, presenting your hand will elicit the bird to lift a foot automatically. Socialization involves thinking and dealing with similar, but not identical, situations in a rational manner. For example, a socialized parrot should come to realize that your yellow ball cap, your son's red knit cap, and your mother's floppy green hat are all the same basic object and nothing to fear. You can't train that, but you can socialize it. A socialized parrot will try different foods even if it has never seen a certain food before. You can't train that, either.

Parrots are hatched with a whole different set of genetic programming than they'll need in an average home. Most baby parrots stay with their parents for several months, even years, learning what to eat, how to eat it, what to be fearful of, where to live, how to bathe, and so on. Your parrot needs to learn all of these same things in your home. Parrots *seem* to be pretty self-sufficient after they're weaned. Yes, they can eat from a bowl of food and find the water dish, but that's not much of a life for a parrot. In general, it's the larger parrots that need the most socialization. The smaller guys — like the keets, lovebirds, cockatiels, and parrotlets — seem to do a little better from the get-go in terms of figuring out what to do.

An undersocialized parrot will spend a lot of its time being fearful. It won't like new people, won't know to eat healthy foods, won't bathe, and will be extremely attached to its cage and become panicky when removed from sight of it. This happens when a young bird is weaned too quickly (as many from large parrot farms are) or when the bird has been abused. Parrots are social creatures that rely on their elders to pay attention to them and offer them mental and physical stimulation. When this doesn't happen, they become mentally or emotionally stunted, just like a human child would be.

Fortunately, parrots mature faster than humans, and their instincts kick in more effectively, giving them a decent shot at surviving a neglectful upbringing. So the parrot survives, but what of its quality of life? That suffers, and so does the bird, unless someone comes along to try to reverse the negative effects of neglect or outright abuse.

Why socialize a parrot? Well, someday you may have to board the bird or even give it up, and you'll want the animal to be accepting of different types of people. The parrot should also be comfortable in its own home, even if strangers are present. Also, an undersocialized parrot is more likely to develop behavioral issues and neurotic tendencies, which can lead to serious health issues.

Hopefully, the breeder will have begun to socialize your baby parrot before you bring it home. If not, or if you have an undersocialized or fearful, recycled parrot, you'll need to use the same socialization methods as you would for a youngster. Here are some ways you can begin to socialize your parrot:

✔ Introduce the parrot to anyone and everyone. Let guests offer the bird treats, like millet spray or almonds. Make sure that everyone who is going to touch the bird washes both hands thoroughly before handling.

✔ Don't allow guests very close to an aggressive bird; instead, have them speak to the bird in an encouraging tone.

✔ Wear different kinds of hats, glasses, jewelry, and clothing around the bird so that it becomes used to these things. If the bird is terrified of an item, show the bird the item as you hold it in your hand, explaining what it is — *don't force the object near the bird too quickly.* My African grey is sometimes fearful of new items that I wear or things I bring into the house (like my big blue inflatable Pilates exercise ball — he didn't appreciate that one at all). I just show him that the item isn't harmful by turning it around and around in my hand, and I explain what it is and then let him touch it if he wants — oddly, this works every time.

✔ If your bird is stuck on eating just a couple of different foods, eat in front of the bird, showing it that certain things are yummy. Lay a whole spread of yummy stuff on a table, and have a feast with your bird.

✔ There will be times when you have to *towel* your bird to give it medicine or examine it (see Chapter 10 for how-to details on toweling). Get your bird used to the towel by playing towel games. Allow the bird to chew the end of the towel, and try to play a little tug-of-war game. Play "get in the tent" with the towel by making the towel into a tent (pulling it into a triangle and hoping it stays) and putting fun items inside, like nuts or millet, and then showering the bird with praise when he enters. Play "toss the towel" by covering your bird with the towel, and then removing it and praising verbally, or by letting him get out on his own (make sure he's enjoying this, or else it's cruel). You can begin all of these games with a harmless washcloth and then progress to a hand towel and finally to a bath towel. Use a solid-colored towel, preferably something light in color.

✔ Socialize the bird to a carrier by placing the carrier near the cage for a few days to get the bird used to its presence. Then play with the bird in and around the carrier, placing nuts and goodies inside.

✔ If the bird won't bathe, try a shower perch to show that a waterfall can be fun (plus it's nice to have avian company in the shower — someone to sing to). Don't dunk the bird — simply allow it to watch you shower, and place the perch closer and closer to the water as the weeks go by, eventually bringing it close enough for the bird to step into the water should it want to (Figure 16-1). Encourage bathing by misting with a water bottle and talking in an encouraging tone (don't spray in the face, or the water may go inside the nostrils — spray up ,and allow the water to shower down). You can also offer a bowl full of wet greens — some parrots like to bathe in them, and it will give the bird something fun to do in any case. A large, shallow dish filled with room-temperature filtered water, colorful plastic toys, grapes, and cranberries will also grab your parrot's interest.

Figure 16-1:
This Goffin's cockatoo enjoys a nice under-wing rub, one way of maintaining the bond between guardian and parrot.

Photo by Patricia Long-Moss

Bonding

The first part of bonding is about creating *trust*. Trust lies at the heart of any relationship, even the relationship between parrot and guardian. There are as many ways to create trust as there are to break it, and a parrot's memory is *long*.

To get a parrot to trust you, move slowly, talk softly, behave gently, and have realistic expectations of your bird. Don't ever tease a bird or treat it with disrespect — these things will only cause the bird to become frustrated or frightened. Ideally, a companion parrot should be a self-directed bird that *wants* to be with you. This means that the parrot is *choosing* to be your companion. A companion bird should call to its owner and come running over to the side of the cage for a head scratch or a treat. You should never have to *force* a parrot to be your pal. Training and taming with slow, gentle methods instills trust in the bird and creates a *companion,* not a *captive.*

You will lose your parrot's trust by hurting it and neglecting it. Training takes time and may frustrate an impatient guardian who wants a tame bird *now.* If you feel that you can't handle training a bronco parrot, buy a youngster who will be more than happy to be cuddled on its first night home.

Even though it's tempting, don't use gloves when handling a parrot. Gloves tend to terrify birds. They're like scary puffy human hands. Instead, if you're truly afraid of a bite, begin by stick-training your parrot, which you'll get details about a little later in this chapter.

Bonding happens when you begin to create a friendship with the parrot. It's not about owner and pet but about a mutual, loving relationship. Bonding happens when the parrot starts to become interested in what the human is doing. It begins to watch its family closely and may even mimic some household sounds and voices. It comes eagerly over to the side of the cage or playstand for petting or treats, and may even jump down and follow the humans or try to find them in the home. The parrot will allow the bonded human to hold it and may even regurgitate for the person in an attempt to bond further by feeding. The bird may try to "preen" the human's hair, eyebrows, and arm hair. I had one lovebird that liked to try to take the freckles off my arm, which was a nice gesture, albeit a futile one.

One warning about bonding: A bird that's *very* bonded to one human and hasn't been well socialized to others may become a "one-person bird." This bird will attack others that come near it or its bonded human. The bird will scream constantly for its bonded human and will even bite the bonded human viciously when someone comes near (in the wild, this would be a protective gesture, forcing the mate to fly away so that no other bird could court her). This behavior is flattering, sure, but what if you have to board or re-home your bird? What if a child visits, and the bird viciously bites her? See Chapter 14 for tips on reversing a one-person parrot.

To begin creating a bond with a baby parrot, all you need to do is spend time with it, snuggling and holding and playing. For an older, less socialized bird, one that's fearful or one that bites, you'll have to approach the situation with a little more caution. Here are some things you can do to begin:

- **Playing peek-a-boo:** Hide around a corner or in a place where the bird can't see you from its cage. Call and whistle sweetly to him from the hidden spot, and see if he responds. Peek out at him, and call him again. Repeat this until he begins to respond to you, which could take days or weeks.

- **Talking and singing:** Talk softly and sing to your new parrot. Show him that you are unthreatening and that you like him. Birds *absolutely* know when we love them and when we don't. Behave in a way that shows your bird that you're on his side, that you're a friend. Parrots love to be sung to — choose a song that's easy for your bird to learn, something with a clear melody, and he might try to mimic you, and it's a great sign if he does. Read to your bird, too — the newspaper, children's books, textbooks, novels, whatever.

- **Food reward:** Find something that the bird really likes to eat, and hand it to him. The food is a reward for trusting you enough to take it from your fingers. Try bits of whole-wheat bread, cereal in fun shapes, sunflower seeds, grapes, and almonds (the size of the treat depends on the size of the bird).

Once a parrot trusts you and you begin to win it over, you can continue bonding with the bird by playing games with it, just like you would with a dog or cat. Some parrots take very well to games; others are less apt to play along. You'll have to judge your individual parrot and choose the right games.

- **Fetch:** Most parrots *love* playing fetch. You give the bird something — a soft toy is ideal — and the bird tosses it on the floor. You praise verbally and give the item back. The bird tosses it on the floor again. You can come up with a catchphrase for this game or a sound, and if the bird is a talking species, he may learn the sound for the game and ask you to play. For example, when he tosses the toy, you say, "Whoops!" and pick it up.

- **Shredding:** Sit down on the floor with your bird, and begin shredding an old black-and-white phone book or some unprinted newspaper. Encourage your bird to shred with you. Packing-and-moving-supply retailers carry unprinted newspaper, as well as brown kraft paper, both of which are great for shredding. Save printed newspaper for the bottom of the cage beneath the grate. Regular newspaper is fine for shredding too, but just the black-and-white parts; some of the colored inks aren't good for your bird. The main reason why I don't recommend that your parrot be allowed to play with too much newspaper is because the ink does rub off onto the feathers and feet, which can discolor a light-colored bird and may cause overpreening in fastidious individuals.

✔ **Dancing:** Play an upbeat song, dance in front of the cage or playstand with your parrot on top, and encourage your bird to dance, too, or sing along. Whatever happens with this game, at least your bird will be amused.

Of course, physical contact is perhaps the most powerful way to bond with your bird. Petting on the back of the neck, head, or under the chin are all things that very tame parrots like — people in the parrot community call this kind of petting *scritches* (see Figure 16-2). I don't know where that came from, but to me, it sounds like a blend of *scratches* and *itches*. Some birds also like to be stroked under the wings or along the back. Most parrots really like their beaks rubbed with your fingernails. This mimics what parrots do in the wild with one another.

Some people like to kiss their birds or allow the birds to eat from their mouth or clean their teeth as a form of bonding. Yes, I used to be one of these people. I allowed all of my parrots to kiss me on the mouth, and I even had one little lovebird that would pick at my teeth, even the molars. Gross, I know. Well, I haven't done that in years. Since then, I've learned that the human mouth is full of bacteria that can be very harmful for a parrot, even deadly. Please resist the urge to make out with your parrot! It can be very entertaining for friends and neighbors, but it's not worth infecting your bird.

Figure 16-2:
A nice head rub or, in this case, a scratch under the chin is another way of bonding with your bird. And birds love it!

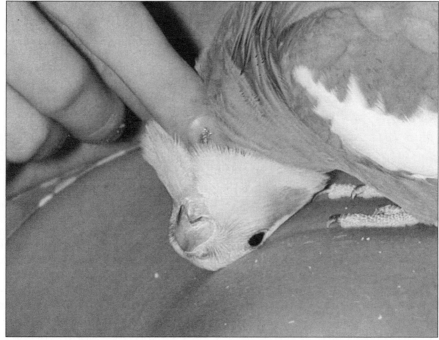

Photo by Priscilla Schmidt

Praising

Parrots learn best from positive reinforcement — when a bird does something you like, you praise. When it does something you don't like, you don't praise. Parrots do not learn well from punishment or negative attention. Direct and loving attention, acting the fool, speaking in a high voice, and singing are all great praise for a job well done. Sometimes, a job well done is simply the parrot's playing on its own with a toy for five minutes. That's a praiseworthy moment.

Unfortunately, quiet parrots don't get as much attention as noisy and misbehaving parrots do. It's also unfortunate that most attention, even if it's you yelling at a parrot to shut up in a mean voice, is also seen as praise to your bird. Yelling *so* does not work to shut a parrot up! The key to praising is to find out what your parrot likes and do just that when the bird is "good" and to ignore the bird when it's exhibiting unwanted behaviors, such as screaming, biting, and the like. I discuss this kind of thing in depth in Chapter 14.

Because a bonded parrot has a giant interest in getting and keeping your attention, it applies learned behaviors to its everyday routine to keep you coming back. If something works, the parrot will do it again. The bird knows that a behavior works when you offer attention — praise. The bird knows something doesn't work when what it's doing doesn't get you to come over, talk to it, or respond at all — no praise. The bird won't keep repeating that behavior, because there's no point in it (unless the bird is truly unhappy or neurotic — see Chapter 14).

The key to praise is to offer it the *second* the bird does something you like. For example, the bird says something you've been trying to teach it, and the second after it says the word, you laugh, say "Good bird!". or respond similarly. *Wow,* the bird thinks, *that got her attention!* So the bird says it again. If you wait too long, even three or four seconds, to praise after a wanted behavior, you've lost the window of opportunity. You'll be praising for whatever the bird is doing just then, which could be nothing more than just standing there (which is fine, but it's not going to reinforce the behavior you want).

This kind of praise-based training is called *operant conditioning.* What that means is that the bird forms an association between a behavior and a consequence of that behavior. If it likes the consequence, it keeps performing the action as long as that consequence happens most of the time when the behavior is performed. This type of training uses *positive reinforcement,* meaning that something is added to the bird's immediate environment (your praise) that reinforces (makes stronger) the behavior.

So the key to any kind of training is finding the exact right type of reinforcer (praise) to add to your bird's environment when it does something you like. Something as simple as turning to the bird, moving closer, and saying, "Good bird, Roxy!" in a high-pitched voice is often enough praise to elicit the response again. Other reinforcers include opening the cage, physical contact, and treats. But whatever you choose as praise, you have to be consistent. It's easy to confuse a bird using this method if you don't praise quickly enough or if you praise only some of the time for the same behavior. Eventually, the behavior will become learned, and you won't need to praise as often as you must in the beginning (before the behavior has sunk in).

The most important thing to remember when using operant conditioning is to not praise behaviors that you don't want. For example, if a bird somehow learns a curse word (but not from you — surely a foulmouthed guest in your home must have taught the parrot that word), and you laugh or yell at the bird for saying it, you have just praised for the word, and the bird will say it again.

If you're trying to teach something that involves two or more steps — for example, teaching a larger parrot to put a whiffleball through a basketball hoop — you have to use praise for each step, not just for completing the whole chain of events that make up the task. This is called *shaping* the behavior. In this case, you'd praise for simply touching the whiffleball with the beak. Then you'd praise for picking up the whiffleball. Then you'd praise for moving toward the basket with it. Then you'd praise only for moving close to the basket but not for picking up the ball. You'd eventually offer praise only as the bird completes more and more of the complex task. Where you once praised for merely touching the ball, you will eventually only praise for touching the ball and moving it toward the basket. This works very well with dogs (and people), partially because rewarding them is easy. You'll have to discover what your bird considers a reward in order to be an effective trainer. For some birds it might be a morsel, and for others it might be verbal praise and a head scratch.

Simple Training Strategies

First, keep training sessions short. You can teach a bird more in two minutes than you can in an hour. The key to training any animal is that the animal should *always* be successful at the task. Animals don't learn from failures the way humans can. So if your two-minute session involves picking up the bird and having it climb up a ladder once, praising, and then ending the session, you've taught more than if you repeated it over and over until the bird didn't want to do it again. Then what have you taught? That hanging out with you is a bore.

Start when the bird is ready to pay attention and is fresh and full of energy. Don't try to train after you've woken the bird up or he's eating. Also, always end training sessions on an up note — on the bird's completing the task with ease. This is why a couple of repetitions are better than a dozen. Do multiple training sessions a day rather than two longer ones.

The best learning comes from inadvertent training. For example, if you want a relatively quiet bird, praise when the bird is quiet and playing alone. If you want a bird to repeat a phrase, praise lavishly when he does. If you like it when your bird snuggles under your chin, make that a pleasant experience all the time.

Teaching Step-Up

Step-up is when your parrot steps eagerly onto your hand or finger when you ask, either by saying, "Step-up," or by offering your hand. This is the most important thing your parrot will ever learn, and it can save his life. Imagine that he's in a dangerous situation, about to be pounced on by a cat or about to fly away — if he knows step-up very well, you can just ask him to step onto your hand and then remove him from danger. Step-up also makes handling your parrot much easier and more enjoyable.

If you're training a very tame or semitame parrot the step-up command, begin by allowing her to come out of her cage on her own by either opening the door and waiting or lifting off the entire top of the cage (if the cage is smallish). It's best if your parrot is standing on a perch or playstand, not a flat surface. It's important that she has good footing and won't slide around when you place pressure on her chest with your finger. If your parrot is a tame youngster, you can gently lift her out of his cage, but because she doesn't know how to step up yet, don't pull too hard, because she will grip the perch or the cage bars.

Once the bird is out of the cage, give her a treat or a head scratch — she gets some positive reinforcement just for coming out of the cage. Next, begin rubbing her chest and belly softly and gently with the length of your index finger, talking to her in a gentle tone and slowly increasing the pressure. Repeat this for several sessions if this doesn't cause her to step up automatically.

As the training sessions go on, or when you feel that your bird is relaxed and responding to you, increase the pressure you place on her belly. Pushing slightly on a bird's chest throws her a little off balance, and she will lift a foot to regain stability. Place your finger or hand under the foot and lift her, if she allows it. If not, simply let her foot remain on your hand until she removes it.

When her foot grasps your finger, ask her clearly to "step-up." Your parrot will come to correlate the action of stepping on your hand with the phrase. Incorporating this training into playtime is ideal.

Once the bird is fairly good at stepping up, you can have her step from finger to finger, repeating the phrase "Step-up," praising all the while. She may hesitate at first, but she will quickly come to realize exactly what you want and have no problem with it. Most youngsters learn the step-up command easily, in one or two short sessions, whereas a wild-bronco parrot may take a little longer. Just be gentle and patient, and continue to praise for wanted behaviors.

Alternate hands when teaching step-up. I learned this the hard way. My African grey parrot is reluctant to step onto my left hand and sometimes hesitates when I offer it. I handle this by offering my right hand because I'm right-handed anyway. Someday, when I have the time (and remember), I'll start socializing him more to my left hand, which shouldn't be difficult. I just wish I had thought of it when he was a youngster.

If you remember nothing else about holding any parrot on your hand, please remember this: Your hand must always be a firm, reliable place to stand. If you get jiggly and nervous or drop the bird, you're reinforcing that your hand isn't a safe place to perch.

Stick training

Stick training is the same as teaching the step-up command, but instead of using a finger or hand, you use a long stick. This is very important and can save your parrot's life someday. Birds tend to find high places to perch when they're flighted or can climb, far higher than you can reach with your arm. If your parrot flies away and is sitting just out of reach on a tree limb, what would you do? Waving a stick or a broom at a bird sitting in a high spot only terrifies it — unless it has been trained to perch eagerly on a stick.

A stick or perch is less complicated-looking and less intimidating than a hand, and it doesn't hurt when a parrot bites it, so there's no big reaction to reinforce the unwanted behavior. Repeat the step-up method described in the preceding section, only use a stick instead of your finger. Using a stick is great for bronco birds to learn the step-up command before you start taming using your hand.

There's a really ingenious product on the market called the Buddy Perch (www.buddyperch.com). This perch is shaped like a "T" so that the parrot can't scooch its way along a straight perch and over to bite your hand, but that's not the ingenious part. The cool part is the piece of Plexiglas attached near the "T" that guards your hand against being bitten.

The whittle-down method

The whittle-down method of stick training is easy and great for bronco birds. Teach the step-up command using a three-foot wooden dowel of appropriate thickness. As the weeks go by, cut the length of the dowel a couple of inches at a time. Eventually, the dowel will be so short that the bird should be used to your hand being near. This gradually removes the fear of your hand, and the bird should learn to step up onto your finger easily.

Taming a Bronco Parrot

An untamed parrot is far different from a newly weaned youngster. The youngster takes to handling very well, while the bronco bird flaps wildly around the cage and makes every attempt to either get away from or bite you. This can be disconcerting, but take heart: The bronco parrot is tamable.

The first thing you have to do to tame an untamed parrot is clip its wings. Even if you later let its wings grow out, which I advocate, a bird being tamed should not have the ability to fly away from you. Training sessions would only last half a second.

Take the bronco bird into a small room, such as a bathroom, but make sure all toxic materials are put away and the toilet lid is down. Each taming session can last 15 to 20 minutes, and you can give up to three sessions a day. More might stress the bird and make it more difficult to train.

If you can, take your parrot's entire cage into the bathroom, and open the top of the cage so that he can climb out. It's not a good idea to begin the training session by grabbing your bird out of its cage, but if the cage is too large, you will have to. Use a small towel, and remove the bird as gently as possible.

Once the parrot is out of the cage or in the room with you, talk gently and whistle to him. You are trying to create a rapport with the bird and make him comfortable. Sit on the floor of the bathroom and just simply *be*. As the sessions progress, moving slowly, get as close to the bird as you can without his becoming startled. Once the bird gives signs of being comfortable, such as yawning, preening, or stretching, you can begin to approach him with your hand. Offer him a sunflower seed or other treat that you know he likes.

After a few more sessions, try to scoop up your parrot in a towel and place him on your knee — I call this the *mountain method* of taming. Sit on the floor with your knees bent up into mountains so that the bird has a place to sit, right on the peak. If he flaps off your knee, simply put him back. Offer him a treat, and talk soothingly to him.

After a few sessions, once you suspect that the parrot feels comfortable on your knee, place your palm flat on your leg, and move your hand upward until it's near his feet. Eventually, after a few more sessions, you will move your finger toward your bird so that you can touch his belly or head and give him a little scratch. If he moves to bite you, *do not* whip your hand away. Just move slowly and pretend like the bite attempt never happened.

This method of *gentling* a parrot will make it a friend, not a hostage. It may take three or four weeks, give or take a few, though some parrots respond much sooner.

If you have a really freaked-out parrot on your hands, try lowering the lighting in the room where you're doing the taming. Some birds respond better when it's "twilight." Also, you can play soothing music or talk radio on low while you're taming. Background noise puts parrots at ease.

Disciplining a Parrot

This heading is actually quite inaccurate. *You cannot discipline or punish a parrot.* You can train, which is a form of discipline, I suppose, but it's not really the same. Disciplining a parrot is passive, meaning you don't really *do* anything. It's what you *don't* do that counts. Here are some "methods" of discipline that don't work:

- ✔ **Hitting:** Never, ever, ever hit, slap, punch, throw, or otherwise hurt your bird in any way. Animal abuse is *not* an effective training tool.

- ✔ **Screaming:** Screaming at your bird only teaches it to be louder and isn't discipline — if your bird were a soldier in the Army, he'd scream back at the drill sergeant and get tossed out pretty quickly.

- ✔ **Pulling away:** A bird that bites knows biting is effective because you get mad, pull away, and cause a scene. The bird wants you to have a big reaction and go away. Pulling away gives the bird what he wants, and he will keep doing the behavior. Instead, *push back*. This not only throws the bird off balance, but it is also exactly the opposite of the bird's intention.

- ✔ **Beak holding:** Holding a bird's beak because it's biting or chewing is akin to holding someone's hands behind their back. The minute the handcuffs are off, the criminal is robbing another bank. Holding the beak doesn't teach anything and is pretty mean.

- ✔ **Time out:** Giving the bird a time out for bad behavior works only if you put the bird back into the cage and close the door the second the unwanted behavior happens, and then turn and walk away. A time out only needs to be five or ten minutes long to be effective. However, the problem with the time out is that you have to pick your bird up in order to enforce it. Praise! By the time you get to the cage, the bird's mind is in a totally different space. So you've taught very little. However, a time out does give you an opportunity to leave the room and cool down.

✔ **Spraying:** Some people "spritz" the parrot with a stream of water when it's being noisy or doing another unwanted behavior. This is a really, *really* bad idea. Water is supposed to be a fun thing for parrots. If you use it as punishment, you'll just make your parrot not want to bathe.

✔ **Ignoring:** Ignoring unwanted behavior is a pretty good method of getting a parrot to stop something, *but only if you're also using positive reinforcement training* as described earlier in this chapter. Also, a screaming, biting, plucking bird may have a health or emotional problem, so ignoring it doesn't do anything but make the behavior worse.

✔ **No:** Giving the bird a sharp "No!" is effective in getting the bird to stop doing what it's doing at the moment — say, eating the drapes — but then the bird will go back to the behavior in a moment. The "No!" is startling and gets the bird's attention, but it really doesn't teach "Don't do that anymore." It just means, "Hey, you, bird, look over here!" Then pick up the bird, which is a nice reward for stopping the offending behavior. However, don't make the "No!" too dramatic; you might reward the unwanted behavior instead.

Simple Tricks Everyone Can Teach

Training your parrot to do simple tricks is easy if you have a lot of patience, ample time, and a clear sense of how to use positive reinforcement (see Figure 16-3). Teach only one behavior at a time, and train using several short training sessions per day rather than tiring out your bird and becoming frustrated with its inability to focus for long periods.

Never, ever starve your bird so that it will respond to food. Some trainers "back in the day" did this, and though it can work, it's cruel and potentially deadly. Don't ever punish your bird if it won't learn something. Be realistic about your parrot's abilities. You might have a really gifted parrot or one that's content to just learn to step up on your finger.

Here are a few easy tricks to get you started:

✔ **Pretty wings:** Parrots stretch their wings frequently, and you can capitalize on this natural behavior. Every time your parrot stretches his wings high, come up with a phrase that you want to associate with that gesture, like "Pretty bird!" or "Show me your wings!" Eventually, he will associate his stretching with the phrase and will do it for you when you ask. You can use this method with other, similar behaviors as well.

✔ **Play dead:** If you begin while your parrot is young, you may be able to train him to lie upside down in your hand or lap. Begin by holding him to your chest with your hand cupped over his back. Make sure he's happy and comfortable with this. Next, lean forward so that he's on his back in your hand but still pressed to your chest. Praise him highly, and scratch his head, if he likes that. Repeat this many times over the period of a few weeks, gradually loosening your hand from your chest. Your parrot may eventually allow himself to be cradled in your palm.

✔ **Wave:** Once your parrot is good at the step-up command, you can teach him to wave. Begin by placing your finger to his feet as if you were going to tell him to step up. When he lifts a foot, say, "Wave!" in an excited voice, and pull your hand slowly away, leaving his foot in midair. Praise him, and give him a treat. Keep repeating this until he gets the idea. Be careful, however, not to make your parrot confused between this and the step-up task.

✔ **Roller skating and other tricks:** You can buy roller skates for larger parrots, little basketball hoops, little phones, and ring tosses, among other props. Each of these should have training directions with it. Remember to capitalize on your bird's natural behaviors with this and to praise highly for even the slightest interest or improvement.

Figure 16-3:
Trick
training can
be good
bonding
time for you
and your
bird.

Photo by Mary Jo Yarberry

Potty Training

Can a parrot be potty trained? Well, to a degree. There will be accidents, and that's okay. But you can certainly learn to recognize when it's on its way and get some mileage out of praising your bird when he poops where you want him to.

When a parrot is just about to go, he will ruffle up slightly, scoot back, lift his tail slightly, and sometimes make a little noise. If you can come to recognize the moment exactly before the poop arrives, you can pick up your bird (who will call off the mission for the moment); move him to a chosen spot; and give him a cue, a word or phrase of your choosing. I like "Go poop." It's simple and does the trick.

Once the bird does his business, praise him wildly, making a huge scene about how great it all was. If you do this enough times, the bird will get the idea. Do not punish for accidents. Simply ignore them, and continue praising the behavior that you desire. Some people use a small paper plate or napkin beneath the bird to catch the results. In this case, the appearance of the plate or napkin will inspire the bird to go.

Teaching Your Parrot to Talk

To teach your parrot to talk, you're going to have to repeat yourself a lot. Birds repeat the words and noises they hear most often. Repeat the words clearly and with regularity. Parrots tend to pick up words and sounds that are said with oomph, like curse words, names, and imperatives (like telling some- one else in the house to "Come here!"). The easiest words for a parrot to say contain the letters (or sounds) b, t, p, d, n, and k. This is why so many par- rots learn to say *pretty bird* and *wanna cracker?*, among other phrases con- taining similar sounds.

Parrots talk and mimic sounds in the household because they're interested in being a member of the family. In the wild, parrots learn the language of the other parrots in their area. In a home, parrots learn the language of the home, which includes the voices of the family members as well as household sounds. They do this largely to get attention and as an attempt at communi- cation, though they sometimes misunderstand the meanings of the sounds. For example, parrot species that are known to be adept at talking will mimic the sound of the phone, microwave, and alarm clock because those are the sounds that make you come running. The parrot thinks, "Hey, if I make that sound, my human will come to me, too!" Well, clearly that logic doesn't work, because a parrot isn't a phone and doesn't need to be answered. But if you reinforce those sounds by responding to them, you have effectively "answered" the parrot, and the sounds will continue.

If you're not a fan of repeating yourself, you can make a tape of yourself saying words and phrases, or buy a professionally made tape or CD and play it while you're not at home. There are also tapes of whistles that are great for parrots to learn. However, unless there's oomph behind the recorded words, there's no real reason for the parrot to learn them. It will more easily learn recorded whistles.

If you want your parrot to talk well, try not to whistle around him when he's a youngster. Parrots take to whistling over talking. Apparently, whistling is easier to do. A parrot can definitely learn words after he learns to whistle, but it's more likely that he'll want to learn more whistles. Some parrots do both very well. Talking and mimicking are very much up to the individual bird.

To teach your parrot to talk, you need to start with a known talking species. However, even one of these parrots isn't guaranteed to talk, though most will at least mimic sounds. They include:

- Budgies
- African greys (both species)
- Yellow-naped Amazons (and their subspecies)
- Quaker parrots (also called Monk parrots or parakeets)
- Indian ringnecks
- Blue and gold macaws
- Scarlet macaws

Though these are the top talkers, most parrots will learn a word or two and mimic other sounds. From the cockatiel to the parrotlet, from the little Hahn's macaw to the giant hyacinth, you'll find talkers in the bunch. Lovebirds aren't known to talk, though I have heard of a couple that have learned a few words. I have one that does the "wolf whistle" and the "charge!" whistle.

Do some parrots understand what they're saying? There is a lot of evidence to show that some do, though you have to actually teach the bird human language — it doesn't always happen on its own. You'll find a lot more on parrot intelligence in Chapter 15.

Most parrots that have the ability to talk will learn without your really teaching. Just talk, and they will pick up the words they feel are important. My

African grey also picks up words and phrases from commercials on television. He tells me to "Call now!" all the time and tells me what kind of car insurance to buy, which carpet company to contact, and what brand of water to have home-delivered. He also tells the dogs to "Be quiet!" and tells me he loves me, because that's what I tell him (though I'd like to think that real love inspires his sweet-talk).

Once a bird starts talking, there may be no way of shutting him up, so be careful what you wish for — and what you say around your bird. There's no off button once your bird learns a choice curse word. Check out Chapter 14 for advice on how to extinguish unwanted words and sounds.

Chapter 17

Breeding Parrots

· ·

· ·

Many people want to breed parrots once they begin keeping them, but it's not as easy as boy meets girl. Sure, many parrots are eager to breed. Some single hens will even lay infertile eggs all on their own, with no male around. Some parrots are easygoing about the breeding process and generally don't mind a meddlesome guardian or noise around the breeding area. Other parrots, however, can be very difficult and cause you more headaches than you bargained for. Also, if you have a hands-on companion, your parrot *may* go back to being friendly after having a clutch of chicks, but others may never want to hang out with you again and can even become vicious.

The raising, keeping, and care of birds is called *aviculture,* and a bird breeder is called an *aviculturist.* Most people who breed parrots are hobbyists — they have a backyard or basement full of their favorite species, and they often breed to show their birds in competition or simply for the satisfaction of creating or recreating specific mutations. These people are often called *fanciers.*

Other people have made a business of breeding parrots, having entire farms dedicated to the endeavor. The backyard bird breeder and the parrot farmer are both valid parts of how birds enter the pet trade — what *really* matters is how the birds are treated. Some large operations are nothing more than parrot mills, and some backyard breeders are simply presiding over torture chambers. Some breeders coddle and spoil their birds, giving each baby a lot of individual attention, offering the parents good nutrition and adequate space, and then finding just the right home for the young birds. If you're reading this book, and you want to breed birds, I'm assuming you're going to take after the latter.

Before You Begin . . .

I would be completely remiss if I didn't issue a warning and a plea. The parrot overpopulation problem has reached an all-time high in the United States. There already aren't enough homes for all of unwanted and neglected parrots, and rescue agencies have reached their spatial and financial limits. It's mostly the larger, noisy, potentially aggressive parrots that get dumped most often — cockatoos, macaws, Amazons — but the smaller parrots find themselves out of homes, too. Though this hasn't been officially documented, it's anecdotal that most larger parrots stay in an average home for 2–3 years before being shuffled along to another home or a rescue. Smaller parrots fare a little better in some areas, but not by much. Some shelters are overrun with smaller parrots, like cockatiels and budgies, because people think of them as disposable pets, which they certainly aren't.

There's a common myth that parrots *have* to be bred or else some species may become extinct. It's true that a great many of the parrots that people commonly keep in captivity are extremely endangered in the wild. But breeding parrots in your home isn't going to help *any* species become less endangered. The critically endangered parrots are species that you won't be able to get your hands on anyway. They are generally being safeguarded in the wild or bred in captivity by trained conservationists and zoos. Some aviculturists are licensed to import very rare birds from the wild to try to breed them for the sake of conservation, but doing this involves a slew of bureaucratic red tape, proof of qualification, and intense dedication.

Another pro-breeding argument is that breeding captive birds will eliminate the smuggling of wild-caught birds. There is very little evidence to prove that because there are captive-raised parrots, poachers will stop capturing parrots in the wild. The wild-caught bird trade continues to thrive, killing and torturing hundreds of thousands of wild parrots every year (see Chapter 11 for more on the wild-parrot trade). Even shutting down the quarantine stations and making importation of parrots into the United States illegal hasn't done a lot to stop parrot poachers.

So I'm writing this chapter not because I'm encouraging you to start breeding parrots, but because I'm realistic about people experimenting with breeding birds. I also know that some people reading this are going to become involved with breeding and showing birds as a hobby. The only parrots that any average person should even consider breeding are the smaller ones: budgies; lovebirds; cockatiels; parrotlets; and possibly Quakers, ringnecks, and some of the smaller conures. Even so, realize that there's an overpopulation problem with these birds, too, and that you should be prepared to keep any babies your birds produce. In any case, this chapter will help you see all the work that went into producing your parrot, so keep reading.

One of the reasons that I cite these particular smaller birds as the only species you could consider breeding is because there's a lively *fancy* dedicated to their color mutations and to showing them. When someone shows birds or becomes involved in the hobby, there's a better chance that they're going to do a lot of research on proper care and that they're going to consult birdy mentors who will help them through breeding difficulties. Also, fanciers tend to care for their birds better than the average bird guardian because their birds have to be in prime shape for breeding and showing. It's in the fancier's best interest to keep the birds healthy and happy. Finally, the smaller birds are a little easier to care for, especially if someone keeps them in pairs or in a colony.

If you take nothing else from this book, please heed this warning: Do not breed birds on a whim. Do your homework, and know the risks. And please, whatever you do, *don't breed the larger birds*. Instead, rescue one from a shelter.

Expectations

Most novice breeders begin with one or two pairs of smaller birds and learn by trial and error. This is fine for the novice fancier but not so great for the parent birds or the chicks. But learning by doing something hands-on is really the only way of discovering all the nuances of a hobby. Unfortunately, this hobby happens to involve living creatures.

Aside from reading all you can on the subject, find a few people already involved in the hobby, and use them as mentors. There are many parrot lists on the Internet where you can meet other people who love your species of parrot as much as you do. These people are often glad to help with your questions or problems. You can also join a parrot society or your local bird club. I can only detail the very basics of the breeding process in this chapter. Asking breeders that you know and setting your parrots up to breed and experiencing the process yourself will fill in the gaps.

Time and expense

Breeding parrots takes more time and expense than just having them as companions. There are more nutritional concerns, medical concerns, and equipment that you have to buy. Handfeeding baby parrots also takes a great deal of time and patience, and often results in multiple trips to the veterinarian and even death for the baby bird or parents. You may have to rush to your veterinarian or stay up all night with newly hatched babies. Are you ready? Are you a patient person? You can't rush breeding birds or weaning babies.

It's crucial to understand that *you will always spend more on this endeavor than you will make on selling the babies.* People often go into breeding thinking that they'll make a quick buck or that selling the babies will pay for the upkeep of the parents. Nothing could be further from the truth. Ask any hobby breeder how much she spends at the veterinarian's office or how much it costs to wean and house babies. You may spend ten times what you paid for the parents on one trip to the vet with a single chick.

Risks

The endeavor of breeding parrots can be precarious. If it seems like I'm trying to discourage you from breeding them, you're reading right. There can be a lot of heartache and disappointment involved, and you have to be prepared for things to go wrong. Finding a clutch of healthy, cheeping babies in the nest is wonderful and miraculous, but it does not cancel out the tragedies that happen in the process. Here are just a few of the situations that you should be prepared to handle:

- **Egg binding:** A hen that's not in fit condition, is living in too small a cage, or has an untreated medical problem can become *egg bound.* That means that an egg is stuck inside of her, unable to come out. This is a serious condition that can lead to paralysis, infection, and death. You can tell that a hen is "eggnant" when her abdomen becomes distended and her droppings are large and watery, like cow patties. If she doesn't pass the egg in a couple of days, you can put her in a warm (98–99 degrees), moist brooder or hospital cage (see Chapter 10 for directions on how to set one up), and see if that helps her pass the egg. You can also put a few drops of mineral oil or olive oil in her beak and in her vent (where the egg will come out — also where waste comes out). If you notice that she has become unable to perch or if you can't handle the situation, take her to your avian veterinarian immediately.

- **Calcium deficiency:** A hen that's calcium deficient can have eggs collapse inside her, leading to a serious medical condition. It can also cause her bones to become brittle or cause her to lay fertile eggs that collapse on the babies, causing them to die. To prevent calcium deficiency, provide your pair plenty of calcium-rich foods and calcium supplements. Your avian veterinarian can also inject calcium into a hen after a few clutches to ensure that's she's not becoming calcium deficient.

- **Too many babies:** Sometimes a hen is so fertile that she lays too many *viable* (fertile and able to hatch) eggs and tries to raise all of the babies. Too many babies, more than five or six, will exhaust the parent birds, and the older babies are apt to crush the younger babies to death. You'll have to remove the first half of the babies and handfeed them yourself, allowing the pair to raise the other half of the clutch themselves. I have had lovebirds lay up to ten viable eggs in one clutch. I had to remove the first five babies that hatched and leave the last five for the parents to raise.

✔ **Mate killing:** Some species — like cockatoos, the larger macaws, and eclectus — are notorious for killing their mates, often the male killing the female. This can happen in any species, and it's heartbreaking.

✔ **Mate death:** If one of the parent birds dies for any reason, you will probably have to take over chick-rearing duties. Sometimes the remaining parent will finish rearing the young, but not always.

✔ **Egg or baby eating:** Some parrots aren't good parents at all, eating or mutilating their eggs and even the babies. Sometimes they're good to the eggs but then kill the babies upon hatching.

✔ **Scrambled eggs:** Nervous parents can inadvertently scramble the eggs inside the nest during feeding time or when you peek inside. Trim the parents' nails before setting them up to breed. Small cracks in eggs can be painted over with clear nail polish and replaced with the parents or put in an incubator.

✔ **Abandoned chicks:** Some parrots are doting parents, but sometimes they abandon their eggs or their babies. This may happen with very new parents, especially if they were handfed as youngsters. In this case, you will have to take over the parenting duties. If a pair isn't great in their first clutch, give them another chance, because they may get the hang of it in the second or third. If they are still bad parents beyond that, you know that you'll have to remove their eggs and incubate them yourself or keep them as a nonbreeding pair. You can also foster the eggs underneath another pair of birds that have proved themselves to be good parents, but only if they're in the same stage of nesting. You can't put a random egg or baby into another nest if the parents don't also have eggs or babies.

✔ **Prolific hen:** Some hens, particularly cockatiels and lovebirds, aren't deterred from breeding by removal of the nest. They just set up shop in the food dish or at the bottom of the cage. These hens are in dire jeopardy of calcium deficiency. Remove anything from the cage that could be considered nesting material, remove the mate and the nest, and put in smaller feeding dishes.

✔ **Dead-in-shell eggs:** Too little moisture and fluctuations in temperature can cause dead-in-shell babies. Offer your parrots a water dish that they can bathe in so that the hen can wet her breast feathers to take moisture into the nest. Illness and pesticides in the parent's food can also be a cause.

✔ **Dead toe:** If there's not enough humidity in the nest box or in your brooder, a baby's feet will become dry, and some of the skin on the toes may tighten, causing the blood to stop flowing to one or more toes. If you notice a "club toe" on a baby bird, take it to the veterinarian to have the skin removed, which will save the toe. If not, the toe will gangrene and fall off.

✔ **Splay-legged babies:** If a baby parrot doesn't have much to grasp on in the bottom of the nest box, it can develop a condition known as *splay leg,* where its legs flare out to the side, causing it to be crippled. This bird will not be able to perch well, if at all, and is considered handicapped, though it can get along quite well in an aviary setting if it's allowed to fly and has flat surfaces to land on. To prevent splay legs in your babies, make sure the babies have something to grasp with their feet, such as pine shavings. Your veterinarian will be able to help you fix splay leg if you catch it before the bird is two weeks old. In any case, a splay-legged baby needs to see a doctor.

Homes for the babies

Your final consideration in breeding your parrots is what you're going to do with the babies once they're weaned. You can keep them if you have the room, but how many can you keep? If you want to sell them, do you have a place that will take all of the babies your parrots produce? Are you sure that you can let your precious babies go to homes where you won't know how they're being treated?

Please also consider the numbers of unwanted and neglected birds already waiting to be placed in good homes. This hobby produces sensitive living creatures, and it is your responsibility as the breeder to make sure that your babies are cared for once they leave your nest.

Paired Parrots

The first thing you need to begin breeding is a mature pair of birds. Some parrots are dimorphic, like budgies and cockatiels, meaning that there's a visual difference between mature males and females, which makes pairing up very convenient. If you have more than one pair of small birds, it's a good idea to allow your parrots to chose their own mates, unless you're pairing up your birds according to color and want a specific result from the pairing. If the birds are monomorphic, and you can't tell the gender just by looking, you'll have to get a DNA test done on your birds to determine sex.

You have to wait until the female is really mature before you set her up for breeding. Males are generally able to breed at a younger age, but that doesn't mean that they'll be great parents. A young pair might have trouble mating and will often tend clutches of infertile eggs. In budgies, for example, the female is ready to breed at 1 year to 18 months, and the male is ready at about 9 months (though it's best to wait till these birds are about 2 years old). In the hyacinth macaw, breeding doesn't begin until the bird is six to ten.

Make sure that your breeding birds are young and in prime condition. They should be eating a highly nutritious diet for many months before breeding and should be healthy and fit. Trying to breed birds that are old or sickly or that have a medical condition is a recipe for disaster.

Breeding Equipment

Begin with a large breeding area, preferably an aviary. The hen needs a good deal of exercise in order not to become egg bound. Flying room is ideal. Next, you need a wooden nest box (some people prefer metal, but I think wood is best for the smaller birds), the size and shape of which is different for different species, as is the nesting material you'll use. For example:

- ✔ Cockatiels like a square nest box 12W×12L×12H (inches) or a rectangular one that's a little higher than it is long. Fill the box with clean pine shavings (from the pet shop) to about two inches below the entry hole.

- ✔ Peachfaced lovebirds like a square box 8W×8L×8H (inches). Fill about halfway with pine shavings.

- ✔ Masked and Fischer's lovebirds like an L-shaped or rectangular nest box that's longer than it is high. Put a handful of pine shavings in the bottom and lots of nesting material in the cage — hay, dried grasses, unprinted newspaper, coco fiber, and palm fronds. These birds build elaborate nests, often consisting of a "living room" and a nesting chamber.

- ✔ Budgies use a box that's approximately 6W×7L×8H (inches), or smaller, with no substrate (pine shavings) in the bottom — instead, the budgie box has a concave area in the bottom where the eggs sit. When the babies hatch, you add a few handfuls of pine shavings so that they have something to grab onto with their feet.

- ✔ Parrotlets use a large budgie box and need a couple of inches of pine shavings in the bottom. (If you do have parrotlet eggs, you will be shocked when you see that they're nearly as large as the parrotlets themselves! They don't look like they could have come from such a small bird.)

Hang the nest box on the outside of the cage, which makes it easy to check on the progress of the eggs and babies. You can hang the box inside the cage, too. Hang the box as high as possible. Make sure that the door to the nesting box is secured shut, because some birds learn how to slide it open. Every couple of weeks, rub a little eucalyptus oil onto all sides of the next box, which helps to keep away mites and pests.

Offer a shallow pan of water every day so that the parents can bathe and take moisture back to the eggs, especially if you live in a warm or dry climate. In very dry weather, you can lightly mist the outside of the next box with water, but don't overdo it.

You will also need to have an incubator and a brooder on hand in case you have to pull the eggs or the babies from the nest (later in the chapter, I tell you how to create your own brooder). You will also need handfeeding equipment and baby-bird formula.

Some parrots — such as lovebirds, cockatiels, budgies, and Quakers — can be *colony bred,* meaning that a group breeds all together in a large aviary. If you're going to attempt this, you have to make sure that all birds are healthy and flighted, that they are all paired properly (male/female), and that you include at least two extra nest boxes to prevent fighting. Also, put all of the pairs into the colony at the same time if you can, especially with lovebirds (cockatiels and budgies are a little more forgiving). People say that birds mate for life, but I can tell you for certain that they have dalliances. When I used to colony-breed lovebirds, I'd get babies in the nest that were genetically impossible to have come from certain pairs. Cheaters!

Nutritional Requirements for Parents

Parent birds need a very healthy, balanced, and varied diet that's rich in protein, calcium, and Vitamin A. Feed well-done hard-boiled eggs, kale, yams, yellow squash, carrots, apricots, cantaloupe, and other dark green and orange vegetables and fruit. Feed spinach and kale sparingly at this time, because an acid in it can bind calcium and make it unusable by the body (see Chapter 8 for a lot more on parrot nutrition). Try to feed only organic produce if you can.

When the babies are first hatching, feed an abundance of soft foods, such as egg food and cooked foods and fruit. Soft food is easier for the babies to digest than plain seeds or pellets. As the babies grow, continue feeding a variety of healthy foods.

The Breeding Process: A Timeline

After you hang up your nest box, your parrots will probably become curious about it. They may peek in and "talk" to the inside of the box. After a few hours or days, they will pop in and out of it, becoming quite excited that the box is there. Depending on the species, the male parrot may begin courting the female loudly and perform a *perch strut,* with lots of whistling or chatter. Eventually, when the time is right, they will mate. During this time, the female or the pair may begin to pull the feathers out in a patch on their chests — a *brood patch* that will allow more heat to reach the eggs.

The hen will begin spending long periods of time inside the box about a week to ten days after mating and will begin laying eggs. She will lay an egg about every two days or so, but this varies. Most species of small to medium birds will lay four to six eggs, though more is definitely possible. Larger birds will lay two or three eggs.

After the first two or three eggs have been laid, the pair will begin incubating them (depending on the species — in some, only one of the pair incubates). If you like, date the eggs by writing numbers on them with a soft felt-tip pen and recording the numbers and the corresponding dates. This is a good way to maintain records, especially if you have more than one pair. Doing this also helps you to know if you have to *pull* and handfeed any of the babies in the clutch. For example, if the first egg is more than 14 days older than the last egg in a large clutch, know that you'll have to handfeed the older chicks in the clutch to allow the younger chicks to thrive.

You can tell if the eggs are fertile by *candling* them (shining a bright light through them). You can buy a commercial candler, a flashlight with a wand and a very bright tip, or you can place the eggs on the face of a flashlight (be careful!). Fertile eggs have veins and a dark spot; unfertile eggs are yellow and clear, and eventually turn gray. Later, you can even see the chick kicking inside the egg! You will also see an air sac (hollow space) in the blunt end of the egg. When the chick is ready to hatch, the air sac will become bigger as the membrane around the chick draws down.

Incubation periods for different species

Budgies: 18 days

Lovebirds: 23 days

Cockatiels: 23 days

Pionus: 28 days

Yellow-naped Amazons: 26–28 days

Umbrella cockatoos: 27–29 days

Blue and gold macaws: 25–27 days

Hyacinth macaws: 28–29 days

If you're using an incubator or have very forgiving parrot parents, another way to tell if your eggs are just about ready to hatch is to place them *very* gently in a plastic bowl filled with warm water. If the egg bobs up and down and moves around, the chick is active and getting ready to hatch. Don't do this unless you're really concerned about the chick's being alive, and use your common sense when it comes to the temperature of the water. Remove the egg from the water and dry it off after less than a minute; then put it back into the incubator.

Infertility in a young pair is normal. Let them take care of the eggs until a few days after you are sure they're not going to hatch; then remove the eggs and let the couple try again. After one or two dud clutches, your pair should be ready for the real thing. Also, it's typical for not all of the eggs in a clutch to hatch. Remove these dud eggs (make sure they're duds first!). If they break, the goo can stick to the parents' feathers and then stick to a small baby, which may then get crushed beneath the parent or dragged out of the nest.

During the incubation period, the parent birds gently turn the eggs over during the day, moving them so that the babies inside can develop properly. If your birds allow, and most parrots will, you can check inside the nest box once a day for a brief moment. Resist checking too often.

At about 18 to 27 days (give or take, depending on the species, temperature, and time of year), the first egg will begin to hatch, followed by the others in the order in which they were laid. The chick hatches using its *egg tooth,* a sharp piece of its beak that eventually falls off (Figure 17-1). A newly hatched chick is wet at first and has a yolk sac (where its belly button would be) that will absorb into its body before the parent feeds it. Some babies have long puffs of down all over their bodies. In some species, the color of the down indicates the mutation color (when it comes to birds, a *mutation* is a naturally occurring variation in appearance). For example, in lovebirds, orange down indicates a green-based mutation, and white down indicates a blue-based mutation.

The parents feed their chicks by regurgitating partially digested food to them. If you check inside the nest box daily, you will see that the chicks grow with alarming speed. Keep an eye on the chicks to make sure they remain healthy. Eager pairs may lay eggs while they're fledging their chicks and may force them to leave the nest by beating them and tossing them out. If they do, you may have to finish the weaning process yourself, which will be tricky if the babies aren't used to handling. Many breeders begin handling young babies in the nest when they are about two to three weeks old, holding and petting them a few times a day if the parents allow (especially in cockatiels and budgies — trying this with lovebirds is a good way to lose a fingertip). This makes the babies very tame and trustful of humans, and is a great alternative to handfeeding them (Figure 17-2).

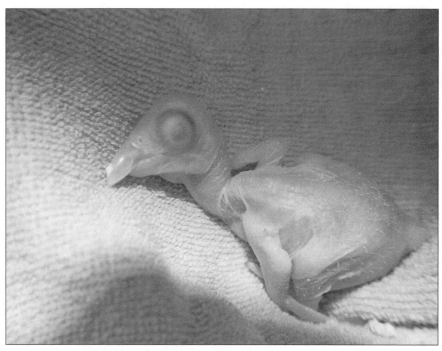

Photo by Essi Laavainen

Figure 17-1:
This is a wonderful photo of a hatchling's egg tooth. The tooth helps the bird remove itself from the shell and then falls off not long after hatching.

Figure 17-2:
This parent budgie is very protective of its fluffy babies.

Photo by Jodi Hillen

Incubation

Occasionally, a pair of parrots aren't the ideal parents, and you'll have to incubate the eggs yourself. Incubating eggs is a tiring and all-consuming task, but the reward is enormous, especially if the babies would have died if you didn't intervene.

Invest in a reliable incubator, one that keeps a constant temperature, though even the best incubators can get too hot or too cool. The temperature should be around 98 degrees, or you risk losing the eggs. This can keep you up all night making minor adjustments, peering in though the little window at the thermometer at 4 a.m., hoping that the mercury reading is correct. Most incubators have a place where you can add water, and you *must* keep it filled. The environment inside the incubator has to be moist, or the babies will dry up in the shell.

You will turn the eggs one-quarter rotation four times a day and more if you're up all night, which you inevitably are. Draw an X on one side of the egg and an O on the other, so that you know where you are in the rotation process. Don't use an automatic rotator, because the slight vibration from it may cause the babies to die inside the shell.

Hatching

After the specified number of days for your species, a baby parrot will begin hatching out of an egg. If you're sleeping when it hatches, don't worry; it will wake you up if the incubator is in your bedroom. Babies are much louder than you think they can be. They will even peep loudly from inside the shell. Never try to help a baby hatch unless you feel that it's having a lot of trouble. If the hatching process is taking over 24 hours, you can chip gently away at the shell with a toothpick, but be very, *very* careful. Babies need to strengthen their neck muscles, and hatching is great exercise, so you don't want to open the egg prematurely.

Most incubators have air holes, and you will now need to open them; raise the temperature to 99 degrees; and place the baby in a container with something soft in the bottom, like white paper towels. Or if you have other eggs in the incubator, invest in a good brooder, or create one yourself.

Making your own brooder

Line a fish tank with paper towels, place an inch or so of pine shaving over that, and place the tank halfway on to a heating pad that's set on low or medium. The babies should be able to roll off the pad should it become too hot. Place small babies on paper towels inside small tubs (clean margarine tubs are useful) inside the tank until they get big enough to be placed inside the tank itself. As the bird begins to feather out, lower the temperature until it's about 85 degrees.

Place a grate on top of the tank and a dark towel most of the way over the top, making sure fresh air can still enter. Babies less than a week old tend to dry up quickly, so create a source of moisture by placing a clean washcloth in a tall glass of warm water and covering it tightly with hole-poked tinfoil ,and place it in your makeshift brooder, making *absolutely sure it cannot tip over* — use tape to secure it. Remove it once the babies are over a week old, a little later if you live in a dry climate.

Invest in a coffee grinder and a good coffeepot. The baby will need to be fed every two hours around the clock, with the first four or five feedings being a drop of something easily digestible, like Pedalyte, and later very thin baby-bird formula. Feed only after the yolk sac on the baby's belly has dried up.

Just like with human babies, you must be *obsessive* about the formula's temperature and about not choking the baby, which can happen if you feed too fast (see the "Handfeeding Baby Parrots" section later in this chapter). I always feed with an eyedropper, because it's easier to control than a syringe. A very small baby needs only one or two drops of food (depending on the species). Some species, like lovebirds, like to be fed on their backs (cradled in your hand, bird's back to your palm, head angled up), and others in their regular sitting position, like cockatiels. As the baby gets older, the time between feedings gets longer, but don't expect to leave the house for at least ten days, or plan on taking the babies with you if you do.

Leg Bands

Many states regulate that all birds being sold must have a closed band on their leg. The bands are also helpful for recordkeeping and are a necessity for showing birds if you want your birds to receive points. The band on a bird's leg is like an identification collar on a dog. The metal band is engraved with the year of hatching, the breeder's initials, the abbreviation of the state where the bird was hatched, and a number that is unique to the band, which allows the breeder to distinguish one baby from another. You can order bands from a variety of companies or through a parrot society or bird club. Bird magazines offer plenty of ads for the bands, so you can shop around.

Band your chicks well before they are two weeks old. The banding process is simple. Lubricate the band with vegetable oil, and slip the two front toes in first, with the two back toes following. Some breeders slip three toes in first, with one following. Whatever way you do it, just don't hurt the baby, and don't force the band onto the foot. The earlier you band, the easier it will be, but don't do it too early, or the band will fall off. Use a toothpick to help the toes through.

If you put the babies back into the nest, watch the parent birds *very* carefully after you band — sometimes they will chew the babies' feet off to remove the bands.

Handfeeding Baby Parrots

Many breeders handfeed their baby parrots. This is not difficult once you know what you're doing, but it is time consuming and can create many problems that are deadly for the babies. Most breeders pull their babies out of the nest box at between two and three weeks of age, or just after their eyes have opened. If you pull them earlier, you will have to feed very often and risk losing a baby if you aren't very experienced with handfeeding. If you pull later than three weeks, the chicks might be fussy, and you may have a difficult time getting them to eat.

Equipment

You need a variety of equipment. First, a brooder (see above to learn how to create one). You have to choose a feeding utensil. I like to use an eyedropper at first because it's easy and there's less of a chance that the food will shoot down the baby's windpipe. When the babies are a little older, you can use a small syringe without the needle attached. Some breeders use pipettes or bent spoons, but I'm still partial to the eyedropper because it's easy to clean and doesn't cause as much of a mess as the other tools, though it does take longer to feed the babies. Some breeders tube-feed their babies, which means that they stick a tube directly into the bird's crop and push the food into it all at once. I do not recommend this method *at all.* Please don't even try it. Not only is it dangerous, but it also doesn't socialize the babies at all. They need to be handled and fed slowly and patiently.

Formula

You next have to choose a handfeeding formula. There are several available on the market that are as easy to make as instant hot cereal. Once you begin with a certain brand of formula, stick with it through the entire handfeeding and weaning process. You can add a probiotic and greenfood (spirulina) to the formula to make it more nutritious.

Before you feed, make sure that the baby is empty. You'll be able to tell by the size and shape of the crop, which is located at the bird's breast. When the crop is full, it's like a saggy bubble. When it's empty, the crop is flat. Don't feed a bird that still has food in its crop (a tiny bit is fine, but aim for empty), especially in the morning. When you feed, you'll be able to tell when to stop as you see the crop fill. *Do not* overfill the crop! This can cause it to become distended, and bacteria may grow in the stretched areas. A full crop should retain its shape and *not* resemble a shiny, hard bubble.

How many daily feedings your baby needs depends on its age. At about two weeks, four or five feedings is appropriate. You can let the bird go six to seven hours at night, but make sure to wake up for an early feeding. As the bird gets older and begins to eat a little bit on its own, you can scale back the feedings. More is not better when it comes to babies. The amount that you feed has to be just right — the bird's life depends on it.

To begin feeding, make a batch of formula according to the directions on the package. Make sure it's not too hot *(please!)*. Stir it with your finger, and test it on your bottom lip as you would food for an infant. *If you don't take the time to do this, especially if you microwave the food, you can kill your babies!* Microwaving isn't recommended because it "kills" the food, making it less nutritious, and creates hot spots. Cold formula isn't good for the bird either — it has to be just right. Stir *very* well to avoid hot spots or clumps.

Take the baby out of the brooder, and place it on a counter or table on paper towels or a towel. Stand or sit in front of the baby, fill your dropper or syringe, and place it up to the parrot's beak. The baby should begin "pumping" at the dropper as you squeeze the food into the beak. The baby should be on a flat surface, sitting on a towel or paper towel, as you hold it gently with one hand while you feed with the other. You might make a mess at first, but that's okay. Just wipe the baby's face and continue. Try to avoid feeding too fast, and don't get the food in the baby's nostrils. If the bird coughs or pulls back, stop feeding, and allow it to recover. After feeding, wipe the baby's face gently with a damp washcloth.

You will know when your parrot babies are hungry because they beg loudly, and you'll see that their crops are empty. Baby parrots with half-full crops may beg too, which might mean that the consistency of your formula is too thin.

I've made it sound very easy here, and it is if you've learned by watching an experienced handfeeder. I wish I could impart to you how tragic and *common* handfeeding accidents are. There are a few things you absolutely need to beware of when handfeeding your babies:

- ✔ **Crop burn:** If the handfeeding formula is too hot or has hot spots, the formula will burn the crop severely, causing a white spot on the crop, which can eventually open up to the outside — a hole in your baby bird! This requires immediate medical attention, can become infected, and is deadly. Please, if you do handfeed, test the formula before you feed it! *If it's too hot, you will kill the baby!*

- ✔ **Slow crop/sour crop:** When there's an infection in the crop, or the food or baby's environment is too cool, the crop can slow down or *sour.* You will notice that food isn't digesting like it used to. This requires flushing of the crop, which you should absolutely not attempt yourself.

- ✔ **Stretched crop:** If you overfeed, and the crop becomes distended too many times, bacteria can thrive in it.

- ✔ **Dehydration:** Dehydration is caused by infection or too little water in the handfeeding formula. When lightly pinched, the skin of a dehydrated baby will stay in a wrinkle instead of springing right back into place. Requires medical attention and generally subcutaneous fluids.

- ✔ **Infection:** Clean all of your feeding implements thoroughly after use, and toss *all* unused formula after each feeding. These items can harbor bacteria and cause a deadly infection in parrot babies. Each feeding should be done with a new, fresh batch of formula. Don't reheat!

- ✔ **Respiratory distress:** It's painfully easy to aspirate (choke) a baby parrot during feeding. Feed slowly and deliberately. Sometimes a novice to handfeeding will force too much food down the bird's beak, causing traces of it to enter the respiratory tract, ultimately leading to pneumonia or *instant death.* It's better to feed with a smaller, slower tool, such as an eyedropper, than risk aspirating a baby bird.

- ✔ **Split breast:** Fledging babies that are just trying their wings, or birds that have been clipped too severely, can split the breast open with a hard landing on a hard floor. Requires immediate veterinary attention.

- ✔ **Scissor beak:** Inexperienced handfeeders can often create *scissor beak* — one part of the beak does not align with the other, making the beak lopsided. If the beak grows like this, the parrot may eventually not be able to eat. A veterinarian or experienced bird expert will be able to "train" the beak over a period of months or years by filing and trimming it. Don't do this yourself! Sometimes, birds have scissor beak even if they were parent-raised, so no one really knows why this happens, but most of the time a handfeeder is to blame.

✔ **Socialization:** The person handfeeding baby parrots should take care to properly socialize the chicks. Feedings shouldn't be a one-two-three-*done* process. The handfeeder should gently caress and talk to the chicks. Believe it or not, the chicks know when the person handfeeding them loves them and will thrive if they are given love and affection.

Figures 17-3 through 17-7 show the growth of a baby bird.

Figure 17-3: Here's the growth of a Ducorps cockatoo. Note how quickly the baby grows. This is the baby at five days.

Photo by Sherlynn Hogan

Figure 17-4: Here's the same baby at nearly a month old.

Photo by Sherlynn Hogan

Figure 17-5:
Here's the
same baby
at about six
weeks old.

Figure 17-6:
Here's the
same baby
at about
ten weeks
of age.

Photo by Sherlynn Hogan

Weaning Baby Parrots

Parent birds naturally wean their babies after they learn to fly. The babies follow the parents to feeding sites and learn to eat by watching and trying. If you handfeed your babies, *you'll* have to wean them, which can be a little more of a difficult proposition than just showing them what they should eat.

First, never, ever (did I say *never?*) force your babies to wean. They need to wean on their own time, not on yours. But this it tricky, because many baby parrots will continue begging and eating handfeeding formula as long as you're willing to feed them. So you have to come to a happy medium (Figure 17-8).

As your babies feather out and begin to explore the brooder, it's time to move them to a small cage. I say *small* because a large cage can intimidate young-sters who haven't learned to climb and perch yet. Offer them seed, pellets, Cheerios, millet, and fresh fruits and veggies — chopped, grated, cooked, and so on. Before you handfeed them, make a shallow dish of their warm formula mixed with oatmeal, and offer it to them on your finger so that they get the idea that it's food. Then feed them their formula. The idea is to get them eating while they're hungry. Always offer a dish of water.

Figure 17-8: This little parrotlet is still a chick, but it won't get much larger than this.

Photo by Donna Dywer

If babies of weaning age are still begging, you can quit the dropper/syringe feeding and move on to spoon feeding. Bend the sides of a spoon toward each other, using a hand wrench; fill it with the baby formula; and offer it that way. Continue to offer the warm foods and a wide variety of other foods. You can cut the feedings down to two — one in the morning and one at night, with lots of soft, warm foods during the day. Eventually, do only one feeding at night, but make sure the babies are eating during the day.

I promise that your babies will eventually wean. Don't *ever* starve them in hopes that they will eat on their own. This is a good way to kill baby birds, or at the very least make them far less socialized than they should be. Babies that are forced to wean can retain baby feeding behaviors, like pumping, well into adulthood and may become insecure and maladjusted adults.

A much-needed rest

After your parrots have blessed you with two or three clutches of babies, give them a well-deserved rest. It is not a good idea to have them continue breeding after three full clutches, because having eggs and tending to babies is very stressful, and the hen will need to replenish her calcium supply. If you live in a hot climate, give your birds a long summer off. If you live in a warm climate, give them the winter to regroup and get strong again. If a pair is particularly prolific, rest them for a year before putting them to nest again.

Very Basic Parrot Genetics

Possibly the most fascinating part of breeding certain small parrots is understanding something about why they show up in so many patterns and colors. This section gives you the very basics of parrot genetics. There's way more to know than I'm going to tell you here. I'm just touching the surface.

If you're computer savvy, you can use one of the many genetic programs on the Internet to help you determine the colors of your offspring before you even set a pair up to breed. In particular, I'm talking about budgies, cockatiels, lovebirds, parrotlets, ringnecks, Quakers, and some conures — the smaller birds that have the more complex *mutations.*

For starters, you should know that the outward color is not always indicative of the other *genes* a parrot carrying (if it's of a species that comes in mutations). A gene is part of the programming that occurs on chromosomes that determines what characteristics an organism has. With parrots, people are mostly concerned with the genes that determine color.

Some genes are dominant, and some are recessive. When a parrot's visual color is the color most often found in the wild — green in lovebirds, for example — we simply call the bird *nominate* or normal. It is showing the genetically dominant color. When the bird is visually showing a recessive color (not found often in the wild but found in aviculture), we call that bird a *mutation* — for example, a blue or yellow (lutino) lovebird.

So how do you come up with a blue lovebird? You actually don't need two blue birds. You can breed two green birds and produce a percentage of blue babies. The color of the babies is determined by the genes of the parents. For example, a green lovebird may be *split to* blue, meaning that it is carrying blue genes, although they are not visually expressed. The word *split* is used to indicate that a bird is carrying genetic traits other than the ones it is visually showing. With sex-linked recessive genes, the female bird receiving a recessive gene will always show that recessive color — for example, the gene for lutino. So she can't be split to lutino, because she will always show the recessive gene — she will be yellow. A green male can be split to lutino, and the genes will show themselves in a percentage of the offspring, all of which will be lutino females.

You never really know what you're going to find in a nest box until you breed the pair. After a couple of clutches of babies, the genetics of the parents should be quite obvious. Some parrot genetics, such as those of lovebirds and cockatiels, are pretty complex because of the number of mutations available.

When you know which genes are dominant, which are recessive, and which are sex linked, and you know with certainty what genes your pair is carrying, you can definitively determine the color of the offspring. Before computers became so popular, people used a Punnett Square to determine sex and color in parrots, and although this method is accurate, it's far easier to find a genetics calculator on the Internet. If you don't know what genes your birds are carrying, you will once you breed them a few times and see the colors of the babies.

Keeping fastidious records will help you keep track of the many mutations in your flock and help you to determine the potential mutations of future babies. You can keep simple records on cards and place them in a card file. Believe me, you will soon forget which of your babies is carrying certain genetic traits or where you sold a particular youngster. Following the genetics is the whole reason why hobbyist breeders enter the fancy and show their birds.

Chapter 18

In the Ring: Showing Your Parrot

Showing small parrots such as lovebirds, cockatiels, and budgies (and of course, other birds, like canaries and finches) is a fun and rewarding hobby that is another aspect of bird guardianship. Single-species shows and all-bird shows draw hundreds of people passionate about parrots, all toting along their well-conditioned show birds in hopes of taking home a prize. The species most popular at shows are the birds that come in a variety of mutations: finches, canaries, budgies, lovebirds, and cockatiels. These are the most exciting classes to watch during the show, and they are surely the classes with the most entries. Cockatiels, budgies, and lovebirds in fact have their own shows around the nation, drawing breeders and exhibitors from every state.

Many serious breeders show their small parrots so that their aviary can claim prestigious prizes and so their babies will bring higher prices — other fanciers will want to purchase offspring from a winning show bird. Some show their birds just to be involved in the hobby and for the self-satisfaction of breeding and conditioning a bird that is close to the *standard* (which I discuss in a moment).

Still others attend shows to mix and mingle with the other exhibitors, to meet other people, and to learn about the species and the hobby. I was involved in bird showing for several years, and I was there mainly to be caught up in the excitement of the shows and to see if I could win prizes with my lovebirds (which never came in above third place, but that was okay with me). I learned a lot and met many interesting and knowledgeable people whom I've kept as friends for many years.

Shows are also great places to trade small birds and to buy and sell birds, if that kind of thing is allowed. Each show has different rules. There are generally tables set up with a lot of great birdy merchandise for sale as well. There may be toy workshops and other types of demonstrations. There are usually also a raffle and door prizes, which are often the best parts of the day.

Words of Warning

I have two major words of warning for you when it comes to showing. First, please don't breed birds just to show them for the sake of showing. If you're going to breed birds, do it because you love the birds and the hobby, and be sure the babies will get good homes. Please stick with the birds that are shown most often and have a lively show presence: lovebirds, cockatiels, and budgies (and canaries and finches).

The reason why these species are shown so often is because they come in hundreds of different mutations and because they're easy to breed. There's a real challenge in *mixing mutations* — using genetics to come up with something really stunning or new, which is what fanciers are after. If that's your passion, great. But I can't advocate entering your companion African greys, Amazons, macaws, or other large birds into a show. These birds are sensitive, and there's no reason to expose them to all the chaos. However, people do bring all kinds of species to shows to win prizes and have a great time, and most of the birds are none the worse for wear, though some individual birds may become frightened by the experience.

The other reason to be wary of shows is health. The birds that hobbyists show most often — lovebirds, cockatiels, and budgies — are prone to a number of diseases and can be carriers without showing symptoms. Some of these diseases are airborne, meaning they can get to your beloved macaw from across the room. Also, most of these shows also allow birds to be sold at vendor tables, and you never know the background or health of these birds. Most shows hire an avian veterinarian to check out all the birds as they come in, but there's no real testing done. The whole thing is kind of on the honor system, which can be compromised when it comes to a competition, no matter how small. Be careful!

The first thing you should do is go to a couple of these shows without bringing any birds. See what it's all about. Watch some of the judging. Talk to the vendors and club members. Stay for the raffle, which always happens at the end. It's a really fun day if you can stick it out till closing time.

If you do decide to bring your birds, make sure you quarantine them when you get home. They should spend 30–40 days in a separate area in case they picked up a bug at the show. You don't want disease spreading to your other birds. Most show people don't quarantine, in my experience. Because it's on the honor system, they assume that everything will be okay. I haven't heard of any show-illness tragedies, but that doesn't mean that it hasn't happened.

Parrot Clubs and Societies

Bird clubs and societies host the bird shows. Most medium to large towns have one or more parrot clubs, either an independent club or a chapter of a larger, national club. They generally hold meetings once a month and have holiday parties, dinners, and other social events. They bring in speakers each month to speak on bird issues, they put out a monthly newsletter, and most have an adoption program. If you love parrots, no matter what species, these clubs are a great place to learn and socialize.

Most clubs have a show or an exposition once or twice a year. A show is where judging takes place; an expo doesn't have a show but has guest speakers and lots of vendors. Some all-species clubs combine a show and an expo, allowing one or two of the "parent" clubs of a species to show there — for example, the American Cockatiel Society, the African Lovebird Society, and the International Parrotlet Society will sanction affiliated local clubs to hold a show within their expo. The judging is done by a qualified and sanctioned member of the parent club.

How a Bird Show Works

Bird shows begin in the morning with the checking-in of the birds and an avian veterinarian viewing the entries for signs of illness. Never, ever bring an ill bird to a show! The birds are entered into classes according to mutation and gender (if gender is obvious, as with cockatiels). For example, male lutino cockatiels are judged against other male lutino cockatiels. The winner of this class goes on to compete against the other birds that have won their classes, and the winner of the division (in this case, the lutino division) goes on to compete against the winners of the other divisions and then on to the competition for the Best in Show title. If you're exhibiting in a cockatiel show, only cockatiels will compete for the Best in Show title. If the show is an all-bird show, the best cockatiel will compete against other species in the final round of judging.

When you check your bird into the show, make sure he's going to be judged in the proper class. Ask a show official to look at your bird if you're doubtful of his mutation or which class he should be judged in. If you're new to bird showing, enter in the novice division. Even birds with clipped wings can enter in novice, and you don't necessarily need a show cage for the novice division either. Novices may show cockatiels that they've purchased — these will have bands that indicate that another breeder bred them. If you want your birds to earn points toward a championship, they must be banded with a closed band carrying your individual code or initials.

Once your bird is checked in, you get a schedule of the show that tells you when your bird is going to be up on the show bench. Try not to become too excited while you watch the judging, because you don't want the judge to know which bird is yours. Also, if your bird sees you and he's a tame companion, he might become agitated and not show well.

Once the judge has selected the top three to ten birds on the bench, depending on how many are entered in the class, he or she might explain why those birds were selected. Be sure to listen carefully. Occasionally, you can speak to a judge after the show is over and ask for details as to why your bird wasn't selected to win (or why she was!). If she doesn't win, remember that there will be other shows and other chances to win. Be a good sport. Bird judges go through a long and rigorous process to get their titles. The judge must be a person of outstanding reputation in the bird community, must have bred and shown champion birds of a particular species, and must have completed an apprenticeship, among many other requirements.

The winners in their class, division, and show, as well as the best novice bird, all receive a ribbon and occasionally even a plaque, trophy, or cup. Don't become disheartened if you don't win in your first few shows, and remember that showing birds is done mainly for the *fun* of the hobby. Your birds are still marvelous, even if they don't go home with ribbons and plaques. If your birds are banded with your personal bands because you've bred them, the winners receive points that will apply toward a championship title. The number of points received is determined by the number of birds entered in the class.

Most shows have a youth class for kids under 18, and some shows even offer scholarship money. In any case, showing is fun for kids and gets them involved. Think: willing cage cleaners and bird feeders!

The Show Standard

Knowing whether you have the "right" bird for showing takes a keen eye for comparing your bird against the *standard*. In a cockatiel show, for example, the birds are not compared with one another, but against a standard written by a particular cockatiel club or the national parent club. The standard explains how each part of the perfect show cockatiel should look and is what the cockatiel judge measures against for each bird on the show bench. Each part of the standard equals a certain number of points, and the winning bird in a class is the one that gets the most points. So to buy or breed show birds, you have to be very familiar with the standard.

As an example, here's the cockatiel standard used by the American Cockatiel Society. Does your bird measure up?

THE AMERICAN COCKATIEL SOCIETY SHOW STANDARD

© The American Cockatiel Society

General Conformation

The Cockatiel is a long bird, with graceful proportions, but of good substance (full bodied). From the top of the shoulder curve to the tip of the wing, from the top of the skull to the vent and from the vent to the tip of the tail (ideally) should measure 7". The goal being a 14" bird with a 3" crest. The total bird being 17 inches.

Crest

Should be long (goal 3"),with good density, curving from the top of the cere fanning out to give fullness.

Head

Should be large and well rounded with no flat spot on top or back of the skull. Baldness will be faulted according to the degree of severity of each bird on the show bench. Our aim is for no bald spot even in Lutinos. The eyes should be large, bright and alert, and placed at midpoint between front and back of the skull. The brow should be well pronounced when viewed from the front, the brow should protrude enough to indicate good breadth between the eyes. The beak should be clean, of normal length, and tucked in so the lower mandible is partially visible. Cheek patches should be uniformly rounded, well defined, (no bleeding), and brightly colored (especially on the males). Adult male Cockatiels will have a bright, clear, yellow head, sharply defined where the yellow meets the border of the main body feathers. A deep bib is preferred. There should be no evidence of pin feathers.

Neck

Should be relatively long- have a very slight curvature above the shoulders and have a small nip above the chest area, giving the bird a graceful outline and eliminating the appearance of a "bull" neck or the "ramrod" posture of some psittacine species. An exaggerated "snake" neck would be reason for fault.

Body

The body of the Cockatiel when viewed strictly from the side angle can be somewhat deceptive, as only a well rounded outline of the chest will indicate whether the specimen has good substance. A frontal (or back) view shows more truly the great breadth through the chest (and shoulder) areas of an adult Cockatiel (more prevalent in hens). It is the strong muscular development that enables the Cockatiel to be such a strong flier. A Cockatiel should have a high. broad. full chest (more prevalent in hens), a slender, tapering abdomen, a wide, straight back (no hump or sway), and be a large, sleek bird.

Wings

Should be large, wide and long, enveloping most of the body from a side view. Should he held tightly to the body,. tips close to the tail with no drooping of the shoulders or crossing of the wings. The wing patch should be wide (goal of 3/4" at the widest point), well defined and clear of darker feathers. All flight feathers should be in evidence. Covert feathers should illustrate their growth pattern clearly.

Legs and Feet

Should hold the bird erect at approximately 70 degrees off the horizontal. Must grasp the perch firmly (two toes forward and two back), be clean, and claws not overgrown or missing.

Tail

The longest flights should be the extension of an imaginary line straight through the center of the bird's body. A humped back will cause the tail to sag too low, and a "swayed" back might elevate the tail higher than desired. The feathers themselves should be straight clean and neither frayed, split or otherwise out of line. All flights should be in evidence.

Condition

A bird in top condition has clean, tight feathers: no frayed or missing feathers, no half grown or pin feathers. The beak and claws must be of suitable length. There should be no unnatural roughness or scaling on the cere, beak, legs or feel. If a bird is in good condition, it will be almost impossible to get it wet. Water will roll off like it does off a duck.

Deportment

In a good show stance, the exhibition Cockatiel should indicate a central line approximately 70 degrees off the horizontal. The bird will present and display well on the perch.

Classification on Types

The following categories concern specific coloration aspects of the Normal and Mutant Cockatiels. While definition is necessary for each type, it is to be remembered that coloration is not as emphasized on the show bench as it may appear to be in the written standard.

Normals
The color should be a dark grey, ideally uniform in color throughout

Pieds
The ideal Pied will be 75% yellow and 25% dark grey. The goal being yellow pied markings over white pied markings. The aim being for tail and wing flights to be totally clear. The mask area should be clear, with no grey to create a "dirty" effect. Symmetry of pied markings are ideal

Lutinos
Ideally a rich. deep buttercup yellow throughout. Long tail feathers and primary flights will not be severely faulted for being a lighter shade of yellow than the body.

Pearl Hens
Extensive "heavy" pearl markings that are well defined, uniform and without splotching. Ideally the pearl markings will be a deep buttercup yellow.

Pearl Males
The same as for hens with less influence placed on the pearl markings.

Cinnamons
The color should be cinnamon, uniform in color throughout

Fallows
The color should be light cinnamon with a yellow suffusion, uniform in color throughout. The eyes should be ruby or red.

Silvers
The color should be a dull metallic silver, uniform in color throughout. The eyes should be ruby or red.

White Face Pearls & Pieds
Same as the Normal but void of all lipochrome. The mask area of the cock will be pure white.

Albinos
Will be void of all lipochrome, a pure white bird, with ruby or red eyes. Primaries and flight feathers will not be severely faulted for being an off shade of white.

Yellowcheek
Cheek patch appears gold with a lemon yellow face color in the male bird.

Pastels
Cheek patch appears peach with a lemon yellow face color in the male bird.

Single Factor Dominant Silver
The body being darker metallic silver than expressed in the silver mutation. Face has an orange cheek patch. Eyes, feet & beak are black, with the exception of Pied; this mutation having flesh colored feet & beak. A skullcap of darker pigmentation is visible on the head. Available in all color mutations, including whiteface.

Double Factor Dominant Silver
The body being a very light metallic silver than expressed in the silver mutation. Face has an orange cheek patch. Eyes, feet & beak are black, with the exception of Pied; this mutation having flesh colored feet & beak. A skullcap of darker pigmentation is visible on the head. Available in all color mutations, including whiteface.

Whiteface Single Factor & Double Factor Dominant Silver
Same characteristics as silver with the exception of being a whiteface mutation.

Olive
Available in all color mutations, including whiteface. This mutation has a green wash and a light feather pattern resembling spangling on the body.

Cross-Mutations
Will be judged by combining the color standards for all mutations involved.

Splits
Markings on Split birds will not be penalized, as these expressions, a genetic factor of birds split to pied and are not a matter of faulty breeding. A bird showing the split mark is split to pied. It can be split to other mutation, but will not show the split markings.

Show Equipment

Birds are generally shown in special show cages that are designed to emphasize a bird's good points. The show cage does not contain anything that would distract the judge from the bird. The cage is solid on three sides, with vertical grating on the front, which is generally painted black. The three solid sides are painted white or light blue, accentuating the bird's color. The show cage is also easy for the show steward to move around on the bench. You can show in another type of cage, but it's not in your bird's best interest to do so. These cages can be purchased on the Internet, and you can find ads for them in bird magazines. Your show cage should be in pristine condition on the day of the show. Paint it each season so that it looks new and does not distract the judge with chipping paint, dried poop, or dirty smudges.

Just before you check your bird into the show, attach a tube-style waterer to the front of the cage, as far to one side as possible, and line the floor of the cage with something that won't get your bird dirty, such as absorbent shredded white paper, chicken scratch, crushed corn, plain seed, or clean rabbit pellets. Newspaper, rabbit pellets, and other litters can cause a light-colored bird to become stained during the course of the show, causing it to lose points, so if you have a white or light-colored bird, use shredded white paper and plain seed.

Conditioning Your Bird for a Show

A bird must be in absolutely perfect condition on the day of the show. This means that you will have to begin conditioning him about 8 to 12 weeks before the show begins. It goes without saying that a good diet is key to a primed and good-looking bird. You should be feeding a nutritious, balanced diet year round (see Chapter 8). Condition a few birds at once so that you can take the finest-looking of your flock to the show and leave the others behind.

Begin conditioning with daily bathing. Mist your bird, soaking him to the skin in warm weather, every day. This encourages preening and makes the feathers shiny and waterproof. You want a bird in good feather condition. Some exhibitors put a little bit of glycerin in the misting water about a week before the show. Don't overdo this, however, because your bird will ingest it during preening. Discontinue bathing a few days prior to the show.

Where the shows are

You can find out about upcoming shows from your local bird club, from a species club or society, and by surfing the Internet. Simply type **bird show** (or the species name) into a search engine, and you should be able to find the information that you need. There are a few large national bird shows each year where you get to see all kinds of birds you wouldn't normally see in your area. These big shows are a lot of fun and very educational.

Next, look for any frayed or broken feathers. These can be pulled 8 to 12 weeks before the show, but err on the side of caution with this, and only pull the feathers that *really* need pulling. Pulling feathers is painful for the bird, and I can't recommend it — I'm just telling you what people who show their birds do to get their birds into show condition. All feathers must be intact, and the tail must be straight, especially in long-tailed species, like cockatiels and ringnecks. You can train the tail to be straight by dipping it in warm water and using your fingers to straighten it out. Keeping your bird in a large-enough cage helps maintain feather quality as well.

If your bird begins to molt before the show, you've just lost your big contender. You can't show a molting bird, because he will not be in peak feather condition. This is why you should be conditioning a few birds at a time.

Show Training

A show can last 8–12 hours, and your bird will need to be patient inside the show cage for that period of time. Buy your show cage early, and begin show training as soon as possible once you decide which birds are going to the upcoming show.

To begin training, place your bird inside the cage for a few minutes a day, and offer him a treat that he loves. Make the experience fun, and praise him. Increase the time he spends in the cage, and move the cage to different locations around the house. The judge will use a wand to move your cockatiel around the cage so that he or she can view every side of the bird. You can use a chopstick to make your bird turn around. It is important that your bird sits quietly on the perch, with good posture, and that he doesn't fight with the judge's wand.

Finally, a few weeks before the show, hold a mock show at a friend's home. Take your bird in his show cage to a friend's house, and set him on a table. If you have several birds or if your friend has birds, this will work very well. Play the radio and the television — it's very noisy at a bird show. If you have a recording of birds, play that too. Have your friend play judge with your cockatiel, using a wand (chopstick) to move the bird around. Do this a few times to get your bird used to the chaos of a show.

Try to keep your birds as calm as possible for the few days before the show. Continue with the usual routine to avoid stress or anything happening to your bird's feather condition. Don't feed anything that will discolor the feathers, such as beets. There's nothing like good preparation to help your bird have the best shot possible at winning. Good luck!

Helping Out at the Show

If you're a member of a club, and you've been around a while and attended a few shows, you can ask to be a steward at one of the show benches (attend the business meetings for the show — you may have to be nominated). As steward, you will put the show cages on the show bench and then move them around based on the judge's indications — he or she will tap a cage and point to the position he wants it in. Eventually, all the birds will be in the order he wants them, from top bench to bottom. The primary show steward is the person who enters all of the birds, keeps track of them, and then makes sure they get back to their owners at the end of the day. This is a big job, and the steward always needs assistants, so pitch in if you can.

Or you can work the raffle table, which is the most fun, because you get to talk to everyone, sell raffle tickets, and answer birdy questions. You can also work the membership table or the coffee and snacks table, or be a runner who does everything from providing basic security to helping vendors. Also, if there's a bird auction going on, you can help bring the birds out and keep everything organized. You'll win major points with your bird club if you volunteer for clean-up crew. They also need people to help set up and break down the show and to help organize the pre- or postshow dinner. Remember, you'll meet more people if you volunteer.

Part VI
The Part of Tens

The 5th Wave   By Rich Tennant

"Of course I'm jittery. I'm here alone, the
lights went out, and now I can't find
the bird."

In this part . . .

Here are three chapters that each contain a list of ten important things. Chapter 19 tells you about the ten things all parrots should know, from how to step onto a stick to learning their own last name and phone number. Chapter 20 is about things you can do to entertain your parrot. Finally, Chapter 21 gives you all the info you need on traveling safely with your parrot — and if you don't want to travel with your bird, you get info here on how to choose a bird sitter as well as a vacation care sheet to photocopy and fill out before you leave.

Chapter 19

Ten Things All Parrots Should Know

Keeping a parrot safe and healthy can be a full-time job. It's a good idea to teach (or socialize, more accurately) your parrot to understand or get used to things that can save its life someday. Here are ten things that all parrots should know.

Step-Up

All parrots should know the step-up directive, discussed in Chapter 16 . In short, when you say, "Step-up," your parrot should become conditioned to put its little foot in the air and step onto your hand. Some parrots become so used to this directive that they will lift a foot if they hear "Step-up" from across the room. Some parrots will even say "Step-up" and lift a foot when they want your attention.

If your bird doesn't know how to step onto your hand, it will be more difficult to remove him from a dangerous situation or retrieve him from somewhere he's not supposed to be. If he flies away, you have a better shot at getting him back if he knows that an extended finger or hand means "Step-up." Even a stranger will be able to retrieve your bird if it's not hand-shy.

Stick Training

After teaching step-up onto the hand, all parrots should be taught to step up onto handheld perches and sticks of various sizes and diameters. This is useful for handling unpredictable parrots or those that like to get themselves out of easy reach, such as on top of the curtain rods. Chapter 16 explains how to stick-train your parrot.

The Carrier

Every parrot should be familiar with a safe bird carrier that is designated specifically for that individual bird. If you have the opportunity, start desensitizing the bird to the carrier when she is young. Allow the carrier to remain in sight of the bird, and play with her on and around the carrier, offering food on top of it. Place the bird inside the carrier with her breakfast or dinner. Don't close the door. You're just giving the parrot the idea that the carrier is something fun and not something scary. You'll be glad you did this when it's time to go to the veterinarian, while traveling, or when there's an emergency.

Socializing the carrier to an older parrot is a little tougher, but not impossible. Use the same method as above. Realize that springing the carrier onto any bird is scary. You have to let the bird see it and live with it for a while in its nearby environment. That way, at least it will be a familiar object when it's time for travel.

Windows and Mirrors

Windows and mirrors can be deadly for fully flighted parrots, who don't understand that they are solid and instead just see more free space in which to fly. Even clipped parrots that can fly a little are in danger of injuring a beak or neck by landing hard against a sliding glass door or full-length mirror.

Walk your parrot around to all of the windows and mirrors, and tap on them, allowing the bird to get very close and tap on them with its beak. Doing this a few times with larger parrots should be sufficient. Smaller parrots may learn by trial and error (and hopefully won't get hurt doing it). All parrots will eventually learn the landscape of the home. Your best bet is to allow your mirrors and windows to become dirty, or to place stickers on them so that the bird can see the difference between the glass and what's behind it.

Name and Phone Number

If you have a talking species, it's not a bad idea to teach the bird your last name and phone number. Some birds will even learn their addresses. Just repeat the information over and over. Making up a catchy song is a great way to teach this information, too. If the bird every flies away or gets stolen, whoever finds it (or buys it) will know whom to call to return it.

But you don't have to teach your parrot its name and number for it to come back home safely to you. Your avian veterinarian can insert a small microchip into your bird's breast muscle — this chip contains a unique number, which you then register with the company. Most shelters and veterinarians own the special scanner that reads these chips. When your bird (or dog or cat) is found, it can be easily returned to you if the information you provide the microchip manufacturer is up to date.

Cage as Safety Zone

A parrot should feel that his cage is a safe place where he can sleep and eat in peace. Don't change the cage around too much once the bird is settled. Leave the perches and toys as they are. You can rotate new/old toys in and out of the cage, but try to keep them in the same basic location.

Don't move the cage around a lot. Once the parrot gets established in one room in one spot, try to leave him there. If you have to move the cage — well, then you have to — but don't do it capriciously.

Try not to place scary things near the cage. Parrots are often scared of things you wouldn't even think twice about, like weird pieces of art; balloons; and large, loud electronic equipment.

If the bird doesn't want to come out of the cage for whatever reason, and you're sticking your hand in there only to bring him out to play, leave him alone and try again later. Don't force or fish him out unless you're taking him somewhere important. If he's on top of the cage, you can persist a little more, but if he's in the cage, allow him to have his space. The only exception to this is when a bird becomes vicious and territorial around the cage. Find out more on cage territoriality in Chapter 14.

Eyedropper or Syringe

If you have the time and the patience, it's a good idea to try to get your parrot to take a few drops of baby food, soy milk, or juice from a plastic eyedropper, pipette, or small plastic syringe. You are *not* going to be handfeeding the bird or even simulating handfeeding. This can cause behavior problems in a weaned bird of any age. What you're trying to do is to get the bird to take a little bit of what you're offering out of the dropper. Make it fun. Eventually, if you ever have to give medicine or vitamins to your parrot, you'll be glad that he likes to nibble out of the dropper.

Trust

You are your bird's best and closest ally, but you're not much good to him if he doesn't trust you. A hands-on avian friend has to come to understand that you're on his side and that you mean only to provide for him and keep him safe and loved. Sure, he may give you a nicely placed nip (or full-on bite) now and again. If you react with anger, you reinforce the bite and begin to chip away at the bond you've built.

Build trust by being consistent. Birds thrive on routine and reliability. If you behave erratically and send your bird mixed messages, he will learn to become suspicious and fearful. Be calm, gentle, and loving, and learn to view your bird as an individual with individual likes and needs. If you understand that you're in a real *relationship* with your parrot, it's easier to treat him as a whole being, not just as decoration for the living room.

Eating Well

All parrots should be exposed to various foods. If you wait too late to offer a variety of healthful foods, the bird may not understand that certain objects are actually food and may ignore them. It's much easier to get a bird to eat well while it's a youngster. However, a lot of older parrots do take to new things with the verve of a fledgling. Discover how to make new foods palatable in Chapter 8.

The Word "No!"

Unlike dogs, parrots will never truly understand the word *no*. However, parrots, like dogs, are mischievous and do get themselves into things they shouldn't — life in the average home is full of interesting and dangerous distractions. A very sharp "No!" does get a parrot's attention. Once you have that, you can stop the bird from doing a behavior by removing it from the situation. Using a sharp "No!" does not work for chronic behaviors, such as plucking or screaming (check out Chapter 14).

Using *no* is better than using *stop it!*, which may sound like *step-up* to parrot ears. It's also preferable to shouting your bird's name — always use the bird's name associated with positive things and praise, never as a reprimand.

Chapter 20

Ten Ways to Entertain Your Parrot

A human becomes bored due to a set routine of dull tasks, doing the same thing over and over every day, with little variation. Life becomes tedious. For a parrot, the opposite is true. Birds thrive on routine, as long as that routine involves having a variety of "jobs," a schedule that's full of activity and mental stimulation. Amusing a parrot does not mean forcing your bird to break out of his routine. On the contrary, a parrot needs a routine, but one that fills his days with play, work, learning, and interesting things to look at and listen to.

When many people think of birds, they think of the cliché of the *bird brain,* the tiny intellect that doesn't think, reason, or have emotions. It is true that parrots do function on a highly instinctual level, but they are intelligent animals, capable of problem-solving and of extreme boredom. You might not believe that a parrot can think, but you have to concede that it can *suffer.* Many parrots suffer from the lack of mental, emotional, and physical stimulation, and this can have terrible consequences for this sensitive creature. A bored parrot will *find* things to do, including feather plucking and chewing, self-mutilation, screaming, and other symptoms of neurotic disorder. Lack of physical activity can also lead to mental *and* physical disorders, such as obesity and aggression.

So what exactly is a parrot's *job?* In the wild, a parrot spends its days flying, searching for food and water, chewing on trees, finding a safe spot to sleep, preening and mutual preening, finding a mate, finding or making a nest and making it suitable for raising babies, mating, protecting the nest, raising babies, and doing it all over again. That's a lot of work. In captivity, your parrot doesn't have nearly as much work to do. His food and water is provided; he has a safe spot to sleep; and he doesn't really need to search for a mate, because either you serve as his mate or you've provided one for him. What a cushy life! So that leaves him with only a few activities in his repertoire: chewing; preening;

nesting (and nesting isn't even part of the package for a single parrot or a pair that is not set up for breeding); and possibly flying, depending on whether or not you have a safe place for him fly. Because the companion parrot is limited in his activities, you have to go out of your way to ensure that he has *plenty* to do to keep him from becoming bored, neurotic, and overweight. This chapter offers some fun activities that you can add to your parrot's routine.

Food

Certain food or ways of presenting food can give your parrot a sense of purpose at mealtime. You can buy a birdy-kabob onto which you thread fruits and veggies so that your parrot has to work to get at the food, rather than just stand at a dish.

Thread leaves of spinach and kale or millet spray through the bars of the cage so that your parrot has to hang onto the bars to eat them. Very wet greens in a shallow plastic or ceramic dish make for some fun eats and a nice bath, too.

Tie up goodies such as popcorn, small nuts, cereal, and other dry foods that your parrot loves, and place them in a white-tissue-paper packet tied up with a bit of sisal rope. Place the packet in the cage, and your parrot will have to tear it open to get to the goodies. You can do the same thing with tiny paper lunch bags or paper towels.

You as Entertainment

The first and foremost activity that will keep your parrot entertained is out-of-the-cage playtime, especially with you. A companion parrot should spend several hours, at the very least, outside its cage daily. A parrot that's cooped up will become crazed to get out of its cage and will become anxious about being confined. Long-term confinement can lead to plucking and other neurotic and health disorders.

If you are your parrot's only pal, hands-on playtime is essential. Give your bird lots of head scratches and time on your shoulder (if you trust him near your face). You can watch television, read, play board games, and do many other activities with your bird present. Include your bird in your daily activities. As I type this, my African grey parrot is sitting on a perch behind me and looking over my shoulder, watching the words appear on my computer screen.

Parrot Toys

Toys are essential for a curious parrot (and they're all curious), which needs the stimulation of chewing and playing. A parrot living in a cage without a variety of toys is like a human living in a home without television, books, magazines, stereo, puzzles, games, knitting, Ping Pong, or any other type of entertainment. How boring! Your parrot can't take itself out to the movies, the arcade, a friend's house, or anywhere else for entertainment purposes. But he can have toys.

Toys are part of a parrot's "job," to chew and to create a custom-made environment for himself. Toys provide your parrot a sense that he can furnish his home the way he wants it. For example, he will slide his toys around and chew them to just the right degree. Toys also provide a sense of security, something to cuddle up to, argue with, and take out his tensions on.

Store-bought toys come in many materials and sizes. It's best to buy one or two of each kind of toy — wooden, rope, leather, preening, acrylic, puzzle, "hidden treat," and so on. This way, your parrot can choose his favorite. Always choose the proper size for your bird — too large a toy may frighten your parrot, and too small a toy can break when he plays with it and cause injury, or worse. When you buy toys from a store, inspect them for potential dangers, such as places where a toe can catch or a ring where the parrot can stick its head through and hang itself.

Making your own toys is also a great way to entertain your parrot. You can buy bags of Popsicle sticks and tie them together with sisal twine (from any hardware store) into all sorts of towers and ladders (small to medium-size birds only). Make sure that you buy only *untreated* sisal rope.

For little birds, take a plastic hanger, and wrap it tightly all the way around with sisal twine. Then, with the same twine, tie plastic buttons all over it. Hang it in the cage or outside as a little play swing.

All handmade toys should be used only under strict supervision. Never, ever leave your parrot alone with a homemade toy.

There are a lot of "instant" fun, cheap toys that your parrot will love:

- ✔ Untreated wooden honey dippers are fun, especially if you put almond butter on the end and roll it in seeds.

- ✔ Remember those straw, woven "Mexican finger-cuffs" everyone had as a kid? You put a finger in one end and your other finger (or someone else's finger) in the other, pull, and then you're locked. These things are really cheap, and they make great parrot toys. It's best to buy the uncolored ones.

- ✔ If you can find those cheap, woven twine or straw drink coasters, they're a lot of fun for medium to large parrots to shred. Even little guys like lovebirds will like them.

- ✔ Untreated wooden spoons make great chewing toys, too.

- ✔ A whole roll of white, unscented toilet paper makes a great shredding toy, but just get ready to clean up! Remove the cardboard roll when the bird is done.

- ✔ When you're done with the telephone book white pages, tear off the glossy cover and allow your parrot to have a ball tearing it up.

WARNING!

Any article that uses any kind of glue or colored ink isn't good for your bird to chew. These items may contain zinc or lead, which can poison your bird.

TIP

If you want to color any of your toys (such as the Popsicle sticks), boil some of them with beets for a red color, and boil others with blueberries for a violet color. Natural vegetable dyes like these are fine to use. Avoid other dyes.

Music and Television

There's nothing more boring than talking to yourself all day, and that's exactly what a single parrot does while its family is away. Leave the television on for your bird, but leave it on low. There is some evidence that some of the frequencies on the television can be annoying to birds.

I leave the TV on low for my birds and put it on one of the nature channels or on public television. I have found that the commercials on regular TV channels are too stimulating for my African grey. Well, perhaps it's not that they're too stimulating for him but that they're more annoying for me. When he "watches" regular television, all he does is mimic the commercials. If I have to hear about new carpet or be told to buy a certain kind of car insurance again, I'm going start making him earn his keep.

Music is also great for keeping birds company, but be careful about the type of music you leave on. Try for something soothing *and* stimulating, like Mozart or jazz. Talk radio is also good. You can also try nature-sounds CDs or CDs made specifically for pets. I have even seen ads for a bird-sitter video, which is a great concept and probably worth a try.

The Great Outdoors

Your parrot will appreciate being taken outdoors on days when the weather is warm and sunny. He will be able to hear and see other birds and to bathe in the sun's rays, which are very good for his overall health. Take the opportunity to give him a misting with water, too. The change of scenery will do him good.

Be careful, however, that you don't place your bird directly in the sun. This can cause overheating and can lead to death if the bird gets too hot. Place the cage so that half of it is in the sun and half is in shade, so that he can move away from the heat if he needs to.

Watch the cage carefully when you put it outside, because predators may become interested in your bird, and many, such as raccoons, can even figure out how to open the cage. Also, there may be objects outside that scare your bird, so it's comforting if you stay with him. If he gets too scared, bring him back inside.

Flying

Flying is the absolute best physical activity that your parrot can do. However, it comes with many potential dangers. The average household contains dozens of items and places that can injure and kill a parrot. Also, an unclipped parrot is far more likely to fly away than a clipped one, obviously.

Fortunately, considerable numbers of people are following the trend of building safe places for their birds to fly. You don't have to house your parrot in an aviary or habitat, though it would be great if you could, but you can build a safe, large area where your parrot can spend a few hours a day flying. You can still house your parrot inside your home, but at least it will have the benefit of stretching its wings in an "exercise flight."

Dancing

Okay, here's where I'll probably lose you, but I'll give it a shot. Dance for your bird. I know, it sounds silly. But parrots love it when you make a fuss and behave like a silly fool. Put on some music, and dance around. Get the whole family involved. What great entertainment for your parrot! I'm serious. Now get out there and dance!

If you like to do aerobics to videotapes, let your parrot watch. Why not? Perhaps he'll become a good coach.

Singing

As long as you're dancing, you might as well sing, too. Parrots love hearing songs, especially if you're the one who's singing. Parrots that are apt to talk will pay close attention to a heartily sung song, especially if you're dancing around too.

I sing a made-up, off-key "la la la" song to my African grey. It's kind of like the scales, but I vary it. He sings it to me all the time and waits for me to sing it back. Then we sing together, a whole off-key symphony of "la la la." I just hope the neighbors can't hear us.

Parrot Pets

If you're away for much of the day, or your lifestyle has changed significantly and you find that you're not playing with your parrot as much, consider buying him a pal. Parrots of the opposite sex are likely to take to each other right away, but this isn't always the case. The parrot "pet" doesn't have to be another parrot, anyway.

If you don't want to get another parrot, you can purchase a couple of para-keets, a canary, or a pair of finches to keep your parrot company. These birds will give him something to watch and someone to talk to in "birdese."

A small fish tank close-ish to the cage makes a nice view, too. Just be sure that the tank is covered well so that your parrot doesn't accidentally fall in when he's out of the cage. One of those little tanks with the fake magnetic fish works too, and they don't croak if you forget to change the water. You can even just buy a bowl or little tank, put an air-stone in the bottom of it. and leave an air pump on during the day — your parrot might enjoy watching the bubbles.

Trick Training

I don't like to call any of the behaviors that you teach your parrot *tricks,* but some behaviors are pretty fun (and funny) and are more like tricks than they are useful. For example, you can buy little parrot roller skates and, with a little patience, teach your bird to use them. You can also buy a ring toss and a little basketball hoop and whiffleballs to dunk. All it takes is time and a lot of persistence. The real deal with this kind of training is the attention that you're giving the bird. This kind of intense, hands-on training is invaluable to creating or maintaining the bond between you and your parrot.

Chapter 21

Ten + Travel Tips

*B*ecause some parrots have the potential to live up to 80 years, chances are that you'll move or travel with your bird several times. Traveling with a bird is not like traveling with a dog or cat. There are a few more details to work out to move these sensitive creatures with care. This chapter helps you prepare for a safe trip, whether or not you take your feathered friend with you.

Your Parrot's Suitcase

You should always have a bag for your parrot packed and ready to go in case of an emergency or impromptu trip. Having a packed "suitcase" for your bird makes any vacation or trip to the veterinarian far easier. If you're not prepared, traveling with birds can be a nightmare and can be dangerous. Your parrot should have at least a little duffel bag where you keep a few important things for traveling. It should contain:

- ✔ Bottled water. Never give tap water to your parrot, especially tap water from places other than your home.

- ✔ A spray bottle filled with clean water in case of overheating.

- ✔ Paper towels for quick cleanups.

- ✔ Seed and/or pellets: Keep in a seal-tight bag.

- ✔ Treat sticks and other treats to keep the bird occupied.

- ✔ Canned fruit with pop-top lid (unsweetened) for a quick sugar rush in the case of an injured or ill bird; the fruit is also a good snack.

✔ Grapefruit seed extract (to disinfect anything that you'll use near your bird, even your hands, one drop per ounce; also good for disinfecting drinking water).

✔ Perches, just in case.

✔ Toys, also just in case.

✔ Clean newspaper (black and white only — no color) to change the carrier lining.

✔ A birdy first-aid kit in case of emergency.

✔ An index card with your veterinarian's phone number and your emergency phone numbers written on it.

Every time you walk out of the house with your bird, you can quickly grab her suitcase. You never know when you're going to need something on the fly. A quick trip to the veterinarian could turn into an hours-long adventure if you get a flat tire or your car breaks down.

You should have at least seven days' worth of food and water in your bird's travel kit. In today's day and age, you never know when you'll have to toss your bird in a carrier, grab her suitcase, and escape from a dangerous situation. Also, should something happen to you, someone who comes in to care for your bird should easily be able to find the bird's kit and take it with them if needed.

The Carrying Cage

The next thing you need for traveling, after a nicely packed birdy suitcase, is a safe carrier for your bird. I like the plastic carriers with the metal grating and sliding door on top for smaller birds, and the grate in front for larger birds. Your parrot will feel secure with four solid sides surrounding him and will like to see out of the slats in the plastic. There's even a carrier that has two grated doors — one on top and one on the front. This type of carrier is ideal for short trips and car travel. If you're putting your bird in the cargo hold of an airplane, use a carrier with only one door on the front.

Some large birds can chew out of a regular plastic carrier. If you have a voracious chewer, take an extra carrier with you. Or invest in an acrylic carrier. These are much more expensive, but they're nice for car travel. For air travel, you'll have to cover three sides with cardboard (with window slots so the bird can see out).

Here are some tips for preparing the carrier for travel:

- ✔ Buy a low-pile, 100-percent cotton bathmat with rubber backing a few days before the trip, and wash and dry it in unscented detergent. Cut it to fit the bottom of the carrier. You should be able to get four or more carrier liners this way. Place two or three of them in the bottom of the carrier. When the top layer becomes soiled, take it off to reveal a clean layer underneath.

- ✔ Place a layer of white paper towels over cotton mat that you've cut according to the directions above. Sandwich them in between the other mats.

- ✔ If you want, you can tear plain newsprint into long strips and put it in the carrier.

- ✔ Loose crocks or cups in the carrier can be dangerous. If you can figure out a way to attach a couple of cups to the sides of the carrier, do so. I drilled a hole into the side of the carrier and then used two washers and a wingnut to attach an appropriate cup to the side. It works beautifully.

- ✔ Place apple wedges, oranges cut in half, berries, and grapes in one corner of the carrier or in an attached cup.

- ✔ Place seed on the bottom of the carrier in one corner or in an attached cup.

- ✔ Do not put perches in the carrier for a short trip. For a longer trip, fashion a sturdy, rough perch onto the front grate of the carrier or drill holes into the sides, and use screws, washers, and a wingnut to secure a perch from side to side. Place any perches low in the carrier.

- ✔ Clip the bird's wings. In case of accident or emergency where the bird is removed from the carrier, you don't want it flying away. A quick trip to the vet doesn't necessitate such drastic measures, but a longer trip does.

- ✔ Write all your contact information and your veterinarian's phone number on an index card, and tape it to the carrier. Include flight numbers and other travel info, along with your bird's personal info and feeding information. If you want to be really sure the info doesn't get lost, write it on the carrier with permanent marker.

- ✔ Tape an additional perch to the top of the carrier, along with a note indicating that if anyone has to handle the bird for any reason, they can use the perch to pick it up. Most people will be afraid to put their hand in a carrier with a bird they don't know, and for good reason.

- ✔ Affix a couple of "Live Animal" stickers to the carrier.

✔ Hang a couple of soft toys from the holes in the sides of the carrier.

✔ Take a towel with you to cover the carrier, should you need to in cool weather — or to keep people from scaring your parrot with unwarranted attention.

Making the Cage Safe for Travel

If your parrot's cage is small-ish, and you're just going a short distance in your car, you can remove the toys and the perches; cover three sides with a towel, blanket, or cardboard; and use it as a traveling cage. Don't forget to clip the doors closed so that your parrot can't escape. If the cage has a removable plastic bottom, tie it to the metal part of the cage so that it can't fall off. Fill the water dish only about a quarter of the way, and put juicy fruits and veggies in the cage for additional moisture.

Air Travel

Most airlines allow you to travel with your parrot in an airline-approved carrier slipped under your seat. There is a fee to take your parrot on board. In general, most airlines will allow one carrier per person. So if you have more than one parrot, you'll have to take other people with you on your trip.

If your carrier is too large, the airline will want you to check your bird with the baggage. This may be fine in certain times of year, but I personally wouldn't do it in winter or summer. Actually, I wouldn't do it at all. The scary stories of the airlines losing pets or of carriers being crushed should invoke caution. But if you *have* to check your parrot into the cargo hold, it's better than leaving your parrot behind if you move. If you're going on vacation, and you can't place the carrier under the seat, consider a bird-sitter instead.

If you're going to another country, and you have to take your parrot, check with the regulations for that country. You may have to leave your bird in quarantine for a period of time, and some countries may not want your bird to enter at all.

Here are some other airline tips:

✔ Try to take a direct flight if you can. If you're going somewhere more than eight hours away, plan a hub in between, and make sure the airline will let you see your bird during the layover (if he's in cargo).

✔ Make sure the carrier you use is airline approved.

✔ Place a "This End Up" sticker or write it on the carrier with clearly visible marker.

✔ If the parrot is being shipped in the cargo hold, USDA has temperature limits for departure and arrival: 45–85 degrees Fahrenheit.

✔ Some airlines require a veterinary health certificate before flying. Call the airline to find out how long before the flight the certificate should be issued.

✔ If the parrot is going cargo, fold a piece of hardware cloth over the front of the carrier, and secure it with plastic ties. This will help deter someone from opening the front of the carrier. Tape a pair of small nail clippers onto the side of the carrier in case someone has to remove the ties. This can be touchy in terms of security, so you'll have to ask about it. In any case, there has to be some way of removing the wire in case of emergency.

✔ If the weather is cold, tape a piece of cardboard halfway over the grating in the front or on the top of the carrier.

✔ Prepare carrier as detailed in "The Carrying Cage" earlier in this chapter.

✔ Prepare to answer a lot of questions about your parrot. The people around you on the plane and in the airport will definitely want to know about your bird.

✔ When on board the plane, don't take the bird out of the carrier, but you can remove the carrier from beneath your seat to interact with your bird. He may be frightened by all the noise, and your presence can have a calming effect.

Road Travel

Car travel is a fine way to transport your parrot, but you will have to be very cautious and prepare well. First, never leave your bird unattended. Someone could smash your window and steal him. If you're traveling alone, and you have to leave your bird to pump gas or use the restroom, park in a safe, visible spot, and be as quick as possible. If it's warm, park in a shady spot. When you stop to eat, park in front of a window so that you can watch your car.

Never, ever leave your bird in a warm car, even for a minute. Keep the air conditioner on, but don't let it blow on the bird directly. Extreme cold is dangerous as well. Make sure your bird is warm enough in the wintertime.

Train travel

You can't legally take your parrot on Amtrak. You can probably take him on local trains in a carrier — most authorities won't stop you. As for Amtrak, I used to take my lovebirds on long train rides all the time. I bought a private room on the train; put my birds in small plastic critter-keeper containers; and then put the containers in a duffle bag, which I kept with me all the time. I only got caught once, when they started chirping away. But the conductor was nice and didn't do anything about them. We could have been put off the train. I was lucky. Today, with all the luggage inspections, I doubt my little trick would work.

Always, no matter what, buckle your bird in when you ride. If you want your bird to be able to look out the window (which many birds do like), place a larger carrier beneath your bird's smaller carrier and then buckle the whole thing in with the seat belt. Use bungee cords to strap down the carrier even further.

Yes, parrots get carsick. I had a blue and gold macaw that used to toss his cookies every time. If you're concerned about carsickness, don't feed your bird for a few hours prior to the trip (but always offer water). You can put a ginger extract in the water as well to settle the stomach. You can also use a few drops of the Bach Flower essence called Rescue Remedy in the water, which is often used to calm nerves.

Water, Water Everywhere, but Not a Drop to Drink

Take bottled water with you when you travel, or fill several bottles with the filtered water that your parrot is used to drinking. Water from other places can irritate your bird's intestinal tract — not something you want to have happen while you're traveling (or ever, for that matter). Bottled water is good because it lasts a long time before the seal is broken and comes in many different-size bottles. If you have to give your bird different water, add one drop of grapefruit seed extract per ounce of water to kill any bugs that may be in it.

Hospitable Hotels

Before you get to your vacation destination, make sure your bird is welcome. Often, you will only have to pay a small per-night fee to bring the bird, but many hotels don't accept pets, and if you don't plan ahead, you could be sitting on the side of the road with your parrot in one hand and your suitcase in the other.

If you're staying a while, ask that the maid service doesn't come into your room. The vacuuming and turning down the bed may frighten your parrot, and some of the cleansers that the maids use are toxic. Instead, bring a handheld vac with you for easy clean up. Make the bed yourself. I know, you're on vacation. But this is the price you pay for having your bird keep you company.

If you're traveling by car and are only staying overnight in a motel, you don't *have* to explain about your parrot if you don't want to. Simply slip in, sleep, and get out in the morning. This advice is for the wearied traveler only. In any case, some motels don't consider birds to be pets the way they do dogs and cats, and most front-desk people will overlook a parrot in a carrier.

Here are some Web sites where you can find more information about pet-friendly hotels:

- ✔ www.petswelcome.com
- ✔ www.travelpets.com
- ✔ www.pettravelleisure.com

Feeding Travel Tips

Of course you're going to bring your bird's base diet with you, but you can also feed your bird the things you're eating on the road if you're careful about what you order.

- ✔ For breakfast, well-done scrambled eggs, buckwheat pancakes, and fruit.
- ✔ For lunch, well-done turkey, whole-wheat bread.
- ✔ For snack, some rest stops have fresh apples and bananas. Wash well.
- ✔ For dinner, veggies, well-done chicken, baked potato.

Finding an Avian Veterinarian on the Road

The Association of Avian Veterinarians is a good place to begin. You can contact them at the Association of Avian Veterinarians, P.O. Box 811720, Boca Raton, FL 33481-1720, phone (561) 393-8901, fax (561) 393-8902, or find them on the Web at www.aav.org.

If you're already at your destination and have an emergency, you can take your chances with the local phone book, but I'd recommend planning ahead and writing down the phone numbers of veterinarians in the area ahead of time.

Hiring a Parrot Sitter

If you've read all of these travel tips and are thinking, "Whew, I'll just leave my bird home!", you're probably thinking clearly. Traveling with a bird is tough and should only be done out of necessity.

If you don't have anyone responsible to look after your bird, contact Pet Sitters International at www.petsit.com or 418 East King Street, King, NC 27021-9163, phone (336) 983-9222, fax (336) 983-3755, or go to the Pet Sitters Yellow Pages at www.petsitters.com.

The next section is a vacation care sheet that you can photocopy and give to your pet sitter to ensure that he or she has all the information needed for your parrot's proper care.

Vacation Care Sheet for My Bird

Phone number where I can be reached:_____

Veterinarian's phone number:_____

Emergency/late-night veterinarian phone number:_____

Family member's phone number:_____

Neighbor's phone number:_____

National Animal Poison Control Center: (888) 426-4435; www.napcc.aspca.org

National Association of Pet Sitters: (800) 226-PETS; www.petsitters.org

Pet Sitters International: (336) 983-9222; www.petsit.com

My bird's name:_____

My bird's basic diet is located_____

Please feed my bird (amount)_____of its basic diet daily.

Other than its basic diet, my bird likes to eat:_____

Please do not feed my bird chocolate; avocado; rhubarb; raw onion; or salty, sugary, or fatty foods.

Please refresh my bird's water cup twice daily and when you notice that the water is fouled.

Please remove all fresh foods nightly or after a few hours in warm weather.

My bird's wings are/are not clipped.

My bird bites/does not bite.

My bird likes/does not like out-of-cage playtime.

Please play with my bird out of its cage for _____ hours a day.

My bird's favorite types of music are:_____

Signs of illness in a bird include:

- Changes in appetite and water intake
- Change in attitude
- Sleeping a lot, especially on two feet
- Change in appearance; bird may look ruffled, and feathers may take on a poor, lackluster condition
- Vomiting and diarrhea
- General weakness or droopiness
- Any type of noticeable discharge
- Changes in droppings: color, smell, consistency, amount
- Favoring one leg/wing
- Lameness
- Seizure

Further instructions:

Index